In the King's Wake

To Lisa,

With gratitude for your support
in bringing this project to completion.

In the King's Wake

Post-Absolutist Culture in France

JAY CAPLAN

The University of Chicago Press
Chicago and London

JAY CAPLAN is professor of French at Amherst College. He is author of *Framed Narratives: Diderot's Genealogy of the Beholder* (1985) and translator of Ludovik Choris's *Painter's Journey around the World* (1975).

The University of Chicago Press, Chicago 60637
The University of Chicago Press, Ltd., London
© 1999 by The University of Chicago
All rights reserved. Published 1999
08 07 06 05 04 03 02 01 00 99   1 2 3 4 5

ISBN: 0-226-09311-5 (CLOTH)
ISBN: 0-226-09312-3 (PAPER)

Earlier versions of some of the chapters in this book have already appeared in print: part of chapter 1, in French translation, as "Un sujet post-absolutiste: Saint-Simon et la politique de l'invisible," *Travaux de littérature* 10 (1997): 163–74; part of the introduction and chapter 4, as "Love on Credit: Marivaux and Law," *Romance Quarterly* 38, no. 3 (August 1991): 289–99; and part of chapter 5, as "Vicarious Jouissances: or Reading Casanova," *Modern Language Notes* 100, no. 4 (fall 1985): 803–14; © 1985, The Johns Hopkins University Press. I would like to each of these journals for permission to reprint this material.

Library of Congress Cataloging-in-Publication Data

Caplan, Jay.
   In the king's wake : post-absolutist culture in France / Jay Caplan.
      p. cm.
   Includes bibliographical references and index.
   ISBN 0-226-09311-5 (cloth : alk. paper).—ISBN 0-226-09312-3 (pbk. : alk. paper)
      1. Louis XIV, King of France, 1638–1715—Symbolism—Influence. 2. Despotism—France. 3. France—Intellectual life—18th century. 4. Intellectuals—France—Political and social views. I. Title.
DC128.C29   1999
944'.032—dc21   99-40561
                                                                                      CIP

♾ The paper used in this publication meets the minimum requirements of the American National Standard for Information Sciences—Permanence of Paper for Printed Library Materials, ANSI Z39.48-1992.

Contents

Illustrations

Introduction

ON SEPTEMBER 1, 1715, the mortal being named Louis XIV passed away, but the elite culture organized around the power of his representation—absolutist culture—had arguably perished long before that date. Absolutist culture revolved around the image, rather than the person, of the Sun King. In a multiplicity of forms and genres—among them medals, portraits, and tragedy ("the royal spectacle")—absolutist culture endowed the image of the king with the power of conveying the theoretically absolute, godlike power of the sovereign. Here the monarch was "the father of the people," endowed with total responsibility for the subjects entrusted to him by God, and his multiform representations made his absolute power manifest throughout the world. Historically speaking, of course, the power of the monarch was never really absolute, except in principle. Even at the zenith of the Sun King's reign, his effective power was limited—by other political agents in France (notably the Church, the nobility, the parliaments, and the guilds), and by international economic trends (the emergence of financial and industrial capitalism).[1] Nevertheless, Louis XIV's powers were officially *represented* as absolute, just as his representations were endowed with the powers of the God who had entrusted those powers to him.[2]

Hyacinthe Rigaud's ceremonial portrait (1701) of Louis XIV epitomizes the aesthetics of French classicism.[3] In a compelling essay, Louis Marin has shown that this portrait aims to display the divine glory of the king's actual body, and to set the absolute monarch above and apart from mortal limits. In principle, the eucharistic "real presence" of the absolute monarch in his portrait consecrates his godlike status, and subjects the mortal viewer to the absolute power of the royal gaze. In Marin's words, "Far from

looking at the portrait of the Prince, from being a subject capable of gazing *at* the prince, the viewer is viewed by the Monarch, he is the object
of his gaze, that is, precisely constituted by this very gaze and subjected
by it as a political subject."[4] The portrait, Marin argues, points to the king
(it says, "This is the King," "This is his body"), and gives him the iconic
equivalent of a proper name (as if to say, "This is Louis XIV," "This is
Louis the Great"). In theory, moreover, the king's portrait performs these
gestures for Louis XIV himself, an audience of one: a mortal onlooker
may be subject to the king's gaze, but he will not dare meet it. The portrait
designates the monarch to himself ("I am the King") and names him ("I
am Louis XIV"), but for himself alone.[5] In sum, the portrait of the king
"transpose[s] the remarkable structure of the theological body into the
juridical and political domain, a transposition that brings to light *the historical gesture of absolutism*."[6]

The king's portrait, however, very quickly lost the power to perform
that gesture. In 1721, twenty years after the portrait analyzed by Marin,
Antoine Watteau depicts in the lower left corner of his great shop sign,
L'Enseigne de Gersaint, a workman crating a Rigaud portrait of the Sun
King—burying it, as it were—and none of the figures in the painting is
paying any particular attention to the king's image.[7] In this book, I shall
contend that the gesture of symbolically "burying" a portrait of the absolute monarch signals the decline (if not the death) of the official elite culture organized around the king's image,[8] and that Watteau's shop sign is
one of many works that reopen the question of the nature and powers of
absolutist representation. After the death of Louis XIV, many artists and
writers inquired into what elite culture could then become, in the king's
wake.

As a political order, absolutism ended with the French Revolution. But
I am not proposing yet another account of the fall of the ancien régime
(which historians from Tocqueville and Taine to Lefebvre, Soboul, Vo-
velle, and Furet have attempted to explain). I am concerned here with the
fate of absolutism as a cultural (not a political) order. The symbolic burial
of the Sun King already testifies, I suggest, to the passing of absolutism
as a cultural order, and to the emergence of new forms—of value, subjectivity, and legitimacy—that would survive the political death of absolutism. These are the forms of what I call post-absolutist culture. Through
analysis of works by five figures who in various ways exemplify the post-
classical, post-absolutist order, this book examines the nature and powers
of representation in a culture that is no longer absolutist or "classical." It

focuses on the changing meaning and status of representation in works by Saint-Simon, Marivaux, Watteau, Voltaire, and Casanova. Changes in a variety of genres and media (theater, painting, memoirs) signal new, specifically post-absolutist relationships between representation and power. All of these "texts" define themselves in relation to absolutist models ("the century of Louis XIV," in Voltaire's words), while imagining new configurations of power and representation. In terms of a common set of issues (legitimacy and illegitimacy, public and private subjectivity, speculation and credit), "post-absolutist" culture asks what kinds of representations should or can be made in the wake of the Sun King.

A Semiotic Crisis: The Case of John Law

One of the most powerful symbols of Louis XIV's absolute power was the louis d'or, a coin whose value was called into question just after the Sun King's death. In 1716, finding it impossible to pay back the already discounted war debt, a desperate Philippe d'Orléans turned to the Scottish financier and adventurer, John Law. He chartered Law's Banque Générale (later the Banque Royale), and authorized it to issue paper notes. The regent later placed Law at the head of the newly consolidated Compagnie Générale des Indes, whose notes were guaranteed by the state. The success of these measures was such that in 1720 Law became controller general of finances and brought the bank and the stock company under his direction. After a frenzied wave of speculation in the so-called "Mississippi bubble," the entire System went bankrupt on July 17, 1720.[9]

Law's System was based upon the proto-Keynesian assumption that the greater the means of payment in a society, the more prosperous that society will become. He expressed this belief in terms of an analogy with the circulation of the blood, which had been demonstrated in 1628 by William Harvey, in *Exercitatio anatomica de motu cordis et sanguinis in animalibus* (On the Movement of the Heart and Blood in Animals). In his *Deuxième Mémoire sur les banques*, Law asserted that "when blood does not circulate throughout the body, the body languishes; the same when money does not circulate."[10] Although Hobbes had already used the circulation of the blood as an economic metaphor,[11] Law was doubtless the first influential monetary theorist to think of the economy in terms of physiology, and we may owe to him the habit of speaking of a "healthy" or "sick" economy. In order to get money circulating in the Scottish system, Law suggested simply printing it, on paper, while guaranteeing its value in land holdings, rather than in precious metals.

Law has been called an adventurer, a man who spent his life imagining various schemes in order to become rich or powerful. Yet his experience of wealth and power was short-lived, in part because he seemed not to distinguish between the schemes that had a good chance of working and those that would need a miracle to succeed. For a number of years he made his living as a gambler, but he was also a rational planner, or "projector." It has been argued that the first loans and resulting note issue by the Banque Générale were perfectly reasonable moves, which considerably eased the financial position of the French state. Indeed, in the judgment of John Kenneth Galbraith, "had Law stopped at this point, he would be remembered for a modest contribution to the history of banking." Galbraith adds, however: "It is possible that no man, having made such a promising start, could have stopped."[12]

John Law's father was a goldsmith, a biographical detail that is not trivial, in the light of Law's lifelong hostility to gold.[13] Indeed, throughout the course of his many adventures in foreign lands, as a monetary theorist Law never varied in his opposition to using precious metals (especially gold) as a standard. As late as 1720 (when the System was beginning to unravel), he urged the king of France to support bank notes and abolish gold currency. Writing in French, he argued that "it is in the interest of the King and his people to insure bank money and abolish gold money."[14]

To get money circulating freely in the economy, Law thus prescribed a severe course of treatment: a radical increase in the means of payment, combined with a drastic cut in interest rates. Underlying this policy was the implicit belief that printing more money would increase the amount of blood in the economic system, and that the blood could be fortified through a simultaneous cut in interest rates. And Law's expansionist monetary policy did put a temporary end to a prolonged recession. Its long-term effects, however, may have been less fortunate. According to Charles Kindleberger, "a traumatic experience with paper money under John Law set back the evolution of bank notes [in France] for a century."[15] By seeking to abolish the use of gold as money, and instead printing guaranteed paper notes, Law's System effected a separation between money as *substance* and money as *function*. (In this case, the notes of Law's bank were guaranteed—temporarily, as it turned out—by the reality of the company's land holdings in Louisiana, and by the promise of gold that the

Louisiana subsoil allegedly contained.) The paper notes of the Banque Générale stood for gold, but were themselves worthless. In other words, John Law's monetary theory had the radical effect of turning money into a form that was itself insubstantial, a mere *sign* of real value.[16]

Edgar Faure, who has written the most detailed historical account of this complicated problem, agrees with Galbraith that Law should have limited himself to a modest increase in the money supply. But Faure portrays Law, and hence his System, in terms of a schizophrenic split between Law the theorist of credit and Law the gambler. He distinguishes between Law's first economic reform package, adopted in late August 1719, ("the wise plan" ["le plan sage"]) and the revised package (or "mad plan" ["le plan fou"]) that Law rapidly put into practice. Faure calls Law's moderate expansionary policy "admirable," and argues that it would have done a great deal of good to the French economy.[17] As for the revised package, the one based on nothing more solid than investor confidence, Faure judges it corrupt and "mad" ("fou"): "In the inventor of System II, we again recognize the adventurer, the breakneck, and if not the immoralist, at least the *amoralist*, a man who takes an insane (and humanly unpleasant) risk for a benefit that can only be derisory or scandalous."[18]

Thomas Kavanagh has recently taken issue with this image of Law's monetary policy as the expression of a split personality. In a book dedicated to gambling and chance operations in eighteenth-century France, he questions Faure's assumption that rational calculation and irrational speculation are contradictory.[19] In fact, Kavanagh argues, Law's monetary theory and his interest in gambling were perfectly compatible. In his view, Law the economic theorist and Law the gambler were the same person: "What Faure refuses to recognize in . . . his analysis is the profound compatibility between Law the gambler's disregard for money as money and Law the economic theorist's fundamental hypothesis that money is never an end in itself, but a tool for motivating individuals and fostering desired activities."[20] From the Keynesian perspective of Galbraith and Faure, it would have been reasonable for Law to stop after having modestly expanded the money supply, instead of adopting a policy whose internal contradictions doomed it to failure. For Kavanagh, on the other hand, Law's System was coherent, and its ultimate collapse was caused by extrinsic, political factors, rather than by any inherent theoretical or moral flaw.[21]

Doubtless there was little reason for financiers, such as the Pâris brothers, to credit notes from a state so heavily burdened with debt.[22] However, I shall not try to determine whether the panic and bankruptcy of 1720 were the inevitable result of John Law's theory (as Galbraith and Faure maintain), or whether the ultimate catastrophe might have been avoided in different political circumstances.[23] For it is the exemplarity of Law's theory that interests me, rather than its merits as economic policy. His attack on gold money and promotion of speculation and credit were typical of a more general semiotic crisis that affected French culture in the wake of absolutism; Law's economic policy exemplified a decisive, "critical" moment in the status and meaning of signs.

In a classic study of the period between 1680 and 1715, Paul Hazard described what he called the "crise de conscience" in Europe at this time. Whether one translates *conscience* as "consciousness" or "conscience," Hazard's term refers to a crisis of *ideas* (progress versus tradition, science versus faith).[24] The crisis that I shall be describing is of a different nature: a "semiotic" crisis is a turning point in the production and coding of signs, in the making and interrelation of form and content. Each of the works I discuss in this book (Law's System, Saint-Simon's *Mémoires*, Voltaire's *Œdipe* and *Commentaires sur Corneille*, Watteau's *L'Enseigne de Gersaint*, Casanova's *Histoire de ma vie*) was, in its own way, the symptom of a semiotic crisis, and also one of several possible responses to it. Each of these works testified to this crisis, and also proposed a way of addressing it. The crisis was not just one of authority, although authority has a semiotic aspect, and although a crisis of authority certainly did beset France (and all of Europe) at the turn of the eighteenth century.

Jean-Joseph Goux's pioneering work on the homology between money and language (and more generally between signs and commodities) may help us to define the historical specificity of this crisis. Goux claims—following Charles Gide—that there are at least four types of money *(monnaie)* or circulating general-equivalent:

> Gold (or silver) money, of fully intrinsic worth; *representative* paper money, with guaranteed convertibility; *fiduciary* paper money, incompletely guaranteed; and *conventional* paper money, sometimes referred to as "fictional" (or fictive) money. . . . The general-equivalent begins as a small ingot, a fragment of the treasury that is realized on the market; in the end, it is a mere paper token whose value is purely fictional.[25]

According to Goux, these types of currency describe a "growing *disincarnation* of the status of value,"[26] and they correspond to precise conceptions of language and literature. Moreover, insofar as language is like gold, it transparently discloses Being itself: "Such a gold-language formulates truth *immediately*, thus dispensing those who avail themselves of it from questioning the linguistic *medium*."[27] In these conditions (which obtained, to some extent, in French classicism), because language is inherently trustworthy, speculation remains only an intellectual exercise, which does not entail any real risks. But when language is conceived of as comparable to representative paper money—when it is no longer a form of reality, but an only an instrument that may represent reality—speculation then becomes a serious risk.[28] Finally, when language is thought of as purely conventional, and completely unrelated to anything outside itself, as in the theory of Saussure, it is beset by a crisis of confidence.

As we have seen, Law's theory separated the substance of money from its function. In terms of Goux's categories, Law's critique of gold money corresponds to a shift from gold currency to representative currency. Indeed, Law would eventually disregard any reliance upon the convertibility of currency, by allowing the value of bank notes to depend exclusively on the free play of credit. This is what Faure called "the mad plan." According to this conception of value, which did not prevail until the onset of modernism nearly two centuries later, the general-equivalent is merely "fictional" money, a paper token.

A Moment of Decision

The following chapters describe a wide range of sometimes contradictory manifestations of this semiotic crisis. In his passionate and theatrical account of the minority *lit de justice* of 1718, the duc de Saint-Simon portrays himself as an aristocratic hero, the man personally responsible for restoring the nobility to the traditional, legitimate rank of which it had been deprived through the tyranny of Louis XIV. However, unlike the heroes he so admired, Saint-Simon could not perform his noble deeds in public, nor could he even have his memoirs published until after his death. Moreover, despite his reactionary aim, he unwittingly shows himself undermining the hereditary basis of aristocratic legitimacy. At the same time, Saint-Simon implicitly recognizes that a fundamental tenet of absolutism has lost its validity: even the king is now subject to the rule of law.

François-Marie Arouet also contributed to the discrediting of bloodlines as a criterion for nobility when, in the dedication of *Œdipe*, he publicly pronounced himself "Arouet de Voltaire." The tremendous success of his first effort at tragedy emboldened Voltaire to lay claim to a new form of nobility, based upon performance, upon actions rather than blood. Until the end of his life, Voltaire would continue to devote much of his prodigious intellectual energy to the task of giving new life to tragedy, without fully realizing that he could only become "M. de Voltaire" because his audiences could no longer believe in the awesome reality of the king's symbolic sacrifice in tragedy. The "king of Ferney" (as Voltaire would be called) could not revive the noble tradition of Corneille and Racine because tragedy, the genre that represented the terrible responsibilities of absolute royal power, had lost all credibility.

Although Watteau's last great painting, *L'Enseigne de Gersaint* (1721), can be seen as the emblem of a mercantile fête galante, in which the image of Louis XIV (and with it, the absolutist system of representation) is symbolically buried, the work also illustrates the ambiguity of Watteau's artistic will and testament. In Goux's semiotic vocabulary, Watteau's signboard remains poised between a "realist" aesthetics and a more modernist, self-referential logic.

The playwright and writer Marivaux was one of the many investors who lost his fortune in the wake of John Law's bankruptcy. Two of his best-known and most successful plays show Marivaux's characters achieving their value in terms of a post-absolutist credit economy, in which one's true worth is also determined (at least in principle) by performance, and not by birth or blood. In both *Le Jeu de l'amour et du hasard (The Game of Love and Chance*, 1730) and *Les Fausses confidences (False Admissions*, 1737), lovers sense each other's inner worth, and feel that despite all appearances, each is worthy of credit; this allows them finally to realize (that is, both recognize and actualize) what they are worth to each other.

Like Voltaire, Giacomo Casanova not only gave himself a noble title (Casanova de Seingalt), but also was a monarchist—in fact a passionate admirer of kings. At least two moments in Casanova's memoirs, *History of My Life*, bring the famous libertine into a relationship with a royal figure. In the first episode, which took place in 1752, an erotic painting mediates Casanova's relationship with Louis XV, the monarch he loved above all others. In Casanova's imagination, however, this encounter causes the divine aura momentarily to vanish from the head of Louis ("le Bien-Aimé"), who is turned into a mere bearer of exchange-value, a louis. In 1760 Casanova finally met Voltaire, and although he had read and admired the philosophe for many years, and would have loved to become the privileged interlocutor of the future "king of Ferney," Casanova found himself treated like an Italian buffoon. He never got over his resentment.

As we shall see, neither Voltaire nor Casanova could have dubbed himself noble, without also implicitly repudiating the symbolic order of royal absolutism.

As in my reading of Saint-Simon's memoirs, I focus here on Casanova's autobiography as a historical text (something he wrote at a particular time), rather than as a historical document (which provides more or less reliable testimony to a number of facts). Scholarly discussions of these works have often used them as a means of reconstructing (and possibly interpreting) historical events, such as the *lit de justice* of 1718 or Casanova's meetings with Voltaire. But these texts, all of which have already been philologically or curatorially established, are also *symbolic acts, performed at specific times and places:* in this precise sense, these acts are indeed "historical."[29]

In various ways, each of these historical acts provides evidence of a semiotic crisis. According to Hippocrates and Galen, a *krisis* is a moment of decision, a turning point in the evolution of a disease. John Law identified reliance upon gold money as the primary cause of the languishing French economy, which he then sought to invigorate with a monetary transfusion. From this point of view, it does not matter why Law's prescribed course of treatment failed to resolve this fiscal crisis, but it is extremely significant that Law, like so many others in his culture, found it increasingly hard to believe that value was "incarnated" in signs, like gold in a coin; that the king's portrait was the king; that with each performance of a tragedy, something real was actually unfolding before their eyes; or that bloodlines, and not actions, were what conferred nobility upon a person. As the following chapters will show, during this period the transition (from "archetype" to "treasury") that now appears to have taken place was neither global nor linear. Post-absolutist culture was fundamentally critical—that is, it corresponds to a prolonged moment of decision, during which absolutist culture itself was being placed in question, and other cultural models were being elaborated.

A Post-Absolutist Subject

Saint-Simon

LOUIS DE ROUVROY, duc de Saint-Simon, has achieved posthumous recognition as one of the greatest writers in the French language. Yet (in part because he could not separate aesthetic questions from moral and religious issues) the duke was not concerned with proving his artistic worth. Rather, he was intent upon establishing his own importance in the world. In 1694 Saint-Simon began keeping a private journal, in the hope of gaining the public recognition that had been denied him on the battlefield: "in the desire and hope of bearing some responsibility [d'être de quelque chose]."[1] He thus conceived of his writing as, among other things, a way of proving that he fully deserved the marshal's baton that Louis XIV had always refused to grant him.

Nowhere in his memoirs is the "desire and hope" to exhibit his own cosmic importance more fully and magnificently displayed than in Saint-Simon's account of the events of August 26, 1718. Early on that morning the regent, Philippe d'Orléans, summoned the Parlement to a *lit de justice*, before which he convened his Regency Council. (A *lit de justice* was a special session of the Parlement, presided over by the king.) At the "Minority" *lit de justice* of 1718 (so called because it was conducted when the future Louis XV was only eight years old), the intermediary rank between the princes of the blood and the dukes that Louis XIV had created for his illegitimate sons was eliminated, thereby depriving them of the right to inherit the throne.

Saint-Simon had begun secretly writing his memoirs in 1694, just two or three months after the Sun King had legitimized his bastards, thus raising them above Saint-Simon and his peers. The close proximity of these two dates suggests that Saint-Simon made a connection between the "scandalous" public promotion of the royal bastards and his own determination to bear some responsibility ("être de quelque chose") in a private journal. The issue resolved at the 1718 *lit de justice* was so fundamental to the way Saint-Simon conceived of his own identity that his self-valorizing project as a memorialist may well have been precipitated by Louis XIV's decision to legitimize his bastards. The haughty duke would later recall August 26, 1718, as a "day of justice and rule" (7:264), when he played a heroic role in healing the "wounds" that a despotic Sun King had inflicted upon the dukes and peers, and upon the nation. Indeed, Saint-Simon would portray this day as the greatest and most glorious of his life, the only day when God's will had been done on earth: it was, in the words of Yves Coirault, "his one day in the Paradise of the peers."[2]

The term *lit de justice* derives metonymically from the bedlike ceremonial apparatus beneath which, during the late Middle Ages, the king would sit during these solemn sessions of Parlement. In Saint-Simon's *Mémoires*, the word *lit* also resonates with the semantic field of *lectura* (reading, lecture, lesson): the *garde des sceaux* informs the Parlement of the king's justice by *reading* aloud the decisions previously announced in the Council meeting, and by *lecturing* the Parlement about knowing its own place. Saint-Simon presents the *lit de justice* as the ritual delivery or publication of a text, which is symbolically imprinted, or impressed, upon an audience. At this *lit de justice*, then, the ceremonial *logos* of justice is once again read aloud, but this time in the presence of the Parlement. By writing down his memories of these events,[3] Saint-Simon means to inscribe them, and himself as well, in a durable and legitimate hierarchical order.

In the vast text of Saint-Simon's *Mémoires*, there are only two episodes of which there exists a next-to-last draft, which can be compared with the final version. This *lit de justice* sequence is one of those two episodes. According to his editor Coirault, the penultimate draft was probably written sometime between August 1719 and March 1720—that is, probably decades before the final draft.[4] What emerges most strikingly (and paradoxically) from Coirault's comparison of the two drafts is how, as Saint-Simon's distance from the events increased, he represented his "experience" of triumph and vengeance with incomparably greater passion and intensity.[5] It was in writing, and as a writer, that the duc de Saint-Simon could achieve the most vivid impression of *being* someone—that is, the exultant, triumphant hero of August 26, 1718. His writing enabled this impassioned supporter of hierarchy and legitimate order finally to put people and events back in their place, and in so doing, to assign a proper place to himself.

In the order of his own narrative, the Minority *lit de justice* occupies a curious and privileged position. The episode is privileged, insofar as it represents the culmination of events that occupy over two thousand pages in the Pléiade edition. And yet (or maybe therefore) its position and mode of presentation are somewhat odd, in terms of Saint-Simon's narrative principles. Time and again, he has the habit of alluding in the memoirs to a given subject, but then refusing to discuss it, in order not to digress—to avoid departing from proper (chronological) order. Instead he normally promises to return to a topic "at the proper time" ("en son temps") or "at the proper place" ("en son lieu") in the "chain" of historical causes and effects.[6] Nevertheless, as soon as his chronological order of presentation brings him to the Minority *lit de justice* (7:73), Saint-Simon embarks upon a forty-page digression into diplomatic history (which he avowedly copies from the memoirs of Torcy).[7] Moreover when he finally presents the long narrative of the *lit de justice* (7:124–293), it is interrupted by two remarkably detailed plans, in Saint-Simon's own hand (7:231, 254–55), which show the arrangement of the participants in the Council meeting and *lit de justice*. These drawings are departures not only from chronology, but from linear narrativity itself. Thanks to these drawings, the reader can see the exact place that Saint-Simon has written for himself in history.

Saint-Simon viewed the elimination of the intermediary rank as a means of restoring the purity of the crown and reestablishing natural hierarchy. For this reason, Coirault has warned against interpreting the Minority *lit de justice* in terms of Saint-Simon's personal vengeance (and still less as a "miniature regicide"):

> The famous *lit de justice* of 1718 was indeed the day "of justice and rule": the degradation of the bastards restored all its purity to the crown, and delivered Saint-Simon from the horrible perspective of a break between royalty and its natural supports. This is the meaning of a ceremony that should not be seen only as the thrilling spectacle of a kill, or the triumph of a strictly personal vengeance, not to mention a miniature regicide.[8]

Whatever Saint-Simon's understanding of this *lit de justice* may have been, his memoirs also suggest a historical reason why this ceremony could not possibly have amounted to a form of symbolic regicide. As we shall see, according to Saint-Simon's own account, by 1718 the king had already lost most of his "symbolic efficacy" (to borrow an expression from Lévi-

DUC
DE SAINT-SIMON

LOUIS·DUC·DE·S·SIMON·PAIR·DE·FRANCE·GRAND   D'ESPAGNE·DE·LA·PRE
L·ASSEC·GOU·DE·BLAYE·GOUV·ET·BAILLY·DE·SENLIS   DU·CONSEIL·DE·REGI
A·LA·MORT·DE·LOUIS·XIV·AMBASS·AD·EXTRAORD·DE·LOUIS·XV·EN·ESPAGNE·172
DU·MARIAGE·CHEVALIER·DU·S·ESPRIT·1728·QUATRE·VINGT·QUINZE·ANS·APR
N·PAIR·DE·FRANCE·SON·PERE·QUI·LE·FUT·A·LA·PENTEC

The duc de Saint-Simon (engraving). Photo: Roger-Viollet.

Strauss).[9] In other words, no one could have committed regicide at this
lit de justice, because the king (as symbolic force, as incarnation of the
nation) was already effectively dead.

There is no doubt about the short-term political effectiveness of the
Minority *lit de justice:* the regent's decisive action on this occasion put an

end to a broadly based conspiracy that had been mounted against him. In his memoirs, the Marquis d'Argenson characterizes these actions as a "most fortunate and daring *coup d'état*," and the historian Philippe Erlanger summarizes the Minority *lit de justice* in terms of the Regent's "awakening."[10] A contrasting view is taken by the historian Sarah Hanley, who argues, in her monograph *The Lit de Justice and the Kings of France*, that Saint-Simon completely misread the events of August 26 ("with characteristic obtuseness").[11] I am concerned not with the meaning of these events, but with the historical significance of the way in which Saint-Simon represents them: in other words, how Saint-Simon reads (or misreads) this historical situation is itself historically (and not just psychologically) significant. I mean to draw out the historical implications of Saint-Simon's self-deluded (and entirely self-styled) heroism. The very fact that there is no evidence, outside his own mind, to corroborate the experience of "triumph," is itself symptomatic of a new historical conjuncture.

This *lit de justice* has also been portrayed as a spectacularly effective display of political theater, and as a "perfect illustration" of the "theatrical paradigm underlying political practice in early modern France."[12] But the drama that unfolds on this day is best understood, not in terms of baroque political action *(coups d'éclat)*,[13] but in terms of a more private and modern theatricality. Most of the drama (or "theater") in Saint-Simon's memoirs will not be played out on a public stage (such as the Tuileries), but on a private one, which only Saint-Simon's reader can see. Saint-Simon's theatrical account of what happened on August 26, 1718, illustrates a modern political and theatrical situation, which exemplifies post-absolutist subjectivity. In that situation, he implicitly recognizes that the absolute monarch is dead.

On the King's Dead Body

The status of the king's body is central to the semiotics of kingship, and hence of regency. This question arises during Saint-Simon's discussion of a ceremony that took place almost exactly a year before the Minority *lit de justice*, on September 1, 1717. The occasion for this ceremony was the anniversary of the Sun King's death, which had occurred on September 1, 1715. This anniversary was duly commemorated every year at the royal necropolis of Saint-Denis. In his memoirs, Saint-Simon indignantly recalls that before the ceremony of 1717, the bishops of France asked for *carreaux*—that is, they requested the honor (not to mention the comfort) of kneeling on cushions during the ceremony, rather than on the hard stone floor. This request was denied, upon which the bishops stormed out of the church and lodged a protest with the regent.

Even though the bishops never got their cushions, Saint-Simon found it appalling that they could dare ask for such an honor. To him, this request betrayed a complete lack of gratitude and respect toward the late king. "Gratitude" *(reconnaissance)*, he testily observes, has long been "out of fashion":

> The anniversary that is observed every year at St. Denis for the late King produced a completely new pretension. *Gratitude has not been in fashion for a very long time:* there were very few persons from the court, M. du Maine and his second son, a few bishops, and the Cardinal de Polignac. *These bishops took it into their heads to want to have cushions.* What is unusual is that only the Cardinal de Polignac was opposed to it, and prevented it, upon which the bishops dared to leave and complain to the Regent. (6:429, emphasis added)

From Saint-Simon's perspective, these bishops should have been so grateful to the Sun King for having protected them during his lifetime that they would willingly genuflect before his effigy at Saint-Denis, with or without the comfort of a cushion.

Of course, Saint-Simon could easily afford to portray himself as the bishops' moral superior, since he (as a duke) already enjoyed the privilege of kneeling on a cushion before the king's funeral effigy. Nor would he have wanted to cheapen the value of that privilege by sharing it. What is interesting, though, is that he immediately connects *reconnaissance* with a political and metaphysical code that he calls "the rule of honors": "The rule of honors is that everyone is in the presence of the corpse and its representation as he was in the presence of this same living person; now the bishops never had or thought of having cushions in any place where the King was" (ibid.). Honors are a matter of etiquette or form, which (as Norbert Elias has shown) was a profoundly serious social and philosophical issue in court society.[14] The "rule of honors" requires that, in whatever form a person manifests himself—whether alive, dead, or represented—he has to be honored in the same way, to enjoy the same privileges, and have the same powers. According to Saint-Simon, this rule requires that one show the same respect for the mortal remains and effigies *(corps* and *représentation)* of the dead as for their living persons. For him, the rule of honors expresses the *unchanging* order of things, and therefore must not be treated as a mere matter of fashion. In principle, one's essence, one's legitimate position in the hierarchy of being, never changes: "everyone is . . . as he was."

In the organic metaphors of absolutism, the king "incarnated" the French nation. Ever since Ernst Kantorowicz's classic work on the subject, the political theory of the king's two bodies has informed our theoretical understanding of medieval kingship in England and ancien régime France. This theory distinguished between the contingent, mortal body of the king (in lowercase letters), and the symbolic, immortal body of the King (uppercase).[15] Although the king's first body was subject to all the weaknesses of mortal flesh, his second, symbolic body (incarnated in the state) could neither err nor die. In this perspective, the famous claim (attributed by legend to Louis XIV), "L'Etat, c'est moi," implies that the absolute monarch temporarily incarnated a symbolic reality that transcended his mortal person. "Absolute monarchy," according to Robert Descimon and Alain Guéry, "can be defined as the dogma of consubstantial union of the king and the kingdom."[16] In *Portrait of the King*, Louis Marin extended Kantorowicz's analyses to "classic" absolutism and argued that, during the reign of Louis XIV, the king's single body was mysteriously composed of three bodies: "The king has only one body left, but this single body in truth unites three: a physical historical body, a juridico-political body, and a sacramental, semiotic body,—the sacramental body, the "portrait" performing the exchange without remainder [sans reste] (or seeking to eliminate all remainder) between the historical body and the political body."[17] In Saint-Simon's narrative, as we shall see, the king's body no longer manifests itself in this "classic," absolutist form. Nevertheless, in the opinion of Louis XIV, the French nation could not exist independently of his body; indeed, no body could incarnate the French nation, except the king's (symbolic, second) body. As Jean-Marie Apostolidès has remarked, the bourgeoisie repudiated this doctrine in the most violent way possible on January 21, 1793, by beheading Louis XVI, and taking the king's place as the true representative (but not, I would stress, the "incarnation") of the French nation.[18]

Although Saint-Simon often alludes, elsewhere in his memoirs, to the king's two bodies,[19] his explanation of the "rule of honors" relies upon still another notion of the royal body. What he means here is neither the living, historical, and mortal body of a particular king ("Louis XIV"), nor what Marin calls the juridico-political body ("L'Etat, c'est moi"), nor even the transcendent, immortal reality that each successive king incarnates ("the King"), but a hybrid of historical and sacramental bodies. According to the "rule of honors," one had to adopt the same position toward another's mortal remains and effigies ("[to be] in the presence of the body and its representation") as toward his "living person." No one occupied a more commanding position in the absolutist hierarchy than "the king": his living person, his effigy, or his corpse. This rule entailed a paradoxical conception of the king's body as simultaneously contingent (belonging to a particular king) and immortal, beyond contingency (a body to whom his subjects are *eternally* "grateful"), one of three identical, imperishable manifestations of a specific king. In principle, all three forms were identical and possessed the same value, the same power to compel respect (if not always belief).

More important, the absolute monarch seems to have wielded this power in practice. In all his manifestations, as noted by many an observer, Louis XIV really had the power to hold his court in check (for example, to make the bishops of France genuflect without benefit of cushions). Thus Orest Ranum notes that "when servants and courtiers at Versailles came and went about the royal bedroom they bowed before the royal *nef,* a gold shiplike vessel containing the king's knife, fork, and napkin. This was done whether the king was present or not. Like the genuflections of the faithful before altars in churches at all times."[20] This example implies that there was a time—how long it lasted is precisely what is at issue here—when representations of Louis XIV commanded the same veneration as his body. When courtiers genuflected before the royal *nef* like the faithful before an altar, they acted as if the king's (metonymical) representation had the power of his living body—as if, like the consecrated Host, it actually *was* his body.[21]

For the bishops to whom Saint-Simon refers, however, the effigy of Louis XIV is simply not Louis XIV.[22] Their only loyalty is to fashion *(mode),* and the rule of fashion requires change. Not only does fashion value innovation (which in Saint-Simon's eyes becomes synonymous with illegitimacy), but it also makes value relative, no longer eternally fixed. By definition, fashion invests persons with a value that has no relationship to their intrinsic worth (or essence), and thus makes it legitimate to think about value as the product of human convention.[23] Hence the heavy irony of Saint-Simon's remark that "gratitude [reconnaissance] is no longer fashionable": it plays upon the contrast between an ideal society that valued *reconnaissance* and a degraded society that values *mode. Reconnaissance,* in the pre-absolutist world Saint-Simon imagines, was a gesture of ritual acknowledgment, whereby one could once again know ("re-cognize") one's place. To be *reconnaissant* was to reaffirm the mixture of gratitude and respect that one felt for a position in the hierarchy ordained by God. *Re-*

connaissance therefore meant to recognize oneself as subjected to those of higher rank—that is, ultimately, as subject to the king.

Indeed, the king stood alone at the summit of this hierarchy, subject to no one, and in absolutist theory responsible only to God. Of all the successive incarnations of the king's immortal body, no one had compelled greater respect than the Sun King, Louis XIV. Yet in 1717, two years after his death, Saint-Simon testifies that even the most solemn representation of Louis XIV, his funeral effigy, no longer has the power to hold all his subjects in check, to bring all his subjects to their knees. To Saint-Simon, however, registering a precipitous drop in the status and powers of this particular king amounts to noting a decline in the powers of "the King," in general. To Saint-Simon, the bishops' obedience to *mode* betrays a crisis of legitimacy: if the rule of honors is no longer "fashionable," to Saint-Simon this can only mean that the legitimacy of absolutist cultural order is already in a state of crisis. The powers of the king's representation are no longer the same, and neither perhaps are the powers of representation in general. In other words, no matter how the king's subjects now behave in the "live" presence of the young Louis XV, they no longer feel any special reverence for a king's dead body or his representations. "The King"—in the ideology of absolutism, that mystical union of a sacred body and its representations—can no longer lay down the law. The miraculous identity of the royal body and its representations has been sundered; the superhuman powers of the representation of the king, and of "the King" as representation, have been irretrievably lost. The absolute monarch, "the King," is dead.

In fact, Saint-Simon implies that the monarch has been dead for a considerable time. To observe in 1717 that gratitude had been out of fashion "for a long while" is to suggest that "the King" has been dead for longer than the two years that had passed since the death of Louis XIV. The duke's remark suggests that, sometime before the passing of the Sun King's mortal body, maybe even long before that date, the legitimacy of the "rule of honors" (and with it the premises of "classic" absolutist representation) was called into question. As we shall see, however, if Saint-Simon believed that "the King" was dead, that *reconnaissance* had been supplanted by *mode*, if he believed that everywhere things legitimate, real, and worthy of respect were being undermined and replaced by degraded, worthless, illegitimate values (such as fashion), he placed the blame for this catastrophic state of affairs upon the shoulders of Louis XIV himself. This particular king, for whose *corps* the bishops of France showed no respect, Louis XIV (his "living person"), bore primary responsibility for the death of "the King."

Genealogy of Illegitimacy

Les écus s'envolent, la crasse demeure. — SAINT-SIMON, *Mémoires*, 7:728

To appreciate how violently Saint-Simon hated Louis XIV for having legitimized his bastards, we must pause to measure the importance of illegitimacy in the duke's understanding of the world. Saint-Simon saw illegitimacy everywhere on the rise, and he lamented the capricious and despotic role of Louis XIV in the process: in the mounting ascendancy of the Parlement of Paris, in the rise of financial capital, and in the ambitions of Louis XIV's illegitimate, but legitimized, children. He repeatedly refers to illegitimately acquired power as a "usurpation" and to the collaboration of legitimate powers in the process as "scandalous." Both Louis XIV and the Parlement claimed to represent the nation, but Saint-Simon viewed both claims as usurpations. In fact, he believed, by usurping absolute power the Sun King had paradoxically become the natural ally of illegitimacy in all its forms.

The duke nursed an implacable animosity toward Louis XIV, not only for having legitimized his illegitimate children by giving them titles, but for forcing his legitimate heirs (such as the duc d'Orléans) to marry them. In his eyes, it was insufferably despotic and callous of Louis XIV to have forced his subjects to recognize the self-contradictory, and therefore "monstrous," legitimacy of his bastards. Saint-Simon held Louis XIV responsible for the "scandalous" claims of the royal bastards, for the decline of France as a European power, and for the general legitimation of bastardy throughout Europe.[24]

At the time of the *lit de justice* of 1718, the duc du Maine, the elder of Louis XIV's surviving illegitimate sons, was still officially responsible for the education of the young Louis XV, while also aspiring to the throne. Saint-Simon calls the royal bastards "the Titans of France" (7:217) and their children "bastardlets [bâtardeaux]" (7:142).[25] In his eyes, the royal bastards had found their most powerful ally (aside from Louis XIV himself, of course) in the *noblesse de robe*, and especially the Parlement of Paris. Doubtless the duc de Saint-Simon's preoccupation with establishing the ancient traditions of the French nobility, and his hostility toward the robe nobility, cannot be explained without noting the relatively recent origin of his family's nobility (fifteenth century) and its dukedom and peerage (1632). For Saint-Simon, nothing better exemplified the Parlement's shameless attack on the traditional prerogatives of the nobility—not to mention Louis XIV's cynical complicity with the *robins*—than the famous "cap affair" *(affaire du bonnet)* of 1714. According to Saint-Simon, traditional parliamentary procedure required the Premier Président (or presiding magistrate) of Parlement to remove his cap *(bonnet)* as a sign of respect when soliciting, first, the opinion of the dukes and peers, and then that of the princes of the blood. As Saint-Simon recalls it, Premier Président Novion (whose very name doubtless suggested novelty, and therefore indecency, to Saint-Simon) began "forgetting" to remove his cap at the proper moments, until the day in 1714 when he dropped all pretense of respect for the dukes ("unmasking himself," in Saint-Simon's words), by removing his cap only when addressing the princes of the blood (V, 54).[26]

Another area in which Saint-Simon saw the forces of legitimacy fighting a losing battle was in the clash between agricultural capital and financial capital, which he discusses at greatest length in the memorandum to the Regent written in 1717 (cited at length in 6:289–334). He calls this conflict the "choc entre fonciers et rentiers" (5:296–301). In Saint-Simon's fairly conventional view, only agricultural capital (land) was real, whereas financial capital was a convenient illusion, and ultimately a catastrophic one: "Landowners consider these establishments of *artificial goods [biens factices]* as the misfortune and ruin of the State" (6:297, emphasis added). For Saint-Simon, financial capital was artificial because it had no substantial, tangible basis; because it was not produced by the land, from which the traditional nobility derived its identity. Financial capital therefore could not be natural or real. One could give power to financial capital only by crediting the disastrously convenient illusion that, like God, a man can miraculously create something from nothing. Indeed, I will suggest below that in Saint-Simon's view, every time an illegitimate value is produced, someone has repeated the original sin of taking himself for God. In his eyes, of course, the most egregious sinner was Louis XIV, whose legitimation of bastardy had turned Paris into the sewer of Europe.

Given Saint-Simon's opinion of financial capital, one might have expected him to oppose John Law's System with the vehemence of a Montesquieu. At first, however, Saint-Simon succumbed to the seduction of "the magician," as Law was called, at least in part (as Thomas Kavanagh has shown) because Law's notes were initially backed by land in Louisiana, and not by the gold and silver of merchants: "Like so many of Philippe d'Orléans's counselors, Saint-Simon was seduced by Law's promise to initiate the realm's economic rebirth by issuing notes backed not by the gold and silver of the merchant class (a practice already operating in Holland) but by land—what the nobility saw as the true touchstone of economic

wealth and order."[27] With this one exception, however, Saint-Simon remained convinced that to place one's hopes in stocks and bonds, in the city
rather than the country, was to invite economic and political catastrophe. A
fiscal policy that relied upon "artificial goods" impoverished the only real
producers of value (the peasants), and also increased the king's power
over the entire kingdom, *rentiers* and *fonciers* included:

> Due to the ease with which they are collected, [these artificial goods] give so
> many persons the opportunity to invest their wealth in them, to *live on them
> in the shade and at rest,* off the sweat of the country people, almost all of
> whose labor returns to the King through the excessive taxes that he needs to
> pay off the loans with which he has burdened himself, and *who thereby puts
> all the wealth of the kingdom in his hand:* the wealth of the landowners in the
> manner just described, that of the loan holders (rentiers) by *opening or closing
> his hand as he pleases.* (6:297, emphasis added)

Thus while *rentiers* idly clipped coupons in the shadows and peasants la-
bored in the sun, all the kingdom's wealth flowed into the capricious hand
of a tyrannical king, for his *bon plaisir.* Saint-Simon repeatedly denounced
this complicity between tyranny and illegitimacy. Yet despite his nostalgia
for a time when a noble's actions displayed and proved his worth (for
what Kavanagh calls "a way of life in which open and public acts of display
. . . proved a nobility of character adequate in itself"),[28] Saint-Simon himself always displayed his own valor behind the scenes, "in the shade," just
like the *rentiers* whose ascendancy he so deplored.

Saint-Simon observed Louis XIV encouraging usurpation and illegitimacy in yet another way: by selling letters of nobility, and thus treating
nobility as if it were a commodity, rather than a state of being. He also
lamented the rise of illegitimacy in the epidemic of misalliances between
impoverished nobles and wealthy bourgeois, and the growing ascendance
of money over blood and honor.[29] For example, after taking note of the
marriage between the duc de Brissac and "a very rich heiress" (7:727)
named Mademoiselle Pécoil, he sarcastically reflects that "the crowns [les
écus] pass, the filth remains" (7:728). His comment alludes to the Latin
proverb, "verba volant, scripta manent" ("words pass, writings remain"),
about the imprudence of leaving written traces of one's opinions—a warn-
ing that Saint-Simon heeded by keeping his *Mémoires* secret during his
lifetime. But the memorialist distorts the proverb to imply that the monstrous, illicit union of honor with filthy lucre bears the indelible stain of
its origins.[30] Although the comment is meant to apply to this particular

case of misalliance, it applies as well to what he considered as the entire sordid, illegitimate legacy of Louis XIV.

In each instance of illegitimacy, something inherently valuable and real to Saint-Simon (nobility, ancestry, land) has gradually been replaced by something of lesser value or no value at all, in precisely the same way that gratitude *(reconnaissance)* had been replaced by fashion *(mode)*. What scandalizes the duke (the word *scandal* continually recurs in this context) is to see legitimate titles cast aside while illegitimate titles achieve currency. For him, it is even more scandalous when these usurpations take place with the complicity of the king (or the regent) himself. It does not surprise him to find unauthorized parties arrogantly making claim to honors they do not deserve: after all, one should always expect dishonorable people to behave dishonorably. What he cannot bear is to see divinely mandated, honorable forces collaborate in their own undoing. Thus he laments the spectacle of Louis XIV brazenly *selling* letters of nobility and that of Philippe d'Orléans agreeing (albeit under pressure) to marry the Sun King's *illegitimate* daughter. Often, as in the cases of the princesse Palatine and Louis XIV, those he saw collaborating with illegitimate parties were his lawful superiors, which made it dangerous for him to voice his opinions in public, much less take any political action.

As he reads the situation, the fraudulent substitution of appearance for reality usually comes about through a combination of naiveté and artifice: naiveté on the part of everyone who should have an interest in preservation of traditional (and therefore) lawful values, and artifice on the part of all the unauthorized "pretenders," who take advantage of what the lawful authorities cannot see. Saint-Simon tends to portray artlessness and artifice, legitimacy and illegitimacy, as mutually exclusive, with one decisive exception: Louis XIV. As the duke saw it, the Sun King had made tactical use of artifice and ruse to undermine the traditional power of the nobility, while remaining fatally blind to the long-term strategic effects of this policy upon the entire social hierarchy.

After the Fall

In the end, Saint-Simon would attribute Louis XIV's catastrophic blindness, and ultimately all illegitimacy, to the corruption of human nature— that is, to original sin, to the ruse of the serpent and the natural pride of humankind. This is why, even in the duke's own eyes, his glorious intervention and triumph at the Minority *lit de justice* would ultimately be of no avail against the forces of evil, at least not in this world. To him, every victory of illegitimacy reiterated the gesture of original sin. For example, when the regent's mother (the princesse Palatine, Charlotte of Bavaria) appears in great pomp at the thesis defense of the regent's illegitimate son (and her illegitimate grandson), the princess seemingly erases the difference between what is legitimate (real) and what is illegitimate (mere appearance).[31] To the duke, this "spectacle" displays an almost incomprehensible denial of reality, and he is convinced that this maddening example of a great noble's folly will now lead others to credit a transparent illusion. It is annoyingly clear to Saint-Simon that by giving a certain credibility to the so-called chevalier, "Madame" also implicitly discredits persons of authentic birth and rank, including herself.[32]

In his eyes, at least two factors make the princess's behavior scandalous, the first of which is its source. Whereas it is in the nature of inferior beings (the royal bastards, the *robins*) shamelessly to aspire to positions they in no way deserve, it should be in the nature (and interest) of superior beings to keep their inferiors in their proper place. Yet time and again (for example, the bishops' demand for cushions), unlawful pretensions elicit not even a murmur of opposition or reproach from those in higher ranks, and worse still, the latter seem to encourage such behavior through their own illicit aspirations. Thus, not only do the parties of legitimacy fail to counter the danger that threatens them, but also, and worse, they delegitimize themselves through their own actions. This is the "scandal" that Saint-Simon struggles to explain. He cannot make sense of the fact that such a notable enemy of bastards and bastardy ("Madame, who was so hostile to all bastards and bastardy") as the princesse Palatine could act in flagrant contradiction to her own principles. When the princesse Palatine sets a poor example for her inferiors, she displays the allegedly natural foibles of women ("Madame . . . had taken a liking for this one *so capriciously*"). It is obvious even to Saint-Simon, however, that she also imitates the much more capricious, scandalous, and corrupting example of her brother-in-law, Louis XIV. Once again, Saint-Simon's argument brings him back to the enigmatic example of the Sun King.

Still more incomprehensible is the undeniable fact that illegitimate practices spread uncontrollably, whereas legitimate ones do not. When Madame appears in majesty ("with pomp, greeted and led to her portière by the cardinal de Noailles, with his cross going on before him") at the Sorbonne, her improper actions certainly call forth more of the same. Moreover—and this is what makes her action scandalous in Saint-Simon's eyes—this improper model has an inexplicably greater mimetic impact than a decent, proper model could have had. For the duke, illegitimacy exemplifies what Hegel would later call "bad infinity": it just never stops.

Although Saint-Simon can find no rational, logical explanation for the contagiously mimetic powers of illegitimacy, his account does allow for a theological explanation of its "scandal."[33] For what he finds so scandalous about the "spectacle" of the princesse Palatine attending the thesis defense of the regent's illegitimate son in great pomp is not just that it tends to confer dignity upon the "chevalier de Saint-Albin," or even that it contributes to the general discredit of a hierarchy ordained by God, but rather that (in his view) a woman has no place in the Sorbonne (just as "Salic law" made it illegal for a woman to succeed to the throne of France). By attending a thesis defense in the Faculty of Theology, the princess implies that a woman has the right to be there. In fact, there is a perfectly conventional explanation for what Saint-Simon found so outrageous and incomprehensible about Madame's actions. For what is original sin, if not the desire to rise above the rank or state ordained by God? Despite the princess's passionate opposition to all forms of bastardy, she apparently encourages it here because of her even more passionate, natural, female desire to rise above her rightful station, the same desire that had seduced Eve into eating of the fruit of the Tree of Knowledge. In this perspective, it is her human nature that blinds the princess and makes her behave in dramatic contradiction to her own interests and beliefs. To ask why the princesse Palatine (or Louis XIV) acts so irrationally, in such flagrant contradiction to her own interest, is tantamount to asking why Eve should have wanted to eat of the fruit of the Tree of Knowledge.

In Saint-Simon's eyes, all innovation is illegitimate, just as everything illegitimate represents an innovation. To him, only by respecting tradition and resisting innovation in all its disguises can one possibly hope to arrest the corruption of all things mortal. Hence his opposition to the principle of *mode,* since without innovation there can be no fashion. To Saint-Simon, the princesse Palatine's "innovation," like everything that is new (such as the cardinals asking for cushions) repeats an original sin.

This theological tradition provided Saint-Simon with strong reasons to doubt that legitimacy could be reestablished through human intervention alone. At times he seems to resign himself, with classic metaphysical pessimism, to the inevitable degradation of all things mortal: for example, when he remarks that "once disorders are established they cannot be reformed" (7:603). In a classic work of literary sociology, Lucien Goldmann argued that the metaphysical pessimism of the *noblesse de robe* was an ideological expression of that group's political decline.[34] Saint-Simon's traditional nobility had also been reduced to a state of political impotence by Louis XIV, and after Louis XIV's death, during the period of government by council, the traditional nobility proved itself incapable of governing. This may also have contributed to Saint-Simon's occasional pessimism. But Saint-Simon's usual mood is not one of resignation or philosophical pessimism, but one of anger. Instead of resigning himself to the corruption of human nature, he rails against the fact that people (especially Louis XIV) have been acquiring powers to which they have no legitimate right. He ceaselessly complains that he and his fellow dukes and peers have been losing the power (or the will) to exercise their long-standing rights.

For some years, however, he did more than complain: he also attempted to regain that power and reassert those rights—most notably on the day of the Minority *lit de justice* of 1718. Already after Louis XIV's death, during the regency of Philippe d'Orléans, Saint-Simon had finally become a political actor. He participated in the regent's brief experiment with government by aristocratic councils (which Saint-Simon had advocated as a means of taking back some of the powers that Louis XIV had illegitimately taken away from the traditional nobility). The Minority *lit de justice* of 1718 marked the high point of the duke's brief, fairly unsuccessful career as a political actor. Here, at least in Saint-Simon's mind and memoirs, was one glorious and heroic exception to the general tendency toward decline of all things legitimate and noble. Of course, in that same year the conciliary experiment was abandoned. And two years later, Saint-Simon refused the regent's offer to make him keeper of the seals, and then (after the death of the duc de Bourbon) he also declined the position of Louis XV's "governor." Finally, after serving as ambassador to the Spanish court in 1721–22, Saint-Simon left the court for good.[35] In the memoirs, he would recall the Minority *lit de justice* as the only time when he had been capable, if only temporarily, of reversing the trend toward greater illegitimacy.

"Ce Jour de Justice et de Règle"

The French Parlements were primarily judicial courts, whose members were appointed by the king. For over a century, however, these bodies had been exercising a form of legislative power, by registering royal edicts before they came into effect. After the death of Louis XIV in 1715, in exchange for supporting the revision of the king's will, Philippe d'Orléans restored to the Parlements the right to refuse those royal decrees they considered contrary to the interests of the nation, the right to "preregistra-tion remonstrances." "A disastrous concession," writes Philippe Erlanger, "for which the Monarchy would continue to pay until its final day."[36]

In close collaboration with his friend Saint-Simon (and others, including John Law), the regent convened the Minority *lit de justice* of August 26, 1718, for the primary purpose of taking back the right to preregistration remonstrances. By the end of that day, Saint-Simon was convinced that the forces of legitimacy (led by himself) had inflicted a crushing defeat upon the dark forces of illegitimacy (represented by the Paris Parlement and the legitimated sons of Louis XIV). He would later recall it as the most satisfying day of his life: "I triumphed, I wallowed in revenge; I enjoyed [je jouissais du] the full accomplishment of the most vehement and continuous desires of all my life" (7:264, translation modified). But what made this summer morning so intensely satisfying for him was that every moment of his triumph occurred twice: first, at a meeting of the Regency Council in the Council chambers, and then at the *lit de justice*, on a stage constructed at the Tuileries Palace. In the text of his memoirs, Saint-Simon reenacts his triumphant *jouissance* twice in a row, on the same morning.[37] Like nearly everything else in the script for that morning, this moment of "voluptuousness," of "transport," repeats itself.[38] Every "act" is repeated, performed, each time on a different stage, before a different audience;[39] in the memoirs, Saint-Simon then replays each performance and makes detailed sketches of the sets and *dramatis personae*.

As mentioned above, an argument has been made for viewing the sec-ond performance of these actions—the *lit de justice*—in terms of what Louis Marin has called "the 'baroque' theory of political action," which "lies between the regime of ceremonial simulacrum, the ostentatious dis-play of signs in rituals and the instantaneous explosion of force, the shat-tering epiphany of violence in an act transcending good and evil."[40] From this perspective, the Minority *lit de justice* can be seen as the successful climax of a high political drama that played itself out entirely on a public stage. Viewed as baroque political action, this "play" can be said to have begun in 1714, when Louis XIV legitimized his bastards and raised them to a new ("intermediary") rank, between the princes of the blood and the dukes, thereby granting his male bastards the right to succeed to the throne. As I have said, however, I am not concerned with the *lit de justice* itself, but with Saint-Simon's representation of it. This representation, I shall contend, is symptomatic of a new historical situation, and of a more private and modern form of theater.

An Empty Chair

The Regency Council had been created in the hope of restoring to the nobility some of the power that it had lost to the (often bourgeois) ministers of Louis XIV. In 1718 there was a conspiracy afoot, centered at the court of the duc and duchesse du Maine at Sceaux, which aimed to overthrow the regent and put Philip V of Spain in his place. The duc de Saint-Simon was the only member of the Council still loyal to the regent. It was therefore of the utmost importance for the regent and his collaborators (Saint-Simon, d'Argenson, John Law) to plan their action with the greatest care, and in total secrecy.

Like the *lit de justice* that would take place later that morning, the Council meeting of August 26, 1718, reads like a heroic drama. The setting of the stage, every word and every gesture that are performed by the regent and his allies, form part of a scenario that has been calculated in advance. Saint-Simon portrays himself and his fellow courtiers as actors on a stage, who work at "composing themselves"[41] and wearing a "mask,"[42] all the while scrutinizing each other from behind these masks. In the framework of his drawings, the duke inscribes the characters' entries and exits, their gestures and words, as well as the reactions of all present to sudden reversals of fortune that evoke the *coups de théâtre* of French classical theater.[43] However, there is no publicly visible action to speak of, and there would have been very little at all for an audience to see. As readers, we know that a succession of blows has struck the allies of illegitimacy (of the duc and duchesse du Maine), but we know this only thanks to Saint-Simon's mediation. Only a small part of the action and conflict in this play takes place publicly, while the essence of the drama remains hidden from outside view. The real drama takes place on a private stage, that is accessible only to a reader.[44]

In fact, this private drama began to unfold before the meeting itself was convened. The meeting was to take place in the room at the Palais des Tuileries where the young king and his governor slept at night: this is why the drawing, in Saint-Simon's hand, bears the notations "The king's bed," "His tutor's bed." At Regency Council meetings, it was customary for the king's armchair at the head of the table to be empty, since the future Louis XV was only eight years old in 1718; the regent sat to the right of "the king," across the table from Monsieur le duc (de Bourbon). On this particular morning, as the drawing shows, the regent ("S.A.R.") placed his chair almost at the corner of the table, closer than usual to the king's empty seat at the head of the table. As Saint-Simon notes, the regent thus meant to draw his audience's attention to the fact that he was now sitting closer to the king's empty seat, and that his new position afforded him a dominating perspective on the assembly: "At the other end of the table the duc d'Orléans moved around a bit toward the king's empty chair, so that he could more easily see both sides of the table—something he never did as a rule. But apart from being able to see his side of the table better, I think he was not sorry to let himself be seen in a prominent position."[45] Before the meeting began, Philippe had privately admitted to the comte de Toulouse (the younger of Louis XIV's two surviving sons by Mme. de Montespan) that the decisions he was about to reveal would not be favorable to him (and even less so to his older brother, the duc du Maine), and that therefore the two royal bastards had his permission not to attend the meeting. This revelation produced the precise effect that the regent had doubtless intended, since the legitimized princes left the room. Moreover, they did so unnoticed, because all eyes were focused on the regent, who had taken a seat near one end of the table, while the duc du Maine and comte de Toulouse made their exit by a door at the other end of the room. This weakened their position and that of their many allies on the Council.[46]

This private drama thus opened with a question, conveyed by twenty-five uncomprehending glances (the entire Regency Council, minus Saint-Simon): "Where are the bastards?" One after another, the members of the Council noticed that the royal bastards were nowhere to be seen: "*One by one everyone failed to see them* [à mesure que chacun ne les vit point] as he went to his seat, *looked around for them* [les cherchait des yeux] and *remained standing* [restait debout], waiting."[47] One after another, twenty-five members of the Council failed to see: the past definite *vit* marks the successive onset of each individual's blindness, while the imperfect tense of *cherchait* conveys the duration of their fruitless search, and *restait debout* the spread of their collective paralysis. At least Saint-Simon's colleagues on the Council could see that something had been going on: but if this action had been performed on a conventional stage, the audience would still be waiting for the action to begin. Saint-Simon's reader, on the other hand, knows that the two royal bastards have already left the room, and why; the reader knows that there has been a dramatic reversal of fortune, a kind of *coup de théâtre*.

While the other twenty-five members of the Regency Council were asking what had become of the duc du Maine and the comte de Toulouse, Saint-Simon proceeded to answer their unspoken question, but in his own forceful way: by taking the seat that was customarily occupied

by the comte de Toulouse, one seat closer than usual to the regent (and
to the king's chair at the end of the table). At this moment, only the prince
de Condé sat between him and the regent. With this move, Saint-Simon
compelled each member of the Council to take a new position, literally—
and therefore implicitly to recognize the illegitimacy of the "intermediary"
rank formerly occupied by the royal bastards.

Each one of Saint-Simon's colleagues is then forced to "see" what he
has not been seeing, and to accept it. The gentleman on Saint-Simon's
right, de Guiche, repeatedly taxes him with taking the wrong seat. More
eloquently than any words, the silent contempt with which Saint-Simon
greets this reproach speaks both of his present attitude toward de Guiche
and of his overall strategy as a writer: "I gave him no answer, while studying the gathering, which was truly a sight."[48] In dramatic silence, the duke
offers himself the "sight" of his own victory, for himself and later for his
readers. His silence also conveys to Saint-Simon's colleagues that he (along
with Dubois, d'Argenson, and Law) is privy to the regent's secret intentions ("dans la bouteille," as he puts it [7:230]). Among other things, his
silence signifies that he deserves to know what de Guiche and the others
have not yet learned.

He alone (and therefore the reader, too) can relish the sight of his
triumph privately, in silence, where it gives him the most pleasure: where
he can enjoy displaying his own superiority, while taking pleasure in refusing to satisfy the curiosity of anyone below him. Saint-Simon finally asks
de Guiche to move up a seat, too; failing to elicit a response, he brutally
pulls the dumbfounded gentleman into the empty seat between them. Paradoxically, it is by making the arrogant de Guiche ("his nose in the air")
occupy an even *higher* rank that Saint-Simon actually forces him to submit.

The beginning of this "play" is thus organized around two highly significant absences. First, as I have suggested, there is no "action" to speak
of—that is, nothing done upon a public stage. Certainly the exit of the
royal bastards amounts to a sudden reversal of fortune, or *coup de théâtre*,
but it is a *coup de théâtre* utterly devoid of classical theatricality. Except
for Saint-Simon, the members of the Council (who are both actors and
audience in this play) do not even see Maine and Toulouse make their
exit. What the Council members do not see, and the fact that they do not
see it, is visible only to Saint-Simon and to his readers. In the second
place, all this action (or absence of action) revolves around a set of empty
seats: at the end of the table, on each side, are the unoccupied seats of
the Sun King's two illegitimate sons, which are taken by Saint-Simon and
the duc de Bourbon, who thereby force everyone else to move into an

empty chair, closer to the end of the table; then there is the seat at the head of the table, "the king's" seat, which (because of Louis XV's age) will remain empty.

"La Captivité de Mon Transport"

In the next "act" of this private drama, the regent strikes another blow to the enemies of legitimacy, by announcing that the first order of business at the *lit de justice* will be to confirm d'Argenson (an enemy of the Parlement) as keeper of the seals. While d'Argenson reads the letters of appointment *(lettres de provision)*, Saint-Simon carefully reads the eyes of his peers: "During this reading, which had no other purpose than to seize an occasion of forcing the Parlement to recognize the keeper of the seals, whose person and commission they hated, I spent my time studying the faces of those around me" (7:232, translation modified). In his account, the interplay of glances is charged with dramatic tension, which would have been invisible to a hypothetical theater audience. All the political drama is in Saint-Simon's representation of the faces *(mines)* of the participants, and in the interplay and interpretation of their glances: what they look at, what they see, and especially their control of their faces and eyes. In a celebrated passage of *Les Caractères*, La Bruyère had remarked that "a man who knows the ways of the Court is master of his gestures, his eyes and his face; he is deep, impenetrable."[49] That is, a successful courtier has to master his facial expressions, for to reveal one's reactions or thoughts is to make oneself vulnerable to manipulation by others. In Saint-Simon's version of the events, only he is "master" of his eyes, while everyone else's eyes are literally "stuck [fichés]" to the regent, by forces obviously beyond their control.

Saint-Simon observes their faces ("I spent my time studying the faces") and savors the spectacle—both of those who are in the know, who can see ("I saw M. le Duc d'Orléans with an air of authority and attention"), and of those who cannot see what is happening.[50] In a gallery of wickedly comic portraits, he reveals the stupefied maréchal d'Estrées, completely blind to what is really happening ("The maréchal d'Estrées had a stupefied air, as though he saw nothing but a mist before him," 7:233), the inordinately pompous marquis de Torcy ("Torcy, three times more pompous [empesé] even than usual, was slyly watching everything" [7:233, trans. Flower]), and the haggard, anxious eyes of the marquis d'Effiat ("Effiat, alert, irritated, angry, seemed ready to fly at someone's throat at every minute; his eyes were haggard, he frowned at everyone and kept glancing

quickly from one side of the room to the other," 7:233). From behind his
mask, Saint-Simon watches them all struggling to maintain their "self-
composure."[51] In the faces of his peers, the duke observes the drama building. He reads there the dawning realization, tinged with fear and spite,
that some calamity is about to befall the royal bastards, not to mention
the Parlement. With the appointment of d'Argenson, the party of illegitimacy has suffered a setback, but now they all realize, to their great confu-
sion, that even more devastating losses are yet to come: "Never have I
seen so many long faces around me, and never such universal and obvious
embarrassment" (7:234, trans. Flower).

   After a dramatic pause ("a short but significant pause," 7:234), the regent begins what might be called "act III," which will strike the most
painful blow to the Parlement and its allies on the Council. He moves on
to the most important item on the agenda of the *lit de justice*, the royal
decree nullifying the Parlement's right to make preregistration remonstrances. In a commanding tone of voice, Philippe d'Orléans praises the
justice of this decree and then (in a significant departure from normal
procedure) asks each member of the Council to take a stand on the question. In that moment, writes Saint-Simon, it was so quiet that "one might
have heard a cheese-mite walking" (7:235). Everyone, including Saint-
Simon, is surprised by the regent's commanding presence. Taken aback
and visibly dejected ("Their faces betrayed the discouragement they
felt," 7:233), the Parlement's allies on the Council realize that nothing can
be done. To their chagrin, the decree regulating remonstrances is unani-
mously adopted.

   Finally, it is time for act IV. The regent assumes an even more authoritative air ("drawing himself up [redressé d'un demi-pied] in his chair" [7:236;
trans. Flower, modified]) to announce the next order of business: the matter
of the royal bastards (whom he calls "the 'legitimized' . . . , without adding
the word 'Princes' "). Orléans explains that he has decided to "render justice"
to the princes of the blood by eliminating the "intermediary" rank (between
them and the peers) that Louis XIV had created for his illegitimate children.[52]
For Saint-Simon, this is the climax of the drama. But he cannot allow his
reaction to show. So he "composes" his countenance, "lays[s] an extra layer
of gravity and modesty [on his face]," 7:237–38), and struggles not to let
his mask fall.[53] As he listens, Saint-Simon is "transported" by the tension he
feels between his public and private selves:

> Contained in this manner, attentive in devouring everyone's expressions, alive
> to everything and to myself [présent à tout et à moi-même], glued to my chair,

my whole body under control, penetrated with the most acute and lively delight that joy could impart, and with the most charming anxiety, with an enjoyment [jouissance] so perseveringly and so immoderately hoped for, I sweated with anguish at the captivity of my transport, and this very anguish was of a voluptuousness such as I have never experienced, before that day or since. How inferior are the pleasures of the senses to those of the mind, and how true it is that the balance-weight of misfortunes is the good fortune that finishes them![54]

Saint-Simon represents himself (his Self) here as divided: torn between a hunger to feed his self-esteem by "devouring" the appearance of defeat on the faces of his enemies, and a need to maintain the appearance of seriousness and keep his exultation to himself. He is drawn at once inward ("contenu de la sorte"), toward containment and mastery of self, and outward ("attentif à dévorer l'air de tous"), toward others. Completely focused both on self and on others: literally, "present to everything and to myself." Saint-Simon is at once overwhelmingly "penetrated" by joy and ferociously intent on holding back, on containing the expression of his feelings. What he discovers, in the manner of a Tantric disciple, is that the very effort of self-constraint ("anguish," literally, "constriction") or self-containment makes possible a "spiritual" *jouissance* ("la plus *démésurément* et la plus persévéramment souhaitée*") that is above and beyond the pleasures of the senses.

But this *jouissance* does know limits. In his chapter on Corneille in *Canonical States, Canonical Stages*, Mitchell Greenberg has demonstrated the role of limits—especially the limit between death and immortality—in the "coming into being of the 'absolute' subject":

> In Corneille we are presented with . . . the coming into being of the "absolute" subject. . . . This dichotomy [death / immortality] . . . is present as the central debate in all of the four canonical tragedies as they elaborate the outlines of a new subjectivity. . . . [T]he subject becomes what we know as the "modern" interiorized, "self-conscious" subject by incorporating in self-interrogation the question of limits, posed in these plays as the problem of mortality.[55]

Greenberg shows that this subject is internally divided and subject to the absolute limit of death. What I am proposing to call the "post-absolutist" subject is similarly divided, and also confronted by the question of limits, but in a way that I shall specify below. Here let me simply note that limits are what make Saint-Simon's ravishment possible: "I sweated with *anguish at the captivity of my transport, and this very anguish was of a voluptuousness* such as I have never experienced, before that day or since" (7:238, emphasis added). The necessity of holding in his "transport" causes intense anguish, and from the very intensity of that anguish comes a "voluptuousness" such as he had never before experienced, and would only experience one more time, at the *lit de justice* itself.

But what is the nature of these limits, and what keeps his "transport" captive? If Saint-Simon were to reveal—that is, to represent—his transport, what difference would it make? In that case, it would be clear for all to see that the duc de Saint-Simon, this champion of legitimacy, experiences these events, above all, as a personal victory, and not as a victory for the ostensibly impersonal cause of legitimacy. By maintaining a façade of seriousness, of indifference—at the costs and with the benefits we have seen—the duke is able to convey his commitment to the rule of law over personal (even royal) pleasure. What keeps his transport captive, and thereby triggers his *jouissance*, is the authority of the law itself. By virtue of that "captivity," by subjecting his public transports to the law, the intensity of the duke's private *volupté* reaches a new peak. The exquisite anguish of his captive transport comes from being *subject to the law*, rather than to the king. Yet the law to which Saint-Simon subjects himself, under which he is a subject, this law is nowhere to be seen.

In Saint-Simon's account of the events, this "act" concludes with yet another crisis, which requires the duke's silent and heroic intervention. As d'Argenson reads the text of the decree eliminating the intermediary rank, the duc du Maine's allies on the Council can hardly contain themselves or their displeasure. Saint-Simon realizes that his enemies may lose control of themselves, and that he must do something about it:

> It took me but a few moments to perceive by the change in the expressions of those around me what was passing through their minds, and but a minute or two longer to realize that some remedy would have to be found for the despair I saw in Villeroy, and the fury I saw in Villars, if they were not to be carried too far astray by the disorder of their present feelings, which I realized it was beyond their power to master. (7:238; trans. Flower)

While d'Argenson is still reading the regent's declaration, the duke silently counters this threat. He removes from his pocket a seven-page document, signed by all the present dukes in February 1717, in which (under pressure of circumstances) they had formally requested that the king eliminate the intermediary rank.[56] Everyone looks at this document containing his signature, but no one dares inquire about it, and those who are seated closest to it once again cannot see what they are seeing: "everyone in turn looked at this strange document though no one else asked me what it was. Indeed it was recognizable enough, and although the Prince de Conti and the Duc de Guiche only asked because they were sitting next to me, I have never seen two men *less capable of seeing what they were seeing.*"[57]

Now that the allies of illegitimacy have been put back in their place, it is time for the regent to strike at them a fourth time. He announces that an exception to the previous ruling will be made for the comte de Toulouse, the duc du Maine's virtuous younger brother. He alone (but not his eventual offspring) will retain the intermediary rank between the peers and the princes of the blood. Just as, a moment before, some members of the Council could not see what they were seeing, now they cannot hear what they are hearing: "The astonishment it caused was general; it was such, that, to judge of those addressed, it seemed that they understood nothing; and they did not recover themselves during all the reading" (7:241). To the intense satisfaction of Saint-Simon, who had pointed to the tactical advantage of making this distinction, this news imprints a confession of guilt upon the faces of the duc du Maine's allies:

> Above all, those who had been particularly distressed by the first declaration seemed now to be even more upset by this panegyric in favor of the comte de Toulouse, as well as by the distinction it made between the two brothers. *In their first involuntary reaction they showed that it was a party matter with them,* since, if personal affection alone had been at work, the second announcement would have been some consolation to them, and not, as it clearly came in this case, as an aggravation of their distress, caused not only by the fact that it seemed to cast the duc du Maine into lower depths than ever, but also by the fact that unless the younger brother should deign from his distinguished position to stoop to his elder's aid, the elder would be deprived in future of his support. I was delighted by the evident success of our plan, *and triumphed inwardly.*[58]

Here again the duke "triumphs," but again he does so privately, in secret *(en moi-même).* Finally, in the last act of this play, his enemies receive what, in Saint-Simon's eyes, are the last, crushing blows: "Villars, Bezons, Effiat bent their shoulders *like people who had received the last blow*" (7:243, emphasis added). Louis XIV's legitimized sons having now become ineligible to inherit the throne, the regent entrusts the education of the future Louis XV to "Monsieur le duc" (Louis-Henri de Bourbon-Condé).[59] This decision marks the final step in the reversal of Louis XIV's last will and testament. "[H]ere are all the dispositions of the late King overthrown" (7:244), laments the maréchal de Villeroi. The regent's riposte to this feeble protest is brutally concise:

> "Monsieur," replied the regent, in a loud and animated voice, "M. du Maine is my brother-in-law, but I prefer an open enemy to a hidden one." At this great declaration several lowered their heads. Effiat kept shaking his from side to side. The maréchal de Villeroy nearly swooned; sighs began to make themselves heard near me, as though by stealth. Everybody felt by this that the scabbard was thrown away, and no one knew where the quarrel might end. (7:44, translation modified)

From Saint-Simon's perspective, these acts—which would be repeated at the *lit de justice*—marked a crushing defeat for the forces of illegitimacy and a glorious victory for legitimate forces, secretly led by him. But as he records for posterity the blindness of the Regency Council and the clarity of his own vision, he himself fails to see that this particular battle has been won thanks to the regent's decisive contempt for the opinion of the Regency Council and, by extension, for the principle of government by council.

More important, Saint-Simon fails to see that this pyrrhic victory also consecrates the triumph of law over blood. The practice of seating the king's illegitimate children between the princes of the blood and the peers had implied the absolute priority of blood over any other form of legitimacy. The regent's decision challenges the principle that blood and bloodlines are a legitimate basis for the exercise of power, if not also implicitly questioning the king's privilege of legitimizing his illegitimate children. As he prepares to savor his greatest moment of personal triumph, Saint-Simon does not see that rule of law, the principle that emerges victorious from this confrontation, will ultimately subvert not only illegitimate royal caprice ("notre bon plaisir"), but also aristocratic privilege. If bloodlines do not legitimize hierarchy, then the hereditary basis of both monarchy *and* nobility is in doubt. In this case, the victory of legitimacy, as Saint-Simon understands it, is also a defeat for the fundamental principle of absolutist monarchy: that while all legitimacy stems from the king (who engenders, fathers, the law), he himself is above the law, and is not subject to it.

Private Transport

Like nearly everything else on the morning's agenda, Saint-Simon's paradoxical experience of triumph is repeated at the *lit de justice*. At the *lit de
justice*, as he had done at the Council meeting, Saint-Simon takes the place
of one of Louis XIV's illegitimate sons, the comte de Toulouse: "The
consternation of the marshals . . . was evident. [N]ot seeing his master,
the duc du Maine, the First President cast a terrible glance at Monsieur
de Sully and me, who occupied exactly the seats of the two brothers"
(7:259, translation modified).

As he listens again to the reading of the text that abolishes the bastards' intermediary rank, and scrutinizes the reactions of his enemies in
the Parlement, Saint-Simon again knows the exquisite tension between
public constraint and private delight. In all senses of the word, it is for
him the *climax* of his life:

> In the meanwhile I was dying with joy; my pleasure was so great that I feared
> I might faint; my heart dilated to excess, and no longer found room to beat.
> The violence I did myself, in order to let nothing escape me, was infinite;
> and, nevertheless, this torment was delicious. I compared the years and the
> times of servitude, the grievous days when, dragged as a victim to the
> Parlement, I had repeatedly served as a pawn to the Bastards' triumph; the
> various steps by which they had mounted to the summit above our heads; I
> compared them, I say, with this day of justice and rule, with this frightful fall
> which, at the same time, raised us by the force of the shock. With rapturous
> delight I recalled what I had dared to tell the Duc du Maine on the scandalous
> day of the cap [jour du bonnet], under the despotism of his father. I could
> see before my eyes that my threat had been accomplished. I owed it to myself
> [Je me devais],[60] I thanked myself that it was through me that this had been
> brought about. I gazed upon the radiant splendor of my triumph *in presence
> of the King* and this august assembly. I triumphed, I wallowed in revenge; *I
> enjoyed [je jouissais de]* the full accomplishment of desires the most vehement
> and most continuous of all my life. (7:263–64, emphasis added)

It is a retroactive, specular vision of the Self as godlike origin, witness,
and recorder of the action. An exhaustive account of the reasons why this
spectacle had such a powerful effect on the duke would require one to
summarize at least the previous three years of his *Mémoires*, starting with
the famous "cap affair" of 1714–15,[61] if not with the earliest real or imagi-

nary slights to his honor that Saint-Simon had suffered at the hands of
Louis XIV, the duc and duchesse du Maine, and the Parlement de Paris.

Saint-Simon, of course, idealized the era of Louis XIII, when his own
father acceded to the rank of duke. It is therefore not surprising that these
passages, which celebrate the reestablishment of the nobility's legitimate
prerogatives, should resonate with what Coirault calls an aristocratic,
"Cornelian" heroism of vengeance.[62] The wounded honor of the peers is
avenged, legitimate hierarchy (that is, before Louis XIV) is restored, and
all of this thanks to a single man: "it was through me that this had been
brought about." Like a moment of divine grace, the "radiant splendor"
of Saint-Simon's vengeance illuminates the entire scene, and with its very
brilliance displays the usurped glory of the Sun King in its true—that is,
illegitimate—light. Imagining himself, anachronistically, as a post-absolutist reincarnation of Rodrigue in Corneille's *Cid* (1636), he celebrates
this reversal of fortune (or *coup de théâtre*) in the presence of the (eight-
year-old) king.

Yet the private character of the noble's triumph and the purely symbolic
status of the king are two departures from the tradition of aristocratic self-
glorification to which Saint-Simon alludes. For this reason, the climax of
Saint-Simon's life contains a paradox: the apparently anachronistic or reactionary *volupté* of personally ending the "despotic" rule of royal *bon plaisir*,
of triumphantly restoring the noble ego to its former splendor and reestablishing pre-absolutist legitimacy, can only be experienced in captivity, by a
self that has already been subjected to the law. As he took the illegitimately
acquired seat of the comte de Toulouse, and moved that much closer to
the head of the table, Saint-Simon may have contributed to the momentary
triumph of legitimacy, but he also hastened the day when the entire noble
order would be subject, not to the absolute monarch, but to the rule of
law. Publicly he is subordinate to the law rather than to the king, while
privately he is transported by joy beyond mortal limits ("I was dying of
joy"). A subject like any other in public, in his silent capacity he rises
above his peers, above even the Sun King: in private, he is a god.

One could say that Saint-Simon is "experiencing," in the anguish of
his divided self, a form of post-absolutist transport, that the structure of
his experience is already that of the modern, political subject, for whom
all *volupté*, all transport is best enjoyed in private. Due to its essentially
private character, such a victory could henceforth be savored only in
memory, in writing; from then on this *jouissance* could be experienced
only vicariously, in private, and alone. In the early eighteenth century
the lines between these two forms of subjectivity are not clearly drawn;

their boundaries remain unstable. What I am proposing to call the post-absolutist subject is divided between the modest (self-effacing) self it presents in public ("I had put an additional layer of gravity and modesty on my face")—the self that is subject to the law—and a private self, one that aspires to the immortal glory of a god, a self that will brook no limits whatsoever, not even death. This private self is constructed (starting perhaps with Montaigne) in the solitary practice of writing.[63]

As Reinhart Kosseleck has shown, the initial division of the subject into public and private halves was a historical achievement of absolutism. Born in the context of the religious wars, absolutism expressed an overwhelming desire to achieve unity and suppress dissension, by any means necessary and at any cost. To Hobbes and other theoreticians of absolutism, the separation of politics from morality was a practical necessity. The fratricidal chaos of the religious wars could only be avoided, they maintained, if individual conscience was subjected to a morally neutral *raison d'État*. The separation of politics from morality thus entailed a complete separation between the public man, or citizen (rationally subjected to the sovereign), and the private man (who kept his opinions to himself): "man is cut in two: a private half and a public half; actions and acts are subjected without exception to the law of the State, while conviction is *in secret free*."[64] To put an end to the religious wars, absolutism required everyone to acquiesce to the moral necessity of abdicating one's conscience to the monarch. In so doing, it profoundly modified the status of subjectivity in the ancien régime, by making everyone equally subject to the sovereign. Before the age of absolutism, the identity of a political subject was defined in terms of multiple and sometimes conflicting loyalties (family, guild, religion, "feudal" obligations), but absolutism reduced the identity of the subject to a single, universal standard: absolute submission to the sovereign. "It is only if all subjects are equally subjected to the sovereign that the latter can take sole responsibility for peace and order. This gesture radically alters the status of subjects, who until then had found their place in a system of responsibility that, even though it had become lax, was multiple: they were members of one of the Churches, dependent upon vassals, in the framework of local political institutions or of States."[65] The advent of the post-absolutist subject is thus marked by two significant departures from the absolutist model. The first of these changes affects the relationship between the king and the law. Under absolutism, the notion of "fundamental" law had been invoked in discussions of royal succession, primarily to dismiss the idea of an eventual interregnum: "Shielding the integrity of concrete sovereignty—the *lex animata*—the law replaced *in extremis* the monarch's will, faltering in death. The law replaced the king only when the king was dead."[66] Under post-absolutism, however, what had been a pragmatic, temporary arrangement became a permanent state of affairs in which everyone (including the king) implicitly became subject to a new principle of sovereignty, equally subjected to a new agency: the law. As the law replaced the king as the transcendent principle to which everyone was publicly subject, in private everyone (regardless of birth) would aspire like Saint-Simon to overcome his or her subjection and occupy the very place that had been occupied by the immortal body of the absolute monarch.[67]

At the Regency Council meeting, when Saint-Simon first celebrates the divine ("présent à tout et à moi-même") *jouissance* of his private vengeance (in the "presence" of the king's empty chair), and later at the *lit de justice*, where he once again (like a new Sun King) savors the godlike, "radiant splendor" of his victory ("in the King's presence"), he also testifies to a kind of historical paralysis. For his own, private representation of these experiences suggests that in the absolute, absolutist sense, "the king" had died with Louis XIV, and that thereafter no king of France would regain the symbolic efficacy of the Sun King; that in fact every "king" of France would henceforth be condemned, by forces beyond his control, to act as a regent.

"Le Poète Roy"

Voltaire's *Œdipe*

My lord, you will be a great poet; I must procure you a pension from the king. . . . Are we all princes? or are we all poets? — VOLTAIRE, *Commentaire historique sur les Œuvres de l'auteur de la* Henriade

THE MAN WHO WOULD become known to his contemporaries as M. de Voltaire and "Roi de Ferney" ("the king of Ferney") was born in 1694 as François-Marie Arouet, the son of a wealthy lawyer. At the age of twenty-four, in 1718, he started calling himself Arouet *de Voltaire* in private correspondence. He did not come out with this new identity publicly until early 1719, in the dedication of the first edition of his play *Œdipe*.[1]

Voltaire would eventually claim to have begun work on *Œdipe* when he was eighteen years old (in 1712), a claim that is probably exaggerated. It is nevertheless remarkable that, unlike most of Voltaire's subsequent plays, *Œdipe* was not rapidly thrown together, but carefully composed and revised over some six years.[2] We shall probably never know precisely what was contained in the manuscript of *Œdipe* that he submitted to the Comédie-Française in 1715 or 1716, and which was judged unacceptable.[3] Apparently the players objected to Voltaire's having written a role for a Greek-style chorus and wanted him to develop the female love interest, by adding a scene for the usual female lead. The idea for the chorus may have come from a performance of Racine's *Athalie* that the young poet had witnessed at Sceaux. His goal, he later contended, had been to return to "*Oedipus* in all its Greek simplicity."[4] In any case, Voltaire seems to have overcome the objections of the Comédie-Française by April 1717, when the first performance of *Œdipe* was declared imminent. The production had to be delayed until the fall of 1718, however, after the author was released from a term in the Bastille.

In the twentieth century, even the best of Voltaire's plays are no longer performed, and are of interest primarily to scholars.[5] His *Œdipe* has not been staged even once in the twentieth century, even though scholars continue to find the play worthy of publication and commentary (it has been published, for example, in the Pléiade anthology of eighteenth-century theater).[6] It is all the more remarkable that the play was (in the words of Theodore Besterman) "an immediate and unique success" with contemporary critics and theatergoers, starting with its first performance (by the Comédie-Française) on November 18, 1718, and that "its record of thirty almost consecutive performances in its first run was not surpassed in Paris by any other eighteenth-century tragedy."[7] Moreover, Voltaire's Oedipus tragedy was so successful that it made audiences forget about the great Corneille's *Œdipe* (a patently "oedipal" effect, to which I shall return below). Voltaire's Oedipus tragedy struck such a powerful chord with its contemporaries that it returned a record 3,000 francs in profits to the young author.[8] Legend has it that Voltaire was also rewarded by the regent with a valuable gold medal (worth 675 livres and 10 sous), with the effigy of Louis XV on one side and that of the regent on the other.[9]

We may think of *Œdipe* as a mediocre tragedy, but Voltaire's first play moved contemporary audiences in a powerful way. As we shall see, the play's political context can account for part of its success.[10] In any case, *Œdipe* marked the beginning of Voltaire's highly successful career both as a poet and as an investor. Voltaire and his audience made significant financial and personal investments in this Oedipus tragedy, and they seem to have derived various types of benefits from it. It is important to note that the first public appearance of "Arouet de Voltaire" occurred in the dedication of a tragedy, that the topic of that tragedy was the Oedipus myth, and that Voltaire's *Œdipe* was a remake of the Oedipus tragedies of Sophocles and Corneille. The poet's gesture of publicly calling himself "de Voltaire" exemplified the post-absolutist agency that is also embodied by the characters in his *Œdipe*. In this chapter we shall see how the Oedipus myth enabled "de Voltaire" to issue his own letters of poetic nobility, assert the struggle of reason against blind superstition, and implicitly define himself (like Saint-Simon) as a post-absolutist subject.

"Le Poète Roy"

The meaning of the pen name chosen by François-Marie Arouet (the word, or letters VOLTAIRE) has been a matter of ingenious and erudite guesswork, primarily because Voltaire seems never to have discussed the subject.[11] However, in a letter written early in 1719 to the poet Jean-Baptiste Rousseau, he does say why he stopped calling himself Arouet. This remark occurs in the dedication to the copy of *Œdipe* that he sent to Rousseau, just below the author's signature ("Voltaire," without noble particle), he writes: "J'ai été si malheureux sous le nom d'Arouet que j'en ai pris un autre surtout pour n'être plus confondu avec le poète Roy" ("I have been so unfortunate under the name of Arouet that I have taken another one, especially in order to be confused no more with the poet Roy," *D* 72). In this elliptical postscript, "Voltaire" thus supplies two distinct reasons for having changed his name: he has been unhappy (or perhaps unfortunate) as Arouet, and particularly unhappy because people have confused him (Arouet [pronounced "ah-roo-ay"]) with "le poète Roy" (pronounced "roo-ay").

The "poète Roy" to whom Voltaire alludes here was Pierre-Charles Roy (1683–1764), a mediocre rival and enemy, whom he also encountered at other stages of his career.[12] Nearly three years earlier, in summer (?) 1716, in a letter written from exile at his father's home in Sully-sur-Loire, François-Marie Arouet had reproached the marquise de Mimeure for favoring Roy with a letter: "Remember that you wrote to Roy, and that you did not write to me" (*D* 40). In 1719, even after the success of *Œdipe*, the possibility of being mistaken for Pierre-Charles Roy was still apparently more than a triumphant young Arouet could bear. By going public as Arouet de Voltaire (or de Voltaire, or simply Voltaire), he could avoid comparison with a mediocrity; by signing this name to an Oedipus tragedy, he put himself in a position to choose his own rivals (Sophocles, Shakespeare, Corneille, Racine) from among the great poets of the past.

Of course, the common noun *roy* also meant "king," and therefore *le poète Roy* also means "the poet king." Eventually, when the name of Voltaire had become celebrated throughout Europe, the former François-Marie Arouet would not mind being called Roy (de Ferney ["king of Ferney"]). In 1719, though, the author of *Œdipe* still felt the need to declare that he was not Roy.

The poet also needed to tell the world that he was not Aròuet: "J'ai été si malheureux *sous le nom d'Arouet* [literally, "under" the name of Arouet,

subjected to this name] que j'en ai pris un autre" (emphasis added). This
refusal to identify himself as Arouet has been interpreted in various ways.
For one thing, the poet could have been repudiating his social class: by
calling himself de Voltaire, he could dignify the common, bourgeois con-
sonance of Arouet. In the second place, he could have used the name de
Voltaire to repudiate the name of his father (or maybe one should say his
putative father, since the identity of his biological father is not certain).[13]
Although Voltaire never drew attention to the fact, it is obvious that he
also suffered oedipally, as it were, from the name Arouet, since it distressed
him to be identified with his father's name. In fact, José-Michel Moureaux
has interpreted Œdipe as "an attempt to exorcise the guilt-inducing image
of the dead father."[14] Voltaire sometimes went so far as to claim ignorance
of his father's identity. On several occasions he claimed that his real father
was a minor poet named Rochebrune ("musketeer, officer, writer"), and
not François Arouet ("who was by nature a very commonplace man"),
or intimated that his mother's husband was not his father.[15] There is also
a certain oedipal register in Voltaire's relationships with women. In the
context of his "psychocritical" reading of Œdipe, Moureaux has shown
how strongly Voltaire was attracted to older women, some of them considerably older than himself.[16]

François Arouet was a narrow-minded and authoritarian gentleman
who wanted François-Marie to become a lawyer, like himself, and certainly
not a poet. In 1713 Arouet père tried to remove his son from the corrupting
influence of the free-thinking libertin environment. So he sent François-
Marie off, first to Caen, and then to the Netherlands. Shortly after arriving
in The Hague in 1713, young Arouet (then nineteen years old) proceeded
to fall in love with a girl named Catherine Olympe du Noyer, and tried
to elope with her. At this point, Arouet père obtained a *lettre de cachet*
and threatened to use it to have his son exiled to the West Indies, if the
affair with Olympe did not come to an immediate end.[17] A few years later,
François-Marie was sentenced to the Bastille, and then to three months of
comfortable internal exile, for publishing a satirical epigraph in which the
regent was accused of committing incest with his eldest daughter Elisabeth,
duchesse de Berry.[18] When the young man was finally released, his father
complained that the regent had treated François-Marie too leniently: "the
Regent has been pleased to recall my son from his exile, which I found
less of an affliction than this far too precipitate recall, which will complete
the ruin of this young man drunk with the success of his poetry and the
praises and the reception he received from the great, who, with all the
respect I owe them, are for him sheer poisoners."[19]

It has also been suggested that Voltaire wanted to reject his family name because its pronunciation evoked *roué*, a term initially used to designate a dissolute companion of the regent. The young poet had been a frequent companion of the freethinking, hedonistic libertins who regularly met at the medieval fortress called the Temple, and perhaps had shown them the first draft of *Œdipe;* in 1718 he may not have wanted to have the name of Arouet publicly associated with *roués*.[20] Certainly, the name of Arouet, with all its associations, was not compatible with the tragic dignity to which Voltaire aspired in 1718.

Many years later Giacomo Casanova (who also invented a noble name for himself) justified calling himself Casanova de Seingalt by citing the example of Voltaire. As he pointed out, the name Arouet had yet another unfortunate association for Voltaire: it sounded like *à rouer* ("to be beaten"): "L'alphabet est public, et chacun est le maître de s'en servir pour créer une parole et la faire devenir son propre nom; Voltaire n'aurait pas pu aller à l'immortalité avec le nom d'Arouet. On lui aurait interdit l'entrée du temple lui fermant les portes au nez. Lui-même se serait avili s'entendant toujours appler *à rouer*." ("The alphabet is public, and everyone has the power of using it to create a word and make it into his own name; Voltaire could not have become immortal under the name of Arouet. He would have been forbidden access to the temple, and the doors would have been closed to his face. He would have felt himself degraded by hearing himself always called *à rouer*.")[21] Casanova is probably alluding here to the famous incident that took place in 1725, when the chevalier de Rohan had Voltaire beaten by his lackeys.[22] Rohan and his kinsman Sully were obviously not disposed to recognize the nobility of de Voltaire's poetic achievements. For them, he remained simply Arouet or *à rouer*— a commoner who needed a good beating to put him back in his place.[23] By having him beaten, Rohan was correcting the noble signature, contemptuously refusing to dignify this bourgeois with a noble particle, or even to address him directly. By having his lackeys administer a beating to the ambitious young poet, Rohan responded to de Voltaire's signature gesture, but he responded indirectly, through his lackeys, thus refusing to dignify a lawyer's son with a personal response. "He is Rohan," he had them say, "and you are Arouet/*à rouer*." In a sense, Rohan had de Voltaire beaten in order to set their names straight and thereby preclude any possibility of dialogue with a vulgar bourgeois.

In sum, there are several plausible reasons why, in early 1719, François-Marie Arouet might have wanted to publish the fact that he was not "the poet Roy." At the very least, the name de Voltaire enabled the poet to say that he was not the son of François Arouet, not a bourgeois, and not a mediocre or common person. Voltaire would not tolerate being confused with Arouet, Roy, or any other "common" name. Moreover, by signing himself Arouet de Voltaire, the poet not only repudiated his father but simultaneously denied one identity and affirmed another.

Noblesse de Plume

The dedication of *Œdipe* concludes as follows: "I am, with deep respect / MADAME, / The most humble and obedient/servant, / OF YOUR ROYAL HIGHNESS, // AROUET DE VOLTAIRE." Since every signature is implicitly dialogic (that is, it validates, or establishes a relationship between interlocutors), it is important to consider the relationship that Arouet de Voltaire defined with his interlocutor, "Madame . . . Your Royal Highness." Scholars have disagreed as to the identity of the royal lady to whom Arouet de Voltaire dedicated his first play. He had first requested permission to dedicate *Œdipe* to the regent himself. However, there is no record of the regent's response to this letter, which the young poet had the prudence to sign without a noble particle, simply as Voltaire.[24] The first scholarly editors of Voltaire (Beuchot, Moland) believed that the dedicatee was the regent's wife, Françoise-Marie de Bourbon.[25] Françoise-Marie de Bourbon was not only the wife of Philippe d'Orléans, but also the illegitimate (and subsequently legitimized) daughter of Louis XIV. As part of the policy of legitimizing his illegitimate offspring, Louis XIV had imposed the marriage between Françoise-Marie de Bourbon, his daughter by Mme. de Montespan, and his nephew Philippe, the future regent. Like her illegitimate siblings, the regent's wife owed her title to royal decree. If Arouet de Voltaire did indeed dedicate *Œdipe* to her, he used this signature to make the implicit claim that having tested his powers with an *Œdipe*, and triumphed, Arouet de Voltaire had earned the right to address his play to the daughter of the Sun King, as one noble to another. François-Marie Arouet de Voltaire would thus effectively have suggested that his poetic nobility was at least as legitimate as that of his legitimized homonym, Françoise-Marie de Bourbon.

More recent Voltaire experts (Besterman, Pomeau) have identified the dedicatee of *Œdipe* with the regent's mother, Charlotte-Elizabeth de Bavière, the princesse Palatine. There does not seem to be enough evidence conclusively to prove either hypothesis.[26] In either case, by signing himself Arouet de Voltaire, the poet was declaring to this great lady (and

OUVRAGES CLASSIQUES

DE L'ÉLÉGANT POËTE

MR. AROUET,

FAMEUX SOUS LE NOM

DE VOLTAIRE.

NOUVELLE EDITION.

Ces Ecrits chez les Hommes éternifent fa gloire ;
Sans d'autres que l'on nomme d'inutile memoire.   I.

TOME PREMIER.

non movent

A OXFORD,

POUR LES ACADEMICIENS.

M DCC LXXI.

Frontispiece to Voltaire, *Œuvres* (1771). Photo: Roger-Viollet.

to the world) that Arouet de Voltaire had been recognized, with the implicit authorization of the regent, as a worthy interlocutor for one of the noblest ladies in France.[27] Under the same signature, Arouet de Voltaire also sent copies of *Œdipe* to other European princes.[28]

In sum, François-Marie Arouet wrote *Œdipe* in order to "make a name" for himself, literally: to make himself known to the world, and to do so nobly, as de Voltaire. In the words of René Pomeau: "*Œdipe* will not be the work of Arouet, but of Monsieur de Voltaire. Does not the dignity of tragedy require such a change?"[29] By coming out with a successful Oedipus, M. de Voltaire portrayed himself as a great (and therefore noble) dramatist, as "the author of *Œdipe*."[30]

Since Voltaire himself said so little about his name, scholars will doubtless continue to wonder about its origins and implications. It is possible that, as Pomeau has observed, the name was above all a theatrical mask.[31] Indeed, the attempt to determine the precise meaning of the name may be fundamentally irrelevant. Perhaps what really mattered to Voltaire was precisely that his name should have no previously determined meaning, that it be an empty symbol upon which only he (through his public actions) could confer meaning. With *Œdipe*, Voltaire issued his own letters of nobility and decreed the nobility of the man of letters. By signing himself Arouet de Voltaire, the poet staked his claim to a new form of nobility, founded upon poetic achievement rather than birth—what might be called the *noblesse de plume*.

Pomeau contends that since Voltaire could not inherit a noble title, he had to elevate his own field of action (poetry) to the level of heroism: "The son of M. Arouet meant to raise himself to the only form of work of any concern to great poetry. In 1718, the author of *Œdipe*, the future author of the *Henriade*, considers himself poised to accomplish this kind of feat, similar to those accomplished by his Philoctète in a different world."[32] In addition, like the Philoctetes character in *Œdipe* (to whom I shall return), Arouet *de Voltaire* asserts that personal worth cannot be inherited, but must be acquired and proved. Voltaire extends the notion of heroism beyond the realm of physical confrontation, to include poetic (and eventually, moral) achievement in the public arena.

Voltaire was convinced that a successful tragic poet (like himself) was worth more than an idle nobleman who had done nothing to deserve his title, and he later claimed to have expressed this opinion as early as 1718. In a "biography" of M. de Voltaire (actually a sort of autobiography, composed by Voltaire himself between 1772 and 1776),[33] the great man confirms a legend that has arisen about himself: that in 1718, he ("the author of *Œdipe*") had asked Louis-Armand de Conti, an amateur poet (and, according to Besterman, "a degenerate nincompoop"),[34] "Are we all princes? or are we all poets?"[35] Whether or not Voltaire actually expressed such bold ideas to the prince de Conti, the regent himself heard similar sentiments proclaimed during the several performances of *Œdipe* that he honored with his presence.

In the dedication of *Œdipe*, the mask of Arouet de Voltaire first entered the public stage. In this dedication, one can applaud the first public act in the nonstop performance that would be Voltaire's life.[36] Theatrical action, and theater in particular, would become for Voltaire a way of asserting the struggle of reason against blind superstition, and of philosophy against the injustice of nature. As we shall see, *Œdipe* also formulates a theatrical conception of human agency—one that I shall call post-absolutist.

Oedipal Investments

To account for the extraordinary success achieved by this interesting, but remarkably undistinguished play, one has to put *Œdipe* in its historical and political context. That context is characterized, first, by a specific relationship between the Oedipus figure and theatrical space. In *Canonical States, Canonical Stages*, Mitchell Greenberg argues that theatrical space under absolutism had a fundamentally "oedipal" character.[37] He suggests that during the historical transition from the Renaissance and Reformation to the age of absolutism, European theater redefined the figure of Oedipus, and used it to mediate between the public and private dimensions of subjectivity:

> The theater, that most "public" form of representation, by mediating the conflicting demands of societal and individual narratives, traces the parameters, in and through the figure of Oedipus, by which the subject of the Renaissance, a subject defined by different familial, corporate, and religious structures, is slowly reconformed as the subject of modernity, the subject defined by and through the internalization of Oedipus's sacrifice.[38]

According to Greenberg, absolutist culture represented its desire for unity with characteristic ambivalence in the patriarchal figure of the king, who was both consciously idolized and unconsciously mocked, at once the object of intense love and murderous hatred: in a word, "the *pharmakos* of emerging, premodern Europe." Since it is impossible to distinguish between individual and collective identity while in the theater, theater is always a fundamentally ambivalent space.[39] Moreover, Greenberg maintains, the powerfully ambivalent feelings of seventeenth-century audiences toward the absolute monarch converged and became bound to the contradictions of the Oedipus myth, which "constantly attempts to replay . . . the journey of the subject away from forces of duality and contradiction toward an attempted (but always unsuccessful) compromise with societal laws."[40]

After the death of Louis XIV in 1715, these ambivalent feelings were transferred from the Sun King to the regent, who was then himself explicitly portrayed as an Oedipus figure. The young Arouet had been condemned to prison (plus three months of internal exile) for allegedly writing a scandalous Latin poem that accused the regent of (among other crimes) incestuous relations with his daughter.[41] Moreover, he had already taken a risk by resubmitting an Oedipus tragedy to the Comédie-Française, in a version that contained explicit allusions to the dissolute morals of Philippe d'Orléans.[42] The rumors of Philippe's incestuous relationship with his daughter (and other alleged crimes) made Œdipe controversial long before the play was performed. The public was therefore convinced that Voltaire's Oedipus play would attack the regent. In early November of 1718, according to Philippe Erlanger, "in Paris, the only subject of conversation was the play written in the Bastille by the young Voltaire, an Œdipe. The title Œdipe suggested incest: but was it the incest of the king of Thebes or the Regent's incest?"[43]

During the rehearsals, "a little Fronde began around the Théâtre Français." Leading this mini-Fronde from her court at Sceaux was the duchesse du Maine, Louis XIV's illegitimate daughter, whose great ambitions had suffered a crushing defeat at the *lit de justice* of August 26, 1718, when (as we have seen in chapter 1) the rank of her husband, the duc du Maine, was lowered by royal edict.

Two further circumstances lent color to the scandalous rumors about Œdipe. First, one of Philippe's former mistresses, Charlotte Desmares, was to play the role of Jocaste; second, Philippe's daughter, the duchesse du Berry, with whom he was alleged to be having an incestuous affair, had become visibly pregnant: " 'Oedipus would not attend the performance alone,' murmured the pedants, 'but the presence of a future Eteocles would also be noticeable.' "[44] Members of the opposition to Philippe's regency figured prominently among the noisy crowd at the first performance. Indeed, rumor had it that someone had dared to cross out the name Œdipe on the bill and replace it with *Philippe*.[45] Nevertheless La Motte, the royal censor, allowed *Œdipe* to appear, and the regent himself attended several performances.[46] The fact that Philippe d'Orléans not only tolerated Voltaire's *Œdipe*, but actually viewed it several times helps explain why, despite all the scandalous rumors about the play, the poet first requested permission to dedicate *Œdipe* to the regent himself.

The oedipal investments of Voltaire's audience (both in their conception of theatrical space and in their images of the king and regent) must have contributed to the success of this play, while the poet himself used his first tragedy to engage in an oedipal dialogue with his father (and by extension, with all guilt-inducing agents of authority). On another level, one might add that when Arouet de Voltaire obtained the regent's permission to dedicate *Œdipe* to "Your Royal Highness . . . Madame," he was defining his identity in relation to a maternal figure, with the tacit permission and mediation of the regent, a "good" (that is, nonrepressive, enlightened) father figure.

Taking Money from a Subject

Not only did this play serve as a vehicle for dialogue with the poet's repressive father, with the permissive regent, and with other representatives of European royalty, but it also enabled Arouet de Voltaire to address the authority of a poetic "father," Pierre Corneille (whose own *Œdipe* had appeared in 1659). Like the Oedipus story itself, the story of Voltaire's relationship to Pierre Corneille is one of troubled, vexed filiation.[47] Voltaire wrote often, and at great length, about the differences between his Oedipus tragedy and the most famous, authoritative versions of the play, especially that of Pierre Corneille. The first public evidence of this Oedipal dialogue can be found in the lengthy "Letters Written by the Author, Which Contain a Critique of the *Oedipus* of Sophocles, of That of Corneille and of His Own," published with Voltaire's *Œdipe* in the first edition of 1719. The letters clearly demonstrate the ambition of Arouet de Voltaire to use the Oedipus story as a vehicle for defining himself as a worthy rival to two of his poetic fathers, Sophocles and Corneille. Just as he composed the play to assert himself as de Voltaire, the poet first wrote the "Lettres sur *Œdipe*" to assert himself as the legitimate heir of Sophocles and Corneille. He briefly returned to Oedipus in the 1730 preface to *Œdipe*, and over thirty years later he came back to the subject in the first edition of the *Commentaires sur Corneille* (written between 1762 and 1765, as part of his edition of Corneille's dramatic works).[48] Voltaire's public dialogue with Corneille concluded in 1775 (three years before his death) with the publication of a second, revised edition of the *Commentaires sur Corneille*. This network of texts testifies to Voltaire's lifelong engagement with Corneille, tragedy, and the Oedipus story. Although the success of his tragedies *Zaïre* (1732), *Alzire* (1735), and *Mérope* (1743) finally established Voltaire as the undisputed master of the contemporary tragic stage, he never abandoned his lifelong determination to rival, if not surpass, Corneille.

In 1719 it had been a bold step indeed for the ambitious young poet Arouet to publish himself as Arouet de Voltaire. By the early 1760s, although so many of Voltaire's contemporaries now recognized his own *noblesse de plume*, the princes of Europe (exemplified by Fredrick II) were still unwilling to consider M. de Voltaire or any man of letters as a worthy interlocutor in serious (that is, political) matters. When Voltaire decided, in April 1760, to prepare a subscription edition of Corneille's plays,[49] as a means of amassing a dowry for an impoverished descendant of the great poet, he meant to teach those princes a lesson about the nobility of men of letters. For this edition (first published in 1765) Voltaire began (in June 1761) to compose his extensive *Commentaires sur Corneille*. In these commentaries, M. de Voltaire passes judgment, not only on the great Corneille, but also on the powerful men for whom Corneille wrote.[50]

It was with a mixture of incomprehension and indignation that Voltaire turned to the dedication of Corneille's *Œdipe*, published over a century earlier, in 1659. His reaction testifies to profound changes that had taken place since the end of what Voltaire himself had called "the century of Louis XIV." Corneille had dedicated *Œdipe* to Mazarin's superintendent of finance, Nicolas Fouquet, the great patron of Molière and La Fontaine.[51] Fouquet apparently suggested that Corneille (after a seven-year absence from the theater) compose an Oedipus tragedy.[52] So it was that in the opening lines of his dedicatory verses, Corneille implored his Muse to scale the heights occupied by the "great genius" who had brought him back into favor: "Let thy flight rise up unto that *great genius* / Who recalls you to the light from which your age had banished you, / Muse, . . ." (emphasis added). In the margin of these verses, Voltaire protested: "This great genius was not *Nicolas Fouquet*, it was Pierre Corneille."[53] And by the time he reached the flattering third stanza of Corneille's dedication, Voltaire was palpably outraged at Corneille's sycophantic willingness to prostitute his talents by taking money from a subject of the king and making him such poor verses in exchange:

[I]t would have been better, in my opinion, for the author of *Cinna,* to live in Rouen on brown bread and glory, than to *receive money from a subject of the king, and to make him such shoddy verses for his money* [emphasis added]. One can never insufficiently exhort men of genius never to *prostitute* [emphasis added] *their talents* in this way. One is not always master of his fortune, but one can always obtain respect for one's modest resources, and even for one's poverty. (7:8)

Of course, Voltaire expected that a poet should be well paid for his work (his own *Œdipe* had been a profitable investment), but he found it degrading for a "great genius" to have accepted money from a vulgar magistrate, a "subject of the king."

In contrast, we recall that Arouet de Voltaire had dedicated his *Œdipe* to one of the noblest ladies in the kingdom, with the implicit approval of the regent, who then is said to have rewarded him with a gold medal. A century after Corneille's *Œdipe,* observes Voltaire, Fouquet is known only for his downfall at the hands of Louis XIV, while "the author of *Cinna* will forever be known to all nations, and this despite his last plays, and despite his verses to Fouquet" (7:16). For Voltaire, Corneille would remain "the author of *Cinna*"—the author of plays that offered princes instruction in the art of governing—just as Voltaire would portray himself as "the author of *Œdipe*"—a man to whom Frederick II (among others) should have been listening.

What especially rankled Voltaire about the dedication of Corneille's *Œdipe* was the poet's willingness to let Fouquet treat him like a tailor or cabinetmaker, with whom one places an order for goods: "It is as if Fouquet had ordered a tragedy from Corneille, to be delivered in two months, as one orders a suit from a tailor, or a table from a cabinet-maker" (7:16). Perhaps Voltaire reacts so vehemently to Fouquet's lack of respect for Corneille's genius because it implies that a vulgar *procureur général de Paris* could treat the noble Corneille like a lackey, as if the great poet were *à rouer.*

Oedipus and the "Defect of the Subject"

In the first edition of *Œdipe* (1719), the text of the play was published with the series of critical letters mentioned above. In these letters M. de Voltaire, the self-styled heir of the greatest tragic dramatists, invokes the principles of French classical orthodoxy (decorum, plausibility, taste) to

pass judgment on the work of his distinguished predecessors, as well as
on his own. Using these criteria, he finds fault with every version of the
Oedipus drama, for reasons both intrinsic to the material and extrinsic,
or contingent, to it (that is, related to the cirumstances in which the various
Oedipus tragedies were performed).

Over the nearly sixty years (1719–75) spanned by Voltaire's comments
on Corneille and the Oedipus story, he gives greater or lesser weight to
intrinsic and extrinsic factors (for example, in the *Commentaire sur Corneille,* composed just after the elimination of onstage seats from the Théâtre Français, he stresses extrinsic factors), without ever deciding if the
basic "defect" in Oedipus plays has been extrinsic or intrinsic to the story
itself. In his eyes, the intrinsic defect of the Oedipus story is in "the subject": "*the first defect . . . is that of the subject.* Normally the *Oedipus* play
should end in the first act. It is not natural for Oedipus not to know how
his predecessor died" (emphasis added).[54] By "the subject," he means the
topic—the basic, irreducible essence of the plot, which no one (not even
Sophocles or Corneille) has been free to change. In Voltaire's judgment,
the Oedipus subject simply does not have enough plot material for a five-
act tragedy. In fact, he suggests, no audience with a minimum of common
sense will believe that King Oedipus has taken so long to inquire about
how Laius, his predecessor, died, and he adds that not even the great
Corneille could have developed such thin material into a five-act tragedy.

Despite the pedantic character of his remarks, Voltaire's criticism of
the Oedipus "subject" also implies a surprisingly modern understanding
of the play as a drama of self-awareness. For he intimates that the core
of the play lies in Oedipus' ignorance of his real situation (past and present) and therefore, ultimately, of who he is. To Voltaire, Oedipus' defective self-awareness, his lack of self-knowledge, is itself a defective subject.
He implies that because there is something lacking in the Oedipus subject,
even Corneille had to fill it out and try to compensate for this intrinsic
fault by inserting a love story into his play.

To look at it another way, the intrinsic defect of the Oedipus subject is
related to what Voltaire saw as the primary extrinsic defect of its greatest
modern versions (Corneille's and his own): namely, the presence of gratu-
itous love stories. Voltaire acknowledges that to flesh out the requisite five
acts, he and Corneille both had to supply something to their Oedipus tragedies. He adds, however, that if they chose to compensate for the defect of
the subject in this particular way—by adding love interest—they did so
primarily to satisfy the audience's miserable obsession with love stories.[55]

The strangest aspect of these comments is Voltaire's refusal to say—

or perhaps his inability to see—that (incestuous) love is inseparable from the Oedipus story (from its "subject"). Instead of noting that love for the mother is at the core of the Oedipus story, he denies that the story has anything to do with love. Like Corneille, Voltaire lamented the presence of love stories in tragedy, and particularly in *Œdipe:*

> It is the height of ridicule to speak of love in *Oedipus, Electra* or *Mérope.* In 1718, when the only *Oedipus* that is still performed today [that is, Voltaire's version] was about to be staged, the actors demanded a few scenes where love was not forgotten; and the author spoiled and debased this beautiful subject by evoking the vapid memory of an insipid love affair between Philoctetes and Jocasta. (*Théâtre de Pierre Corneille*, 7:130)

In the first place, he complains (like Rousseau) that it is for the sake of women and effeminate values that French audiences and actors insist on weakening a virile genre ("this manly and fearsome style," "the manly and harmonious energy of the Greek verses"),[56] by adding love interest to tragedy. But he instructs his readers that tragedy—and especially *Oedipus*—has nothing to do with love ("our contemptible habit of always introducing a love plot, or rather a galant plot, into subjects that exclude all love" [*Théâtre de Pierre Corneille*, 7:82]).

Voltaire recalls how in 1718 the actress (Charlotte Desmares, the regent's mistress) who had played the *amoureuse* in Corneille's *Oedipus* had forced him to insert a minimum of love interest into his own *Œdipe*, thus repeating Corneille's mistake.[57] Despite the box office success of the play, he acknowledges that it failed to achieve a true tragic effect, and attributes this failure to other factors (the design of French theaters, presence of onstage seats) extrinsic to the basic Oedipus material. These extrinsic elements, claims Voltaire, severely limited the scope of what an audience could accept as "reality."[58] Ever since the French theater has been encumbered by such conventions, he argues, not even the great Corneille has been able to write a great modern version of Sophocles' *Oedipus*. Voltaire deems these elements extrinsic to the Oedipus material itself, even though they were (like the *parterre*) essential components of French classical performance practice. In his view, like the demand of his contemporaries for love interest, the performance conventions of the previous century have nothing to do with theater itself. Indeed, these conventions have been determined only by Parisian fashion—that is, ultimately by women.[59] In other words, Parisian women have deprived the Oedipus subject of whatever power it could have had—despite its intrinsic defect.

Since Voltaire considers women responsible for much that is wrong
with various versions of the Oedipus tragedy (including his own), it is
all the more striking that in his *Œdipe*, Queen Jocaste is morally faultless.
She is arguably the most powerful character in the play, and maybe also
(as I shall suggest below) the most "Voltairean." While the presence of
Jocaste and her former suitor, Philoctète, nominally satisfies the audience's
desire for romantic love interest, Voltaire has the characters lecture the
audience on the inappropriateness of romantic love to authentically noble
concerns—that is, to tragedy. In the first scene of the play, after Philoctète's friend Dimas has told him about the death of Laius, his former rival
for the hand of Jocaste, Philoctète tells Dimas that his constant companion
during four years of absence from Thebes, Hercule ("the greatest of hu-
mans"), has also died, depriving Philoctète not only of a friend, but also
of a model for true (that is, ascetic) heroism. For Hercule has inspired
Philoctète to overcome his love for Jocaste; his friend Dimas tells him
that "[Love] is the first tyrant that you have overcome" (I, 1). And Philoctète responds that it was only by joining Hercule/Heracles in his labors
that he was able to understand the nature of true heroism:

> L'amitié d'un grand homme est un bienfait des dieux:
> Je lisais mon devoir et mon sort dans ses yeux;
> Des vertus avec lui je fis l'apprentissage;
> Sans endurcir mon cœur, j'affermis mon courage:
> L'inflexible vertu m'enchaîna sous sa loi.
> Qu'eussé-je été sans lui? Rien que le fils d'un roi,
> Rien qu'un prince vulgaire, et je serais peut-être
> Esclave de mes sens, dont il m'a rendu maître.
> (I, 1, 120–28)

> A great man's friendship is a blessing from the gods:
> I could read my duty and fate in his eyes;
> With him I served my apprenticeship in the virtues;
> Without hardening my heart, I strengthened my courage:
> Inflexible virtue enchained me beneath its law.
> What would I have been without him? nothing but a king's son,
> Nothing but a common prince, and perhaps I would be
> The slave of my senses, of which he made me the master.

I shall return to the last three verses of this speech, which explicitly decry
the value of nobility based solely upon royal ancestry (and which were

not included in the original text of the play). The rest of Philoctète's speech is consistent with the notion that there is no higher law than "inflexible virtue" and that a concern with romantic love tends to undermine real tragedy.

Likewise, when Jocaste informs her confidant that she has felt only dignified, sober friendship for Œdipe ("I felt a stern friendship for Œdipe"), she confirms the belief (already expressed by Philoctète) that the true Oedipus story has nothing to do with love, and weakens the feelings of horror that the story traditionally had provoked. Indeed, Jocaste avers that she has never felt real passion for anyone but Philoctète ("I did not recognize that burning flame / That only Philoctète has kindled in my soul" [II, 2]). Nevertheless, she claims, like Philoctète, to have heroically sacrificed her love to a higher law ("[A] supreme law / Has always used me against my will" [II, 3]). Thus Voltaire goes so far as to suggest that when Jocaste committed the "crime" of incest, she was merely obeying "a supreme law." Voltaire portrays both Philoctète and Jocaste as characters who hold their passions in check and are able to sacrifice the "tyranny" of love to the highest law. Voltaire could not yield to the audience's desire for love interest in tragedy (in fact, he seemed completely uninterested in any form of romantic love, whether in poetry or in life) without making several additional points: that desire is out of place in an Oedipus story; that in his Oedipus story, desire is not really desire; and finally, that the incest of Jocaste and Œdipe is ultimately legal.

Since Voltaire could not see the essential horror of the Oedipus story, he concluded that either something was lacking in "the subject" of the Oedipus tragedy, or the play's power had been emasculated by various extrinsic (ultimately feminine) factors, to whose power even the great Corneille had been forced to submit. In the end, he held women responsible for all the extrinsic defects that had marked French remakes of the Oedipus tragedy. Voltaire particularly regretted the fact that French audiences had refused to give credence to characters in *Œdipe* (such as Oedipus and Tiresias) who are both male and thematically linked to the sacred (he does not discuss whether the audience failed to credit Queen Jocaste). Nevertheless, what mattered most to Voltaire was not the virility or effeminacy of characters, but what he imagined as the virile power of tragedy, of which the Oedipus drama was the greatest example. Voltaire passionately wanted to establish the full (uncastrated) gender of Oedipus, and therefore of the tragic genre, without ever realizing that it was "he" (a subject blind to specific historical and biographical forces) who had actually diminished the genre.

A "Philosophical Tragedy"?

In 1718 both the implicitly oedipal character of absolutist theatrical space
and the explicitly oedipal public image of Philippe d'Orléans made Voltaire's audience willing to invest itself in a new Oedipus tragedy. However,
to account for the extraordinary success achieved by Voltaire's play, one
has to consider not only the context, but also the text itself. As commentators have noted, this text not only alludes to rumors of the regent's alleged
incestuous relationship with his daughter, it also criticizes the hereditary
basis of monarchy in very explicit terms. Doubtless the success of Voltaire's *Œdipe* derived in part from the transgressive pleasure of hearing
such criticism voiced on the stage of the Comédie Française (the king's
theater), and sometimes even in the presence of the regent.

Not only did Arouet de Voltaire explicitly address his first play to royalty, but he also used it implicitly to legitimize himself as royal adviser.
Voltaire clearly saw his *Œdipe* as part tragedy and part "philosophical"
drama, and it has been termed a kind of "manual" for the enlightened
monarch.[60] The play is filled with maxims, such as "It is a king's duty to die
for his country" (II, 4), political allusions (for instance, to the annulment of
Louis XIV's will [I, 3, 185–92]), and other bits of didactic material, all
of which are meant to instruct the prince.

As we have seen, in the opening scene Philoctète acknowledges his
debt to Hercule for having shown that a prince can make himself into
something more than "a king's son": "Qu'eussé-je été sans lui? rien que
le fils d'un roi, / Rien qu'un prince vulgaire" ("What would I have been
without him? Nothing but a king's son / Nothing but a common prince"
[I, 1, 126–27]). These lines were not included in the two 1719 editions
of *Œdipe*, although legend has it that they were greeted with applause
at the play's first performance in 1718 (when an eight-year-old king was
on the throne of France, and the regent was under attack). Pomeau calls
such sentiments "theatrical republicanism" *(républicanisme de tragédie).*[61]
Whether or not one takes these ideas seriously, they echo Voltaire's own
rejection of the hereditary basis of personal worth. For Philoctète (and
Voltaire), true nobility is the product of actions, rather than blood or birth.
By vanquishing monsters, Prince Philoctète claims to have given meaning
to an otherwise empty noble title ("a king's son"). By calling himself
"nothing but a king's son," Voltaire's philosophical spokesman also reiter-
ates the typically oedipal gesture of trying to diminish the power of the
father. Likewise, Arouet de Voltaire (who vigorously denied that he had
inherited his poetic gifts from François Arouet, "who was a very common

man as for genius")[62] proclaimed that he had *earned* his noble title by emerging victorious from the first performances of *Œdipe*.

Certainly there is much about *Œdipe* that is "philosophical," in the Voltairean sense. For one thing, *Œdipe* expresses what Theodore Bester-man has called "an increasing disgust with all forms of absolute authority, and in particular with that of the church and the throne, a disgust of which the regency was an *unconscious* and impermanent expression."[63] The fact that Voltaire had been authorized by the regent to dedicate *Œdipe* to the latter's wife or mother conferred legitimacy upon ideas that never would have been tolerated by Louis XIV. For example, in act II, scene 4, Philoc-tète affirms: "Un roi pour ses sujets est un dieu qu'on révère; / Pour Hercule et pour moi, c'est un homme ordinaire" ("For his subjects a king is a god to be revered; / For Hercule and me he is an ordinary man").[64] Under Louis XIV, no one would have dared to declare, on the official stage, that a king was "an ordinary man," and doing so in the presence of the Sun King would have been even more dangerous. At the same time, these are not exactly revolutionary sentiments. Philoctète relies upon the traditional (aristocratic) distinction between knowledge, derived from the exercise of reason by the enlightened few, and popular opinion, which comes from prejudice and superstition. When he says that for Hercule and him a king is "an ordinary man," Philoctète is not suggesting that a king is "ordinary," in the sense of "common" or "inferior" (in the sense that Pierre-Charles Roy was an "ordinary" poet). Rather, he is saying that a king is a human being, a mortal, and not a god. For his subjects, a king remains a god ("un dieu qu'on révère"), but the noble Philoctète and Hercule can see that a king is human, "an ordinary man."

Œdipe himself explicitly denies royal omniscience: "Dans le cœur des humains les rois ne peuvent lire; / Souvent sur l'innocence ils font tomber leurs coups" ("Kings cannot read human hearts / They often strike the innocent with their blows" [II, 5]). In addition, Araspe, Œdipe's confidant, disputes the High Priest's supposedly inspired revelations with a typically "Voltairean" anticlerical argument. He argues in favor of "using our own eyes" to look for the truth, instead of giving blind credence to priestly authority:

Ne nous endormons point sur la foi de leurs prêtres;
Au pied du sanctuaire il est souvent des traîtres,
Qui, nous asservissant sous un pouvoir sacré,
Font parler les destins, les font taire à leur gré.
Voyez, examinez avec un soin extrême

Philoctète, Phorbas, et Jocaste elle-même.
Ne nous fions qu'à nous; *voyons tout par nos yeux:*
Ce sont là nos trépieds, nos oracles, nos dieux.
(II, 5; emphasis added)

Let us not be lulled by faith in their priests;
At the foot of the sanctuary there often are traitors;
Who, enslaving us beneath a sacred power,
Cause destiny to speak or keep silent, at their will.
Judge them, examine with greatest care
Philoctète, Phorbas, and Jocaste herself.
Let us trust only ourselves; *let us see everything with our eyes:*
These are our tripods, our oracles, our gods.

In fact, Œdipe spends the entire play actually trying to follow Araspe's
advice—trying to "trust only [himself], see everything with [his] eyes."
Later on, in the most famous lines of *Œdipe*, Jocaste decries the way in
which priests take advantage of the people's ignorance: "Nos prêtres ne
sont pas ce qu'un vain peuple pense, / Notre crédulité fait toute leur
science" ("Our priests are not what a vain people thinks / Our credulity
is their only form of knowledge" [IV, 1]). Here Jocaste is trying to re-
assure Œdipe that he has not really killed his father, despite what the
high priest claims to know. Although Jocaste's "philosophical" couplet
has become famous, and although she remains morally in the right, both
she and Araspe are sorely mistaken about the facts. Jocaste's anticlericalism
(her "science") leaves something to be desired, since the priest is right
about at least one thing: it was Œdipe (his "hand," impelled by the gods)
who killed Laius.[65]

Philoctète and the Riddle of Voltaire's *Œdipe*

[T]he beauties of a work are sometimes born from a defect.
— VOLTAIRE, *Lettres sur* Œdipe, V

The most obvious difference between Voltaire's *Œdipe* and Sophocles' or
Corneille's version of the play lies in the presence of a Philoctetes character
(who already appeared in the 1715–16 manuscript). Of course, Sophocles
also wrote a *Philoctetes* tragedy, but his *Oedipus tyrannos* contains no references to this character, who traditionally had nothing to do with the Oedi-

pus story. Yet in *Œdipe*, Philoctète is not only the principal spokesman for enlightened monarchy but also Jocasta's love interest. In fact, Voltaire made Philoctète into as important a character as Œdipe himself, turning the prince of Euboea into Oedipus' rival (in politics and love) and his designated successor as king of Thebes.[66]

If only because Philoctète is such an important character in the play, the plot of Voltaire's *Œdipe* is quite different from the familiar version of the Oedipus story in Sophocles.[67] In the first published edition of Voltaire's play, Philoctète's friend Dimas opens the play by asking him what he is doing in Thebes:

> Est-ce vous, Philoctète? en croirai-je mes yeux?
> Quel implacable dieu vous ramène en ces lieux?
> Vous dans Thèbes, seigneur! *Eh! Qu'y venez-vous faire?*
> (I, 1, 1–3; emphasis added)

> Is it you, Philoctète? Shall I believe my eyes?
> What implacable god brings you back to this place?
> You in Thebes, my lord! *Ah! What brings you here?*

By raising this question immediately, Voltaire apparently meant to anticipate the audience's concern with the *vraisemblance* of meeting Philoctetes (who was traditionally associated with his wound, and with the magic bow and arrow given him by Heracles) in the context of the Oedipus story. What indeed was Philoctetes doing in an Oedipus tragedy? Although he quickly revised this passage,[68] Voltaire was never able to find a satisfactory answer to the question raised by the presence of Philoctète. (Both Philoctetes and Oedipus were often portrayed as having been wounded in the foot—that is, symbolically castrated—but Voltaire does not allude to this fact.)

In the fifth of his *Lettres sur Œdipe*, Voltaire acknowledged that he had failed to assimilate Philoctète into the Oedipus material, so that his tragedy ended up looking like two plays, rather than one: "One has the impression that these are two tragedies, one about Philoctète and one about Œdipe."[69] Yet from the outset, *Œdipe* appears to have been a hybrid—part Philoctetes play and part Oedipus play. By Voltaire's own admission, *Œdipe*— a play that he had spent at least four years writing—had an incoherent plot and violated the most basic principle of Aristotelian poetics: unity of action.

Although Voltaire repeatedly acknowledged the glaring *invraisemblance* of so much Philoctetes material in an Oedipus tragedy, in subsequent revisions of the play he never did anything to rectify the problem. For this reason, one can infer that the unresolved conflict between a Philoctetes play and an Oedipus play was fundamental to the conception of Voltaire's first attempt at tragedy. It has escaped no one's attention (starting with the author's) that Œdipe is a composite: both a "virile" tragedy and an "effeminate" love story, an Oedipus play and a Philoctetes play. Like the Sphinx, Voltaire's Œdipe is a hybrid, and its composite nature proposes a riddle: Where did this strange creature come from? And why was Voltaire unable (or unwilling) to correct its obvious defects?

From a psychoanalytic perspective, chronic, unresolved conflicts in behavior are symptoms of powerful unconscious desires. According to the psychoanalytic critic José-Michel Moureaux, the answer to the riddle of Œdipe can be found in Voltaire's own "oedipus complex." As we have seen, young François-Marie Arouet got on very poorly with his authoritarian father, who twice sent him into exile and even threatened to have him sent to the West Indies with a *lettre de cachet*. François-Marie did not get along either with his elder brother, Armand, who would eventually become a fanatical Jansenist. On the maternal side, we have already taken note of Voltaire's attraction to older women, such as "Pimpette" (Catherine Olympe du Noyer), whom he met in The Hague in 1713. Although she was only two years older than François-Marie Arouet, she addressed him maternally as "mon haimable anfan" ("my lovable child").[70] Two years later, while he was composing Œdipe, Arouet fell in love with Mlle. Duclos, a distinguished actress some twenty years his senior, and unsuccessfully sought to obtain her favors. Following one of the first performances of Œdipe, de Voltaire became fruitlessly infatuated with the maréchale de Villars, another member of his mother's generation.[71]

In light of these (and other) biographical considerations, Moureaux claims that Voltaire saw himself in Philoctète, "the character in which the creator probably put the most of himself."[72] Like the young Arouet, he argues, Philoctète was forced to flee the hostile father-figure (Laius) who had separated him from the maternal Jocaste. Moureaux contends that in the first part of the play, Œdipe represents a judge for Philoctète, a repressive older brother and/or father figure, who has replaced Laius as the paternal rival for Jocaste's love. Philoctète/François-Marie refuses to subject himself to the judgment of this "bad" father; like the young Arouet, Philoctète wants to be judged on the basis of his deeds, and not in terms of his inherited social position ("nothing but a king's son / Nothing but a common prince"). Moureaux argues that Philoctète fled from Thebes to conjure away the hostile father's threat and achieve a positive identification with a "good," protective father figure, represented by Hercule.[73] (Philoctète mourns Hercule in these words: "L'innocent opprimé perd son dieu tutélaire; / Je pleure mon ami, le monde pleure un père" ("The oppressed and innocent man loses his tutelary god / I mourn my friend, the world mourns a father" [I, 1, 87–88]). This good father is above all the protector of the people, while the evil father is primarily committed to judging (and punishing) in the name of the law. Philoctète credits his friendship with a great man for enabling him to overcome his filial subjection to authority and renounce his love for Jocaste:

Il fallut m'arracher de ce funeste lieu,
Et je dis à Jocaste un éternel adieu.
. . . .
Je marchai près [d'Hercule], ceint du même laurier.
C'est alors en effet que mon âme éclairée
Contre les passions se sentit assurée.
L'amitié d'un grand homme est un bienfait des dieux.[74]
(I, 1, 111–21; emphasis added)

I had to be torn away from this ill-fated place,
And I bade Jocaste an eternal farewell.
. . . .
I marched with [Hercules], crowned with the same laurel.
It was then that my enlightened soul
Felt itself proof against the passions.
A great man's friendship is a blessing from the gods.

Friendship with a great man would become an important theme in Voltaire's thought, and Moureaux interprets this motif in ultimately oedipal terms.

Moureaux finally argues that the real protagonist of this play is neither Œdipe nor Philoctète, but the dead father/king.[75] In his view, the plot unfolds in a way that eventually gives the castrating father figure a justification for preferring his younger son (Philoctète/François-Marie Arouet) to his older one (Œdipe/Armand Arouet): by refusing to become the father's rival, the younger son makes himself worthy of ultimately taking the father's place. Moureaux concludes that *Œdipe* seems to be essentially "an attempt to exorcise the guilt-inducing image of the dead father."[76] For the same reasons, he claims, Voltaire would devote his life to exorcising the arbitrary, guilt-inducing image of the dead father, in all its forms (gods, priests, . . .).

I would take issue with at least one part of Moureaux's interpretation. Philoctète was Jocaste's suitor before she was forced to marry Laius (and give birth to Œdipe), and is therefore at least one generation older than Œdipe. But Moureaux's desire to exploit the parallelism between the brothers in Voltaire's family (François-Marie, Armand) and the "brothers" (Philoctète, Œdipe) in Voltaire's play leads him to suggest that Œdipe, by initially adopting the role of judge, plays the role of older brother to Philoctète, although the latter is actually much older than he. In psychoanalytic terms (representation of a term by its opposite), this interpretation can be justified, but it seems forced in this context.

A scene from Voltaire's *Œdipe* (engraving). Photo: Roger-Viollet.

Whether or not one is convinced by all the details of Moureaux's argument, he certainly makes it difficult to maintain that Voltaire wrote an
Oedipus tragedy only because Sophocles and Corneille had written one,
or that he introduced a Philoctetes character simply for didactic, "philosophical" reasons. Although such conscious factors certainly played a role
in Voltaire's "choice" of topic, Moureaux shows that there were other
reasons that escaped Voltaire's conscious control. In what follows, I would
like to propose another, historical reason for the patently unresolved conflicts in Voltaire's first play.

The Death of the King

At the beginning of *Œdipe*, Dimas asks Philoctète why he has returned
to Thebes, and then makes a stunning (but apparently unrelated) an-
nouncement: the king (Laius) is dead. "[D]epuis quatre ans ce héros ne
vit plus" ("This hero has been dead for four years" [I, 1, 22]). This is
wonderful news for Philoctète, since it means (or so he thinks) that he
will finally be able to marry Jocaste. News of the death of King Laius
awakens hope in Philoctète, just as (also four years earlier) news of the
death of Louis XIV (on September 1, 1715) had given some of his subjects
reason for hope: "Il ne vit plus! quel mot a frappé mon oreille! / Quel
espoir séduisant dans mon coeur se réveille!" ("He lives no more! What
is this I hear! / What seductive hope awakens in my heart!" [I, 1, 23–
24]). In *Oedipos tyrannos* Sophocles suggests that around twenty years had
elapsed since Laius' death. In 1718–19, however, Voltaire changes that
interval to four years. Although he may have done this in order to make
Oedipus' ignorance of Laius' death somewhat less implausible (to remedy
the "defect of the subject"), it seems more likely that Voltaire was deliberately alluding to the death of Louis XIV in 1715 (even the names, Laius/
Louis, are similar).[77] In any case, Philoctète does not know the circumstances of Laius' death, or that Jocaste has again been forced by reasons
of state to marry someone she doesn't love. He soon learns that for the
"empire," the king's death has been a catastrophe. As Dimas explains: "Ce
fut de nos malheurs la première origine: / Ce crime a de l'empire entraîné
la ruine" ("This was the origin of our misfortunes: / This crime led to
the empire's ruin" [I, 1, 35–36]). At first, Philoctète sees the king's death
only as an individual. But the death of Laius does not have the same
meaning for him that it does for the empire: to Philoctète it gives new
reason for hope, but to the empire it has meant pestilence and ruin. More-

over, if Laius (like Louis XIV) had simply died of natural causes, there
could be sadness or rejoicing, but there would be no tragedy. The an-
nouncement that his death is a crime, for which someone (or something)
must be held responsible, introduces the tragic element.

From this point on, the play is conducted like a criminal investigation,
as Œdipe interrogates witnesses and examines testimony, to discover who
is responsible for the king's death.[78] He impulsively leaps from one explanation of Laius' death to another, never stops to think, and always makes
the arrogant assumption that the guilty party is someone other than himself. At first, when "the people" (for Voltaire, an inexhaustible source
of error and prejudice) accuse the noble Philoctète of Laius' murder,
Œdipe refuses to defend him. Through weakness or hypocrisy, he claims
to want "heaven," speaking through the high priest, to name Laius'
murderer:

> Et bientôt, retirant *la main qui nous opprime*,
> Par la voix du grand-prêtre [le ciel] nomme la victime;
> Et je laisse à *nos dieux, plus éclairés que nous*,
> Le soin de décider entre mon peuple et vous.
> (III, 3, 731–34; emphasis added)

> And soon, removing *the hand that oppresses us*,
> Through the high priest's voice may [heaven] name the victim;
> And I leave to *our gods, more enlightened than we*,
> The task of deciding between my people and you.

At the beginning of act V, Œdipe suddenly remembers an earlier manifestation of his arrogance, a scene to which "the hand of the gods" had
blinded him until this very moment, and he recounts it to Jocaste as follows:

> Enfin je me souviens qu'aux champs de la Phocide
> . . . .
> (*La main des dieux* sur moi si longtemps suspendue
> *Semble ôter le bandeau qu'ils mettaient sur ma vue*),
> Dans un chemin étroit je trouvai deux guerriers
> Sur un char éclatant que traînaient deux coursiers;
> Il fallut disputer, dans cet étroit passage,
> Des vains honneurs du pas le frivole avantage.
> . . . .
> Inconnu, dans le sein d'une terre étrangère,

Je me croyais encore au trône de mon père;
Et tous ceux qu'à mes yeux le sort venait offrir
Me semblaient des sujets, et faits pour m'obéir.
(IV, 1, 1056–71; emphasis added)

At last I recall that in the fields of Phocis,

. . . .

(*The hand of the gods* that has long been suspended over me
Seems to remove the blindfold that they put on my sight),
In a narrow path, I met two warriors
In a brilliant chariot drawn by two steeds;
In this narrow passage, one had to vie
For the frivolous advantage of the vain honor of passage.

. . . .

Unknown, in the midst of a foreign land
I imagined myself still on my father's throne;
And all those who appeared before my sight
Seemed to me like subjects, meant to obey me.

Of course, when Œdipe recalls this fatal scene, the hand of the gods has
not shown him the whole truth. At this moment, he and Jocaste are becoming aware of the fact that he did kill Laius, but they do not yet see that
Laius is his father.

Philoctète, however, has a cooler head than Œdipe and a more "philosophical" idea of justice. For him "honor" is a higher and more reliable
standard of justice than the strict letter of the law:

Votre équité, seigneur, est inflexible et pure;
Mais l'extrême justice est une extrême injure:
Il n'en faut pas toujours écouter la rigueur.
Des lois que nous suivons la première est l'honneur.
(III, 3, 735–37)

Your equity, lord, is inflexible and pure;
But extreme justice is an extreme injury:
One should not always listen to its rigor.
The first of the laws we obey is honor.

For Philoctète (as for Voltaire), one becomes worthy of honor by performing noble deeds, without concern for the dubious judgment of the
local gods or the pitiful superstitions of the people:

C'était, c'était assez d'examiner ma vie;
Hercule appui des dieux, et vainqueur de l'Asie,
Les monstres, les tyrans, qu'il m'apprit à dompter,
Ce sont là les témoins qu'il faut confronter.
De vos dieux cependant interrogez l'organe:
Nous apprendrons de lui si leur voix me condamne.
Je n'ai pas besoin d'eux, et j'attends leur arrêt
Par pitié pour ce peuple, et non par intérêt.
(III, 3, 743–50)

Indeed it was enough to examine my life;
Hercule, champion of the gods, and conqueror of Asia,
The monsters, the tyrants, that he taught me to subdue,
These are the witnesses that ought to be summoned.
But question the spokesman of your gods:
He will tell us if their voice condemns me.
I do not need them, and I await their decree
Out of pity for this people, not self-concern.

In the end, of course, Œdipe will learn that the truth is even more horrible than he has imagined: Laius, the man he killed in that "narrow path," was his father, and Jocaste, his wife, is his mother. Nonetheless, in his final soliloquy (V, 4, to which I shall return) Œdipe continues to maintain his essential virtue: "Et je me vois enfin, par un mélange affreux, / Inceste, et parricide, et pourtant vertueux" ("And I finally see myself, through a dreadful mixture, / Incestuous, and a parricide, and yet virtuous" [V, 4, 1333–34]). Likewise, in the last scene of the play, when Jocaste finally kills herself (more from anger and despair than from remorse for her "crimes"), she insists: "I have lived virtuously, and I die without remorse" (1402).

What this conclusion means, according to Eric Van der Schueren, is that "in this early work Voltaire announces his intention of reconciling men with themselves, and acts on behalf of 'civilization' against the morbid wrath of the gods or uncultivated nature, which now replaces them in the eighteenth century."[79] Unlike Racine's most tragic characters—Néron, Bajazet, Phèdre—who even on stage are powerless to avoid doing evil, the virtuous protagonists of Œdipe are as innocent as Candide. Before the decline of absolutist culture, the crimes of Oedipus (incest, parricide, regicide) were themselves absolute, as it were: they were crimes for which responsibility could not conceivably be limited, of which no one could in any way be absolved. In the king's wake, however, Voltaire is impelled to diminish Oedipus' responsibility. Despite the innocence of Œdipe and Jocaste, these enlightened characters are so blinded by philosophical prejudice that they cannot see the truth until it has destroyed them. In *Œdipe* only the gods (who speak through the high priest, their "organ") speak the truth. Taken out of context, the anticlerical, rationalist ideas that virtuous, "philosophical" characters propose to the rulers of Europe seem eminently Voltairean, but in the context of the tragedy these ideas are wrong. Likewise, although Voltaire was consciously determined to prove that actions, and not blood, are the true criterion by which personal worth should be measured, his Oedipus play presents characters who are innocent, precisely insofar as they are not responsible for their actions, which are determined by forces ("the gods") beyond their conscious control. It therefore remains to be seen whether tragic necessity can be reconciled with philosophical responsibility.[80]

Post-Absolutist Agency

When Œdipe cuts out his eyes (offstage), he is presumably still a blind "instrument" in the hands of an inscrutable "god." In *Œdipe*, all a virtuous man or woman can ever see or know of this god is the "hand" that carries out its will. Thus Œdipe tells Jocaste: "On m'avait toujours dit que ce fut un Thébain / Qui leva sur son prince *une coupable main*" ("I had always been told that it was a Theban / Who laid *a guilty hand* upon his prince" [I, 3, 201–2; emphasis added]). Later Œdipe conveys to Philoctète the hope that "heaven" *(le ciel)* will designate the guilty party, thus "removing *the hand* that oppresses us" (III, 3, 731; emphasis added). When he begins to see the truth about himself, Œdipe claims that *"[t]he hand* of the gods that has long been suspended above me / Seems to remove the blindfold that they put on my sight" (IV, 1, 1059–60; emphasis added). Voltaire's characters need not know whose hand this may be, so long as they know it is not one of their hands. In Act I, scene 1, Dimas tells Œdipe that "an enemy hand" was responsible for the death of Laius: "A peine vous quittiez le chemin de l'Asie, / Lorsque, d'un coup perfide, *une main ennemie* / Ravit à ses sujets ce prince infortuné" ("You had scarcely left the road to Asia, / When the treacherous blow of *an enemy hand* / Ravished this unfortunate prince from his subjects" [31–33, emphasis added]). One may wish to view this "hand" as a mere cliché, an overinflated vestige of tragic diction. But in *Œdipe*, the hand is more than a cliché, it is also a recurrent figure of post-absolutist agency. Unlike Œdipe and Jocaste, Racine's Phèdre always believed that, although she had little control over "[*her*] homicidal hands [*mes* homicides mains]," she (and not Venus) was ultimately responsible for her actions. Indeed, the actions that separate Phèdre's initial reference to her innocent hands ("Grâces au ciel, *mes mains* ne sont point criminelles" ["Thank heaven, *my hands* are not criminal"; I, 3, (221)]) from her subsequent admission that "her" hands yearn to become guilty of Hippolyte's death ("*Mes homicides mains,* promptes à me venger, / Dans le sang innocent brûlent de se plonger" ["*My homicidal hands,* eager to avenge me / Burn to immerse themselves in innocent blood"; IV, 6, (1271–72); emphasis added]) illustrate both absolutist and tragic agency. The first, because Phèdre (like an absolutist subject, according to official doctrine) recognizes that she has little control over actions ultimately determined by a transcendent source (the Sun King, "the gods"). The second, because Phèdre also *accepts* her necessary complicity in a "fatal" (tragic) sequence of events. In post-absolutist culture, however, one can no longer see or accept that necessary complicity, even when one also recognizes how little responsibility one ultimately has over one's own actions. This representation of agency will place Voltaire, if not his Œdipe, in a paradoxical position.

At the end of what Pomeau has called "Voltaire's "first philosophical tragedy,"[101] Œdipe tries to understand how it can be that an invisible, "enemy" hand has made him look (even to himself) like the most horrible of criminals. He "sees" himself "incestuous, and a parricide, and yet virtuous" (V, 4, 1333–34). In other words, he cannot help seeing himself as a man who has committed incest and parricide (he knows that these are the only words for his present situation), and yet he himself has done nothing to deserve these terrible names. Œdipe does not say that he has committed incest and parricide, he simply acknowledges a *fait accompli*. But a fact accomplished by whom?

Toward the end of his soliloquy, Œdipe still cannot name the agents responsible for the death of the king (and therefore for his fate), except in the vaguest of terms ("a god stronger than [virtue]," "an unknown power"). Phèdre knew the name of her divine persecutor (Venus), unlike Œdipe who, at his moment of greatest lucidity (when he laments the futility of devoting one's life to virtue) cannot even see who has been victimizing him:

Misérable vertu, nom stérile et funeste,
Toi par qui j'ai réglé des jours que je déteste,

A mon noir ascendant tu n'as pu résister:

. . . .

Un dieu plus fort que toi m'entraînait vers l'abîme;
Sous mes pas fugitifs il creusait un abîme;
Et *j'étais, malgré moi, dans mon aveuglement,*
D'un pouvoir inconnu l'esclave et l'instrument.
(1335–43, emphasis added)

Miserable virtue, sterile and fatal name,
Thou on whom I have modeled a life I detest,
Thou couldst not resist *my dark ascendant:*

. . . .

A god stronger than thou was dragging me into the abyss;
Beneath my fleeting steps he was creating a gulf;
And *I was, despite myself, in my blindness,*
The slave and instrument of an unknown power.

Phèdre ultimately recognized the necessity of sacrificing "even virtue" (III, 3, [908]) to her incestuous, fatal passion. In contrast, Voltaire's Œdipe can only see that virtue—the (philosophical) cause to which he claims to have devoted his life—is feeble indeed, for it has been overwhelmed by a stronger ("plus fort que toi") and darker power ("mon *noir* ascendant"). Arrogant King Œdipe, who has always believed that everyone else was subject to him ("[T]ous ceux qu'à mes yeux le sort venait offrir / Me semblaient des sujets, et faits pour m'obéir" ["All those who appeared before my sight / Seemed to me like subjects meant to obey me," 1070–71]), has actually been nothing but a "slave," an "instrument" in the hands of an "unknown power." He concludes his soliloquy by railing against the gods ("Impitoyables dieux, mes crimes sont les vôtres," 1344), by claiming that the crimes of Œdipe are also, or perhaps really, the crimes of the gods. Nevertheless, as soon as Œdipe has been compelled to punish *himself* for "[his] crimes" (1360), "the god of heaven and earth" (1379) tells the people (with thunderclaps and flashes of lightning) that their misery has come to an end.

In *Œdipe*, the "hand" is a synecdoche, a part for a whole that cannot be represented or known in any other way. The hand conveys an impersonal notion of agency: action—especially evil, destructive action—for which no individual can be held responsible. The hand is a trope for evil, but evil detached from any personal responsibility. In *Œdipe* it is ultimately not persons who do evil, since people are only the "blind instrument[s]" of abstract, impersonal powers that far transcend them. Absolutist action (and the absolutist theatricality of Versailles, as well) had revolved around the king, around his solar person. But when the absolute monarch had lost his symbolic efficacy, one could no longer believe that all human action proceeded from his demigodly royal "person," as all life proceeds from the sun.

With Voltaire's *Œdipe*, one enters the contradictory realm of post-abso- lutist agency. As we have seen, despite all the "oedipal investments" of which he may not have been aware, Arouet de Voltaire laid claim to a noble title on the basis of his individual performance as a poet, as an "author," the person ultimately responsible for an exceptionally successful tragedy. We have also seen that in *Œdipe*, the play whose success legiti- mates the poet's public claim to a title, the main characters attribute ulti- mate responsibility for their actions to abstract, impersonal forces. This would seem to be an inescapable contradiction of post-absolutist agency, which places new emphasis upon both personal and impersonal (the law, chance, the market, heredity) responsibility as explanatory principles.

In Voltaire's *Œdipe*, Jocaste has the last word. Like Œdipe, she protests that the gods are responsible for the crimes of her hand. But she adds that *she is responsible* for having put the gods themselves to shame: "*J'ai fait rougir* les dieux qui m'ont forcée au crime" ("I have made them ashamed of themselves, these gods who forced me into crime," 1408). Perhaps the Voltairean lesson here is that in the face of apparently implacable forces (earthquake, pestilence, superstition, war: forces both in "nature," and in human nature), one can always refuse to recognize the necessity of those forces; with whatever powers one has, one can publicly deny that all is for the best, or that things cannot be otherwise. Perhaps this very sign of opposition, this public display of refusal—this civilizing gesture—will put to shame all those who would glorify natural "order" or simply resign themselves to natural disorder. If tragedy requires its audience to recognize the overwhelming "implacability of the world," that "there is *ultimate* in- justice in the world,"[82] then there is a fundamental contradiction between tragic action and Voltaire's actions as poet and philosophe.

The Death of Tragedy

"[D]epuis quatre ans ce héros ne vit plus" ("This hero has been dead for four years"): with these words, Dimas announced that Laius was dead, and Voltaire registered a historical fact: that the symbolic order of which

Louis XIV had been the center, absolutism, was no more. Laius/Louis
was dead, and had been effectively dead for even longer than the four
years since his actual passing. The symbolic order that revolved around
the representation of the king had become irretrievable; it had become
impossible to invest oneself fully in tragedy, to "credit" the "royal spectacle." To announce the death of the king was tantamount to announcing
that it had become impossible to write, or give credence to, a genre that
(as Jean-Marie Apostolidès has shown)[83] reenacted the death of the king:
that tragedy itself was dead. "Philosophical tragedy" is therefore a contradiction in terms.

Voltaire's *Œdipe* plays out a question (Who is responsible for the king's
death?) that has everything to do with the hybrid nature of the play itself.
Just as the plot of *Œdipe* is torn between the story of Philoctète and the
story of Œdipe, so the play itself is torn between the tragedy that Voltaire
wanted to write and the more philosophical drama he actually wrote.

Voltaire's *Œdipe* records the passing of the king as the center of a
symbolic order, the death of the king that is tantamount to the death of
tragedy. Who is responsible for the death of tragedy? And can tragedy
(like Thebes) be saved? Voltaire continued this investigation throughout
his career as a tragic poet—that is, for the rest of his life. Throughout
his career, he would pursue the project that he began with *Œdipe:* that
of announcing the death of the king, and hence of vigorously pursuing
the responsible parties, while doing one's best to bring "the king" (and
with him, tragedy) back to life. But tragedy was dependent upon values (the implacability of the world, absolute monarchy, the authority of
priests) that Voltaire and his enlightened contemporaries could not possibly endorse. In the end, it would turn out to be impossible to reconcile
Enlightenment (which recognizes only the authority of reason, of evidence, and which clings to the hope of making things better)[84] with
tragedy.

In this post-absolutist context, *Œdipe* asks questions about legitimacy
(Who is my real father? Where does real nobility come from? What confers nobility and/or legitimacy upon a poet or a political ruler?) and about
agency (Who or what makes us act as we do? Should we be held responsible for our actions?). In the process, the play also reflects on what it means
to be a subject in the wake of absolutism and why, in these changed circumstances, it has become impossible to achieve a tragic effect. Certainly
Voltaire's play attained unprecedented success with its audience, a success
that enabled him to forge a new, noble identity for himself. However, it
may be that the play produced its effect, and its author succeeded in declar-

ing himself Arouet *de Voltaire*, precisely because *Œdipe* was not really a tragedy, and because the conditions of possibility for tragedy (the "royal drama," par excellence) no longer existed.

The Real "Poète Roy"

For Voltaire, writing an Oedipus play was itself an oedipal gesture—symptomatic of his mixture of admiration for established authority and his desire to replace it (with himself)—a gesture that both recognized legitimate authorities and sought to redefine the nature of legitimacy. With *Œdipe*, he aimed to present himself both as legitimate adviser to the king (like Philoctète, a "philosophical" spokesman) and as illegitimate rival to the king (like Œdipe). At the same time that he respectfully asked permission to dedicate his new play to the regent's wife (or mother), he was threatening to usurp the position of the king ("father of the people"). In the course of the eighteenth century, the century of Voltaire, he would ultimately impose his own legitimacy as the prince of European Enlightenment. Long after *Œdipe* announced the death of the absolute monarch, M. de Voltaire became known throughout Europe as the "king of Ferney." On his own terms, the poet Arouet had finally become "le poète Roy"!

III

The King's Insignia

Watteau, *L'Enseigne de Gersaint*

WATTEAU'S LAST GREAT PAINTING, *L'Enseigne de Gersaint* (1721), is a signboard that displays a scene in the shop of his friend, the art dealer Edmé Gersaint. Across the foreground of the signboard stretch the cobblestones of the street, where a contemporary viewer would presumably have stood. According to the conventions for signboards, the front wall of the shop has been painted away, like the fourth wall of a stage, to reveal the scene inside. One sumptuously dressed couple enters the shop, whose rear walls are covered with paintings, while the staff show art works and luxury items to other elegant clients. In the background, and almost in the center of the signboard, a door opens onto the rear of the shop, which is empty.

When Watteau began the work in late 1720, on his own initiative, he was already greatly weakened by tuberculosis and knew that he did not have long to live. As far as is known, he did not undertake this painting in fulfillment of a commission or in response to market demand. According to Gersaint, Watteau made the signboard simply to keep his fingers supple ("pour se dégourdir les doigts").[1] Whatever the artist's intentions may have been, his last large project doubtless had the highest personal and artistic significance for him. Indeed, it has become customary to treat the *Enseigne de Gersaint* as Watteau's artistic will and testament.

In a classic article on the history and provenance of the painting, Hélène Adhémar expresses this view of the painting as Watteau's artistic summation: "Watteau was so insistent with Gersaint about painting this vast canvas, because he wanted to transmit to us, through this magisterial synthesis, the message of his life, his art, his reason for being."[2] Adhémar refers to this painting as a "synthesis" because of the various strands of the European artistic tradition (Italian, Flemish, French) to which the paintings in Gersaint's shop refer, and which Watteau draws together under one roof and in a single frame. Not only does *L'Enseigne* assemble several schools of painting, it also brings together "high" and "low" art. It is, as Donald Posner remarks, "at once a commonplace sign advertising a mercantile establishment, and a painting of great monetary value embodying a vision of high culture."[3] In that vision, Watteau not only synthesizes various artistic traditions, high and low, he also (as Mary Vidal has pointed out) brings them into "conversation," or dialogue, with aestheticized forms of elite social ritual.[4] One has then to ask why Watteau, knowing that he did not have long to live, used an enormous shop sign, representing the business in an art dealer's shop, to make a statement about his art, or perhaps to raise a question about it.

    L'Enseigne de Gersaint, which now hangs in the Charlottenburg Palace, Berlin, is 163 centimeters high and 308 centimeters wide.[5] The *Enseigne* was originally painted on two separate canvases, which were joined in an arched frame (whose outlines are visible on the picture surface) and displayed for two weeks in the upper section of the storefront of Gersaint's art shop, located on the Pont-Notre-Dame, Paris. In Watteau's original conception, the painting was a so-called *enseigne de plafond* (a "ceiling" shop sign, as distinguished from the "gallows" shop sign, or *enseigne de potence*):[6] it fit into the arched upper storefront of the shop, like a tympanum.

    Although the shop sign was a lowly genre in the academic hierarchy, Watteau had made other shop signs early in his career, when he desperately needed any kind of artistic work.[7] This sign was meant to be viewed by spectators standing well below it, on the sidewalk whose fictional extension crosses the bottom of the painting. Since Watteau intended it to occupy an arched space, its original shape was somewhat different from the rectangular dimensions of the work currently on display in Charlottenburg. The original was also about 49 centimeters wider and shorter. The modifications to Watteau's painting have been attributed to his student, Pater.[8] X-ray analysis suggests that beyond the present left edge of the painting was the image of a cart filled with hay.[9]

    During the fortnight in 1721 when the sign was hung above Gersaint's shop, Au Grand Monarque, a prospective client would have beheld three successive planes receding within an arched frame: the pavement, the shop properly speaking, and the back room. At first glance, the work may seem to adhere to the conventions of central perspective, but it departs from them in two important ways. In the first place, the room and horizontal picture frames have one vanishing point, while the human figures have another. The vanishing point of the room and the picture frames is in the middle of the painted door, not in the middle of the painting (which is located farther to the right); this deviation from central perspective is underlined by the central seam that divides the two canvases. The people in the shop have a much higher vanishing point (around the fourth cross-bar of the door) than the shop and the paintings.[10] In a second, remarkable deviation from central perspective, the left wall is much more dramatically foreshortened than the right, even though the vanishing point of the room is so close to the center of the painting. As a result, the wall with windows in the back room of the shop is made to look completely unrealistic. Whether or not this apparent disparity was deliberate, Martin Sperlich is right to emphasize that it removes the entire shop from the realm of every-day, measurable reality.[11] These built-in inconsistencies also suggest—or so I will argue—that there may be no single, unified perspective from which to interpret Watteau's last great painting.

Before entering the shop itself, viewers (or prospective clients) were separated from Watteau's representation of the shop by the first plane, a fictive extension (drawn to scale) of the very pavement on which they were standing.[12] This foreground is drawn in rapid, heavy brushstrokes,

Antoine Watteau, *L'Enseigne de Gersaint* (oil painting, 1721, Charlottenburg Castle, Staatliche Schlösser und Gärten, Berlin). Photo: Roger-Viollet.

perhaps as if to underline that these are not real, everyday cobblestones, but cobblestones transformed by art (on the far right, the dog searching for fleas recalls a painting in Rubens's Maria de Medici cycle). They cross the bottom of the *Enseigne*, like a symbolic threshold between daily life (outside the painting) and the graceful world inhabited by the figures in the middle ground, where everything and everyone is obviously a work of art. In contrast to the shop itself, the cobblestone pavement is nearly empty, and the few details on its margins are emphatically trivial: on the left, a cart filled with hay; on the far right, the dog from Rubens.

The King's Portrait

In the lower left corner of the shop sign, a workman is crating a portrait of the Sun King. This portrait is clearly recognizable as one of Rigaud's portraits of Louis XIV,[13] or a copy of it; in Rigaud's image, the king displays (upon his jabot) a medal of the Ordre du Saint-Esprit. Another workman holds a heavy mirror, which he is waiting to put into the crate, while a third figure in workman's clothing holds a pitchfork (which he will presumably use to fill the crate with hay). The portrait of "the Great Monarch" also names Gersaint's shop (Au Grand Monarque ["At the (sign of the) Great Monarch"]) on the Pont-Notre-Dame,[14] which is why the work has been called a signboard within a signboard.[15]

Beyond naming Gersaint's shop, what else (if anything) is the king's portrait doing there? Robert Neuman, who has documented the extensive use of portraiture within contemporary entombment images and funerary literature, has argued that the crating of Louis XIV's portrait is also a gesture of entombment. He notes that Watteau used the Sun King's portrait as an ironic emblem of succession—that is, to entomb Louis XIV, while suggesting that art dealers and collectors (rather than Louis XV) are the true successors to "the Great Monarch" as patrons and protectors of the arts.[16] The crating of Louis XIV's portrait has also been interpreted in terms of the older emblematic tradition of *vanitas*, which rehearses the transitory character of human glory. Among the other conventional images of *vanitas* in the shop sign, one may cite the clock—which (as others have pointed out) has been placed almost directly behind the portrait of Louis XIV—and the mirrors, one of which is about to be crated along with the portrait.[17] The crate can thus be seen as a sort of coffin, and the dead king's portrait as a *gisant*. In fact, Gérard Le Coat has argued that even Watteau's use of color forms part of a traditional allegorical program.[18]

In contrast, Paul Thibaud has interpreted the king's portrait in the light
of a more modern and celebratory religious context. In "Adieu lumière
de ma vie," he situates these same images in a Christian spiritual tradition
(associated with Erasmus, Rabelais, and Marguerite de Navarre) in which
the prospect of death confers the highest value upon life, and hence love,
in this world.[19] Mary Vidal also takes issue with those who would interpret
the king's portrait (and the painting it names) in terms of *vanitas:* "[This
interpretation] ignores Watteau's sensitive celebration of the things of this
world and his evident delight in beauty and youthfulness. Shimmering
satin dresses, silvered and suavely curled wigs, the flash of brocade linings,
the nape of a woman's neck caressed by a few strands of loosened hair—
everything contributes to the pleasure of the eyes and anchors the image
firmly in the present and in life."[20]

Although one may find it more plausible to view *L'Enseigne de Gersaint*
as a celebration of the fleeting pleasures of art, love, and life than as a
statement about the vanity of images and human glory, one cannot just
foreclose other interpretations. For example, what does one make of the
fact that the back room of Gersaint's shop is empty? Is it empty, simply
in order to highlight the shop and its customers? Or to reiterate the emptiness of all things human? Or perhaps to emphasize the urgency of celebrat-
ing human life and love? Then there is the matter of the light that pours
through the windows of that back room. It would seem that this light
cannot come from the same place as the light that casts shadows across
the front of Gersaint's shop. Does this curious light imply some kind of
divine or artistic transcendency? Or does asking this kind of question
amount to "overloading" a detail, such as the king's portrait, "with too
much significance"?[21] The most radical position against interpretation of
L'Enseigne de Gersaint has been taken by Kenneth Clark, for whom this
work is merely a frivolous genre scene of exceptional dimensions.[22]

Whatever Watteau's last signboard means, the king's portrait stands
for *L'Enseigne de Gersaint*, just as the signboard itself stands for the shop.
The portrait is a part that stands for the entire painting and also for the
shop, Au Grand Monarque. The portrait is a synecdoche for the entire
signboard, and it has itself been literally "troped" (turned) at a ninety-
degree angle. By the simple gesture of having a workman turn the portrait
on its side, Watteau makes the king's gaze seem lifeless and empty, almost
disembodied.

Under the reign of Louis XIV, the king's terrifying gaze had been the
center of attention, just as his portrait had imposed the Great Monarch's
theoretically "absolute" power. Louis Marin has argued that Rigaud's full-
length ceremonial portrait of the Sun King (now in the Louvre) epitomized

Detail of Watteau's *L'Enseigne de Gersaint*. Photo: Roger-Viollet.

the premise of absolutist representation, according to which the king's gaze was endowed (in principle) with the power to subject the onlooker.[23] By 1721, however, the king's portrait has been turned on its side, and its relationship to his subjects has been turned around as well. Although little more than five years have passed since the death of Louis XIV (and two decades since Rigaud's ceremonial portrait was painted), the beholder can now look at the portrait freely. For example, the viewer can imitate the young lady in the vibrant pink satin dress, who glances at the picture as she enters the shop. He or she can also inspect it at leisure, or even (like the gentleman in the center of the shop sign, offering the lady a hand) ignore it altogether.[24]

The gesture of turning the king's portrait on its side testifies to a dramatic turn of events, of which the overturning of Louis XIV's will is another symptom. In Watteau's artistic will and testament, the royal portrait is still important, because it names Gersaint's shop. It retains the special function of *naming*, except that this name no longer has the unique status that Louis ("Louis le Grand," "Le Grand Monarque") had enjoyed.[25] Au Grand Monarque names a place of business, where expensive art objects (this particular portrait among them) are for sale.

Just as the Sun King's eyes have ceased to radiate light, so the large mirror behind his portrait (which another worker is preparing to put in the crate) reflects almost nothing. As Mary Vidal points out, the combination of portrait and mirror modifies the mimetic function of art:

> The mirror-portrait combination is a commentary on the mimetic function of art, and at the same time transforms that function by the manner in which the two objects are represented. Easy identification of Louis XIV is prevented by the partial, overturned presentation of the portrait, while the mirror reflects nothing but a shadowy blur. . . . Watteau avoids the *trompe l'oeil* effects of the realist image—effects that are essential qualities of the mirror and the portrait—in order to display and consider the two forms of art in relationship to one another.[26]

The "shadowy blur" reflected by this mirror hints at what I shall call Watteau's "specular" vision. The term *specular* (from the Latin *specere*, "to see") is appropriate here, because it underlines the connection, in post-absolutist culture, between mirroring *(speculum)* and (economic) *speculation*. In the next chapter (in the context of Marivaux's theater and its kinship with John Law's monetary policy), I shall discuss the relationship between these two sorts of "specular" or "speculative" activity.

At this point I shall simply anticipate that discussion, by alluding to the ties among Watteau, Marivaux, and the financial bourgeoisie—and, in particular, the Crozat brothers.[27] Pierre Crozat, who maintained an elaborate pleasure park outside Montmorency, protected Watteau for some years (his relationship to Watteau's fêtes galantes has been the topic of a suggestive article by Thomas Crow).[28] Watteau's enigmatic, specular vision[29] is not presented directly or immediately in the *Enseigne*, but indirectly, through the mediation of other images. Everything in Watteau's shop sign is a sign of art and stands for a determinate form of cultural mediation. Through the mediation of the various signs of art and artifice that compose it, the *Enseigne de Gersaint* displays Watteau's specular vision of art in the post-absolutist future.

Commodification

By turning the king's portrait on its side, and turning it into one art object
among others (a portrait of the king and not "the king" himself, part of
a series of objects offered for sale to the general public), Watteau undermined its unique mimetic and ontological status. In a way, this was a
revolutionary gesture. It implied that although "the king" (his timeless,
eternal body) still lived in official doctrine, he had become marginalized
and irrelevant as an ontological or aesthetic standard. This glorious shop
sign suggests that the classical hierarchy—in which the divine ruler stood
high above all political subjects, the shop sign was a very "low" genre,
and certain subjects were inherently valuable—is dead. The king's portrait in the shop sign continues to raise questions about its own status
and meaning, but these are the same questions elicited by every other
commodity on the art market. Rigaud's ceremonial portrait of Louis XIV
was commissioned by the king, while the version (or copy) of that portrait
displayed in *L'Enseigne* is now meant, like every other painting in the
shop, to satisfy the demands of an anonymous market.

In the corner of *L'Enseigne de Gersaint*, the king's portrait names Gersaint's shop and also makes an implicit comment on French classicism and
the status of art in France after the death of "the Great Monarch." Art is
beginning to emerge from the patronage system, and artists need no longer
cater to the desires of noble patrons, the greatest of whom was Louis XIV.
Art is becoming a luxurious commodity, offered for sale, not to known
individuals, but to an anonymous market. Insofar as it lays no claim to
any special status, the king's portrait now typifies the commodity status
of post-absolutist art works.[30] Unlike the original Rigaud portrait, the Sun
King's portrait in *L'Enseigne de Gersaint* subjects no one, and it proposes
neither a political nor an aesthetic model. In its place, in the king's wake,
Watteau's shop sign proposes a different notion of subjectivity and another
standard of value.

By turning the portrait of the "Great Monarch" on its side, having it
crated and "buried," Watteau implicitly raises the question of succession:
who (or what) will now be authorized to determine the direction of society
and art? In the previous chapters on Saint-Simon and Voltaire, I noted
how post-absolutist culture tends to discredit blood as a principle of succession and to replace it with a more abstract or impersonal standard, such
as the law. The Minority *lit de justice* of 1718 had denied Louis XIV the
power (asserted in his will) to transmit his authority to his illegitimate
children. Likewise, in 1719 a poet who called himself Arouet de Voltaire

Hyacinthe Rigaud, *Louis XIV* (oil painting, Musée de Dijon). Photo: Roger-Viollet.

had issued his own, poetic letters of nobility. By turning over the Sun King's portrait, Watteau registers the end of an era of artistic patronage (organized around the image of Louis XIV) and affirms the birth of a new age, in which art and artists are subject, not to individual noble patrons, but to the more abstract demands of a market for refined luxury goods.

An Enigmatic Invitation

The people in the shop are divided into four groups, two on each panel. These four groups are arranged symmetrically, two to a panel/side, in "wave-like arabesques."[31] Considered as a single form, these groups have

the shape of an S, a form that (as René Huyghe notes) often recurs in
Watteau's work.[32] In this analysis, I follow the line of that S by reading
it (like a European language) from left to right: from (on the left) the
group organized around the king's portrait, to the couple that is entering
the shop, to (right of center) the couple examining an oval portrait, and
finally, the group organized around a mirror. This left-to-right S sequence
is not only a compositional pattern, but also a significant narrative principle in Watteau's shop sign. In terms of both composition and narrative,
it is remarkable that the S of *L'Enseigne* is traversed—crossed out, as it
were—by the line that connects the young couple entering the shop with
the open door at the rear of the shop (more precisely, with the seam that
separates the two canvases). It is as if this couple (and once again, the
viewer) were being drawn in two different, conflicting directions: into the
shop (following the S) and away from it, into a utopian space where beautiful people and luxury goods are the sole subjects and objects of desire,
and somewhere else beyond (or simply behind) that world.

The viewer's attention is drawn into the middle ground of the shop
sign (the shop itself) by the lady in the lustrous pink dress, just left of
center. Her dress is a so-called *robe volante* ("hoop dress"), the latest Paris
fashion in 1721; she also is wearing a green bonnet, fashionably tiny, with
white lace.[33] This young lady steps up into the shop itself, with the assis-
tance of her companion (wearing a three-piece suit, which was also a new
fashion),[34] while casting a sideways glance at the king's portrait. This couple composes what may be the most frequently reproduced detail of the
painting, one that has become part of a "visual cliché" for refined society.[35]
The young lady's rear foot and the bottom of her pink dress have not yet
left the pavement and entered the world within, just as the viewer has not
yet entered the shop. Posner sees the pose of the lady in pink as an invitation to enter the higher realm of art: "The picture's main theme is introduced by the lady at the left. We are invited to follow on her heel, up
from the real, everyday world of the cobblestone street and flea-ridden
dog, into the enchanted realm of beauty and culture. It is a realm where
the senses and intelligence sharpen and brighten, and where existence is
given justification."[36] Mary Vidal counters this interpretation by maintaining that nothing in the painting distinguishes the inside from the outside of Gersaint's shop or suggests that the lady has been transformed by
stepping up into it: "On the contrary, the high fashion of her clothing
and the polish of her manners already materializes for us the meeting of
the outside and the inside. Her appearance and behavior links the social-
aesthetic spectacle of the Parisian street, and its parade of ladies and gentle-

men, with the social-aesthetic institution of the luxury boutique, and its fine goods on display."[37] We have seen that within the shop sign itself, both the inside and the outside of Gersaint's shop contain references to art: even the dog looking for fleas in a corner of the painted sidewalk is an allusion to an art work. But Vidal makes a more radical argument: that the inside of the shop sign's frame was socially and aesthetically continuous with the aestheticized world of the painting's elite viewers. To the extent that Watteau's contemporaries were part of the same "social-aesthetic spectacle" as the *trompe l'oeil* painting, Vidal argues, there is (or was, in 1721) no difference, aesthetic or ontological, between the shop sign and the world of its customers standing in the street. According to this interpretation, elite viewers of the shop sign had already turned themselves into art objects, before the lady in pink invited them to enter the shop and follow her gaze: from the portrait of Louis XIV that names the shop to the heavy mirror that another worker is waiting to crate, up and across the painting to all the other art works that the figures in the composition are admiring.

As we have noted, the rapid, heavy brushstrokes in the foreground underscore the fact that the cobblestones, like the dog on the far right, are not part of any banal reality, but signs of reality transformed by art. However, there is also a marked contrast between the rough brushstrokes of the cobblestones and hay in the shop sign's foreground and the more carefully, delicately applied paint within Gersaint's shop. Doubtless everything within the shop sign has been transformed into a sign of art, but not everything has been transformed in the same way, or perhaps to the same extent. To maintain that there is no qualitative difference between the world of Gersaint's shop sign and the world outside it, one has to minimize the significance of the artistic contrast between the foreground and the rest of the painting.

There is no question that the lady in pink satin is inviting viewers to enter the shop: she is, after all, part of a commercial advertisement. Yet it remains to be seen whether she is inviting viewers, however fashionably dressed, to enter the world of the painting itself. After all, this "invitation" is being tendered by a lady who has her back turned. Norbert Knopp has remarked that despite the intensity of the relationships among the characters in Watteau's paintings, they hardly ever concern themselves with anything or anyone outside of their own group, and especially not with the viewer. As he points out, in *L'Enseigne de Gersaint* the viewer's gaze is actually met only by the lifeless eyes of Louis XIV.[38] The world within the frame of Watteau's painting, in and out of the shop, is filled with

elegant people (fashionably dressed clients, attractive and solicitous employees) and art objects. But if the beholder or prospective client has the
impression of being invited into the "enchanted realm" inhabited by these
people, he or she is also manifestly excluded from it by the characters'
absorption in their own activities. One may therefore wonder if the lady's
pose is an unequivocal invitation to follow her into the realm of Watteau's art.

This enigmatic invitation is related to the dual status of *L'Enseigne de
Gersaint*, to which I have already referred—its status as both a shop sign
and a work of art, representative of both low culture and high culture.
Gersaint himself implicitly recognized this ambiguity by removing Watteau's work after only two weeks' display, to protect it from the elements.
For one thing, the shop sign and the work of art do not convey the same
message: as a shop sign, the work clearly invites us to enter the shop
below, but as a work of art it does not unequivocally invite us to do
anything. Donald Posner formulates the painting's ambivalence in this
way: "Because the painting has been reshaped and framed like the usual
kind of museum picture, one can no longer fully or easily appreciate its
intended duality as an object. It is at once a commonplace sign advertising
a mercantile establishment, and a painting of great monetary value embodying a vision of high culture."[39] Adopting a different perspective, Julie
Anne Plax places this "meeting" of high and low culture within a social
context. She argues that by breaking down the boundaries between high
and low culture, *L'Enseigne de Gersaint* makes a case for the "nobility"
of an emergent social class of art dealers and art collectors, while also
creating a new genre:

> In *L'Enseigne*, Watteau creates a new genre of painting, as he did in his *fêtes
> galantes* and *Départ*, by playing the cultural conventions and assumptions of
> official "high" art against those of popular "low" expression; . . . he creates
> a new genre of painting which simply did not fit into the traditional institu-
> tionally determined categories. . . . In *L'Enseigne*, Watteau redeems and tran-
> scends pure genre by embedding allusion to larger, more important mean-
> ings—the stuff and substance of traditional history painting—within the
> specific time, space and experience of modern life.[40]

The dog and the lady in pink have both already entered the frame of
Watteau's painting, and have thus become art objects on display, but it
is not so obvious where the viewer stands. The position of the viewer and

her or his relationship to the painting (in a word, the status of the beholder) is precisely what remains to be seen.

Entering the Aesthetic Dimension

In Kant's classic formulation, the experience of the beautiful is that of a "disinterested pleasure." However, in *L'Enseigne de Gersaint* the customers are obviously looking at each other (each of them a beautiful luxury object), and at the inanimate art objects in the shop, with an extremely "interested," erotic intensity. Consider, for example, the two groups of figures on the right side of the work; in each group a shopkeeper shows a work of art to a group of clients. The first group is next to the back door of Gersaint's shop: the shopkeeper displays a large oval painting of female nudes in a vaporous landscape, and an older couple carefully scrutinizes it. The woman in this group (who is using her lorgnette to examine a presumably savory detail) wears an old-fashioned dress, which recalls fashion in the time of Louis XIV.[41] Kneeling on the floor while supporting himself with a walking stick, her companion is also giving his full attention to the nude female figures. Indeed, as Plax remarks, "he is as close to the painting as he can get without touching it," even though, as Vidal notes, "at such close range the man sees as much paint as he wants to see flesh."[42] In the second group, a young female salesperson is showing a small framed object (probably a mirror, part of a "vanity set") to a lady and two gentlemen.

In both these groups, Watteau focuses upon the relationship between art and desire, which had been a central preoccupation of the fête galante.[43] There is a general consensus that the fête galante is, as Thomas Crow puts it, "the culminating and defining product of Watteau's artistic project."[44] But not enough attention has been paid to the thematic and formal continuity between Watteau's fête galante and his last shop sign. Watteau's fête galante, which typically shows elegantly attired men and women, often in theatrical costumes, in the context of a beautiful park or similarly "natural" context, was not just a figment of the artist's imagination. As René Démoris has shown, these paintings are based upon the actual behavior and costumes of certain members of the aristocracy, activities to which Watteau then added yet another layer of artifice.[45] Despite the increasing austerity at court after 1684, these fêtes galantes enabled members of the aristocracy to continue playing the essentially theatrical role that Louis

XIV had assigned to them. Their behavior expressed a resurgence of aristocratic values that culminated during the Regency of Philippe d'Orléans, when members of the higher nobility attempted to regain some of the political power that they had lost to the crown. These political ambitions played themselves out during the brief experiment (1715–18) with aristocratic monarchy or "polysynody" (discussed above, in chapter 1), in which Saint-Simon played a role.[46] After the failure of this experiment, the nobility was forced to continue asserting itself primarily in the cultural sphere.[47]

Démoris establishes a suggestive link between Watteau's painting and many novels written during the period between 1700 and 1720. At this time, he contends, French novels were suffering from a sort of "narrative *malaise*."[48] He shows that the novels of Watteau's contemporaries emphasize their own artifice and contain little substantive action, just as Watteau's painting is stylized, passionless, and practically devoid of action.[49] In Watteau, the impression of artifice is compounded by the fact that his characters do not participate in any common dramatic action; rather, they all stand theatrically apart, both from each other and from their implicit audience. In the *Enseigne de Gersaint*, as the characters examine works of art (looking at art is their only common "action"), each seems to remain isolated in his or her individual consciousness.

Watteau's fêtes galantes are coded performances, whose action is limited to the gestures with which one sex pays courtly attention to the other, in such a way that desire and artifice seem to reinforce each other. Each of these gestures is like a mask: it uses artifice to entice the beholder and invites her or him to uncover the mystery that it openly conceals. In Watteau, the mask is a sign of artifice, of art, and art is an invitation to desire. Everywhere in the fêtes galantes, art and desire court each other, so to speak, in mask: in music and dance, movement and speech, as well as in signs of artifice. At times the characters wear theatrical costumes (just as members of the aristocracy sometimes disguised themselves on such occasions), but they always carry themselves as if they were "onstage," in front of an audience, displaying their own artifice. The characters of the fête galante speak of desire in poses and gestures, clothing and glances, but always in coded, culturally mediated form, and that very theatricality is what seems to make them desirable.

Despite its theatrical form of presentation, the fête galante displays almost no human action, and even less conflict.[50] The relative lack of action has the effect of drawing one's attention to the fête's stylized natural setting. French classical doctrine had devalued nature, because the latter belonged to the inferior ("ignoble") realm of material necessity. By "correcting" and masking it, Watteau ennobles nature and makes it into a dignified (that is, playful) object of desire. Nature itself becomes a *mask* for the desire that motivates the fête.[51] The fête galante simultaneously masks desire and solicits it, from its participants and from its viewer. Like a mask, Watteau's fête galante points to itself and invites the beholder to discover what it is concealing. In contrast, when Rigaud's absolute monarch pointed to himself, he did not claim to stand for (to represent) anything, but simply to impose the fullness of his own being: "*I [Moi]*." He asserted the miraculous presence of his own being, transubstantiated, as it were, into art. From the standpoint of the Port-Royal theologians, this was a heretical claim, since it transgressed the boundary between politics and the eucharist. As Louis Marin notes: "This is the boundary that is crossed by power's desire for the absolute, through the fantastic representation of the Monarch in his portrait and his name, the portrait legitimized by the representation of the prince; a portrait named, the name of an image that is the presentation in which the king is seized by the absolute, as he seizes himself as absolute by gazing at himself in it."[52] Like the eucharist, the absolute monarch theoretically is the fullness of Being itself, not a mere sign; his portrait does not stand for anything else. In contrast, the characters of the fête galante point to the fact that they do stand for something else, that they are masked—in short, that each of them is a sign.[53]

Thematically and formally, therefore, the fête galante and *L'Enseigne de Gersaint* form part of the same artistic project, the same "specular vision." Just as the regent had moved the official center of cultural life back to Paris in 1715, Watteau's *Enseigne* transfers the antinatural, theatrical (and ultimately semiotic) aesthetics of the fête galante to an urban stage. He also carries the logic of the fête galante to a more abstract, if not theoretical, level. Instead of continuing to mask nature as art, he frees himself almost entirely from "nature" and concerns himself, in an almost modern way, with art and the desire for art.[54] In Watteau, nature is always transformed by artifice, it is masked.

It is for this reason that, as Vidal has remarked, the three large mirrors in *L'Enseigne de Gersaint* suggest their reflective function, rather than representing it.[55] In his last shop sign, Watteau imprints not only nature, but art itself with the mark of artifice. Donald Posner has argued—convincingly, I believe—that the paintings that cover the walls of Gersaint's shop are not reproductions of actual paintings, any more than the people in the shop are imitations of actual people. In the first place, it is inconceivable that the walls of Gersaint's shop could really have been filled with Venetian, Flemish, and French masterworks. Further, a careful look at these pictures reveals that none of them (or at least none painted by Watteau) is a copy of an actual masterwork. None of the people represented in the shop is based on a "real" person, either, although a great deal of energy has been invested in discovering "real life" models for them. In fact, Watteau seems to have been more interested in delineating the folds of a dress than in painting the faces of recognizable individuals.[56] He readily copied faces from one work to another, and it seems safe to say that the people portrayed in *L'Enseigne de Gersaint* have no specific models in "life."[57]

Neither the paintings nor the people are copies of specific models, but they are signs of certain artistic and social types. The paintings stand for artistic traditions (Flemish, Venetian, French) or types, just as the people in *L'Enseigne* are masked or idealized social types (workers, salespeople, customers, young and old, lovers), signs of a reality that has been transfigured by Watteau's art. Even the dog looking for fleas, in the lower right corner of the painting, is an allusion to art and not just an imitation of nature. Ironically enough, this dog is the shop sign's only certifiable reference to a specific painting.

The fête galante had previously been a vehicle through which the marginalized "counter-court" aristocracy (at Sceaux and other places) could justify its own uselessness and enact its superiority to the wealthy bourgeoisie. During the latter half of the seventeenth century, this theatrical form of conspicuous leisure had been the exclusive province of the aristocracy. But on the urban stage of Gersaint's shop sign, what distinguishes the "noble" from the vulgar is the ability to endow one's leisure with an artistic quality. If not for the fact that two of the gentlemen are wearing swords, one would not be able to tell if his fashionable clients were members of the nobility or rich bourgeois. What defines the superiority of these art lovers is not their birth, but their distinctive gift for fashionable self-display.[58] Gersaint's clients demonstrably belong to the elect few who can publicly transform desire into art and art into desire. They seem somehow to have achieved a state of grace, though how they have reached that exalted state remains their secret. As Julie Ann Plax has noted, "Watteau's fêtes challenge the viewer to recognize and understand the hints and suggestions he deploys: they demand, are you one of the elect or are you one of those that has to be told things directly?"[59]

It is equally obvious that the workmen and shopkeepers in Gersaint's shop are not among the elect. For them, art is work, not play. These wage laborers need art to make a living, whereas the clients are ladies and gentlemen of leisure, to whom the coded nuances of art are second nature. By our day, all these "suggestions" have become part of the culture that one must laboriously acquire through research. Yet now, having worked through the relationship between the fête galante and *L'Enseigne de Gersaint*, we can define the status of the shop sign's beholder.

Museum Theatrum

As Mary Vidal has shown, in *L'Enseigne de Gersaint* Watteau continues the primarily Flemish tradition of *cabinets d'amateur*, in which collections of art objects are theatrically displayed, and he transforms that tradition by integrating aristocratic figures into the display. In this way, Watteau makes the represented figures into aesthetic objects that are just as important as the works displayed on the walls of Gersaint's shop. At the same time, Vidal argues, he creates a space in which art becomes continuous with a broader, aestheticized system of elite social exchange.[60] In her view, the theatrical absence of a store front (or "fourth wall") underlines the continuity of the shop with the street, and hence with the world.

However, the *cabinets d'amateur* and the aestheticized, theatrical world into which Watteau seems to have transformed them must be placed in a historical context. Until the seventeenth century, works of art had not been considered as collector's items. Indeed, as Giorgio Agamben has shown, the very appearance of *cabinets d'amateur*, and of their representations in words (catalogues) and images, testifies to the onset of the separation between art—and the aesthetic, in general—and the rest of the world.[61] Although art collections have become part of our modern environment, they did not exist in the Middle Ages (or a fortiori, in the ancient world), since at that time what we now call ("fine") art had no specific or autonomous mode of existence for a contemporary viewer:

> As he looked at the tympanum of the cathedral at Vézelay, with its sculptures representing all the peoples of the earth in the sole light of the divine Pentecost . . . medieval man did not have the aesthetic impression of observing a work of art, but instead got what for him was the most concrete measure of the limits of his world. The marvelous was not yet an autonomous sentimental tonality or an effect belonging to the work of art, but an indistinct presence of the grace that, in the work, put human activity in harmony with the divine world of creation, and thus kept alive an echo of what art had been at its beginnings in Greece: the miraculous and disturbing power of bringing forth, of *producing* being and the world in the work.[62]

There is a vast gap between medieval man's experience of the tympanum at Vézelay and the early eighteenth-century beholder's experience of the secular tympanum that is *L'Enseigne de Gersaint*. In the context of this chapter, I would like to emphasize two of the most obvious differences between these experiences.

First, unlike the Vézelay tympanum, Watteau's "tympanum" (like the fête galante) is addressed to members of the social elite, not to everyone. Second, and more radically, although *L'Enseigne* is a glorious *sign* of art—and therefore of an elevated, noble state of being—it is unlikely that many beholders have ever perceived Watteau's shop sign in the way contemporary viewers saw the tympanum at Vézelay—as a manifestation of Being itself. Moreover, unlike Rigaud's ceremonial portrait of Louis XIV, which theoretically incarnated the fullness of Being, Watteau's painting does not even claim to be anything more than a sign. At best, *L'Enseigne de Gersaint* represents for us an exquisitely true world, but it cannot literally *be* that world for us.

In fact, precisely because Watteau's work of art now posits the aesthetic dimension as the highest (and therefore as a separate) mode of human existence, because it represents art as the means of acceding to that higher, truer world, it separates its beholders from that world. In this situation, notes Agamben,

> all the viewer can ever find in the art work is now mediated by aesthetic representation, which is itself, independently of any content, the supreme value and most intimate truth, which deploys its power in and from the work itself. The free creative principle of the artist stands between the viewer and his truth, which he could obtain from the work of art, like a precious veil of Maia that he will never be able to grasp concretely, but only through the image reflected in the magical mirror of his own taste.[63]

In the history of Western art, the notion of "taste" would eventually require the beholder to occupy a position that was completely detached from the work of art, so that he or she might enjoy the "disinterested pleasure" of aesthetic judgment (in the Kantian sense). But the beholder of Watteau's *L'Enseigne de Gersaint* occupied an unstable, transitional position in the emergence of the aesthetic dimension. At this moment, desire and aesthetic pleasure have not yet been separated. Watteau's beholder is invited to enter a higher and truer, artistic world, which art itself prevents him or her from really entering.

Let us take a closer look at the attitudes that the figures in Watteau's shop sign adopt toward works of art. All four groups in this painting are linked by a common activity: looking at art that is for sale. Either they work for the shop or they are viewing its wares, they are either employees (dependent for their livelihood upon the sale of art) or potential consumers, but all are joined by a common visual preoccupation.[64] Of course, they are not all looking at art with the same intensity or "interest." The laborers and salespeople—that is, the characters who are not customers—look at the objects operationally (as objects that need to be taken down, stored, or sold). For the laborers on the far left of the painting, the art works are simply pieces of furniture, and for the staff of the shop (on the right) they are just commodities. Neither group looks at the paintings very carefully, nor should they be expected to. The paintings matter to them only as a source of livelihood. Nor would it be appropriate for them to look very attentively (that is, like persons of a higher social class) at the works of art. The art-sellers stand or sit behind the art works, while the art-lovers examine the works from the front. From their class perspective, the elegant customers pay no attention to the workers and salespeople. For example, the lady in pink is drawn to the portrait of Louis XIV, but she seems not to notice the men who are packing it. For the elegant clients ("customer" would be too common a label for them), the laborers and shopkeepers do not exist: it is as if they were pieces of furniture, parts of the scenery.

Conversely, the shopkeepers and workers do not look at the art-loving clients, either. Consider the beautifully detached, distracted gaze of the young female salesperson on the far right. Like her fellow employee, she offers a work of art for examination by the clients, but she does not look at it or at them. She seems to be looking at no one and nothing in particular, as if her gaze were meant to express her engagement in a potential transaction. Her gaze looks strangely abstracted; everyone else is looking (either operationally, or as art-lovers / voyeurs) at something tangible. She, however, seems to convey nothing but her participation in the sales situation. In her subordinate position, it would not be suitable for her to signify complicity; rather, she should suggest that she is at their service. In Watteau's shop sign, the only gaze that has less "presence" than hers is the dead gaze of Louis XIV.

The young lady behind the counter is showing a small framed object to a group composed of a lady and two gentlemen. One can see only the back of this object, but critics have inferred that the object is a mirror, part of a so-called "vanity" set. The inference is justified both by the presence of other, visible mirrors in the shop sign and by the manifestly narcissistic pleasure that Gersaint's customers take in their own images, even though one could also imagine that the customers in this group are looking at a painting. If these customers are "intently" studying a mirror, as Posner believes, the spectacle of their self-adoration presents an ironic contrast with the scene of Adoration of Christ that hangs behind this group on the shop wall.[65] The figure of the Christ child in the latter scene is almost directly behind the mysterious object on the counter; within the painting, He is the object of everyone's attention. Yet while on the wall everyone is looking adoringly at the Holy Child, around the counter the customers are intent on what seems to be a mirror. The attitude of the three viewers betrays a mixture of aesthetic and erotic intensity, but it is certainly not religious. The clients are appreciating, and not adoring, this "mirror," along with what they see in it. Vidal remarks: "In the context of the art gallery, their narcissism takes on a positive, aesthetic meaning. It is celebrated and put on display, like the paintings on the walls, for the pleasure of those who are displaying themselves and for the delectation of those who pass by or who visit the shop."[66] Whether or not it is the contemplation of their own image that gives these people such pleasure, one can be sure that they are looking at an object, something delightfully part of this world. A sacred work, such as the tympanum at the Vézelay cathedral, was believed to disclose Being itself and was therefore not really an object. In traditional religious terms, object-ness belongs to the profane, not the sacred:[67] the sacred is "no thing," it points to the nothingness of all things worldly. In these customers' eyes, the mirror (or whatever it may be) is an erotically charged art object.

What are these people really looking at? One asks this question, even though one knows that the entire painting is an illusion, and that the customers are not really looking at anything. But rather than dismiss this question as vain speculation, let us consider what it means to have asked it, to have believed that the characters in this painting can see something that we cannot. The rapt quality of their gaze is no illusion, nor is the fact that all we can see is the back of a frame. Insofar as *L'Enseigne de Gersaint* is a shop sign, an advertisement, it invites us to imitate a model— but by desiring what? If we are invited to model our behavior on this lady and two gentlemen, the apparent object of our mimetic desire has its back turned to us, just as the young lady who "invites" us into the shop also turns her back to us. Once again, the status of this image and of its beholder is called into question. If *L'Enseigne de Gersaint* is an image of transcendent beauty, does it imply that this transcendence, this state of grace, is available to us (perhaps through the love of art)? Or is Watteau's shop sign, like the mirrors in the shop, an image that ultimately reflects only a "shadowy blur," in Vidal's words? Maybe all we now can see is an enigmatic sign of transcendency and grace, and indeed the object of our desire is (literally, a) "vanity."

Let us recapitulate the S-shaped sequence that we have followed from left to right, examining four groups of figures, each of which is organized around a work of art. On the left, we noted that the king's portrait had been turned on its side in a crate, that it names Gersaint's shop and also registers the end of an era organized around the image of "the Great Monarch." The couple just to the left of center also seems emblematic, as it tenders an enigmatic "invitation" to the viewer. With the group just to the right of center, Watteau seems to have emblematized the relationship between art and desire, just as in the last group he may have suggested the vanity of both art and desire.

In this left-to-right order, these four "emblems" tell the viewer a story. In the first scene (or episode), the old king is being buried: the viewer may register the passing of the old artistic order and the emergence of a new one. Having noted this change, the viewer is then invited (in the second group) to step up into the (post-absolutist) world of art and artifice. The couple to the right of center has already taken that step and is poised to discover the secrets of art and desire. And then, in the most enigmatic scene in Watteau's last will and testament, we are faced with an emblem of the impossibility (or perhaps simply the vanity) of redeeming life (overcoming death) through art.

Emptiness

If we consider *L'Enseigne* from front to back, outside to inside, we also find ourselves confronted by disquieting images of emptiness. Gersaint's shop (the crowded middle ground of the signboard) is chock full of art, but it is bounded, front and back, by spaces that are nearly empty: in the front, the cobblestone street; in the rear, the back room. The last and narrowest of these receding planes is located in the center of the shop sign. Visible through glass doors in the rear, and illuminated by the light that streams through the windows on the left, is the empty back shop, devoid of both people and art works. At the center of the painting is a seam, and around that seam an empty, open space: a hole. The border separating the two canvases at the center neatly bisects the back door of the shop, whose back wall seems to be made of "French" windows or doors: in any case, nothing can be seen in the rear of the shop, except an empty room (or the empty part of a room) and empty, transparent window frames.

The viewer's attention is drawn to this vacuum by its central position, by its elevation (in Watteau's original conception, the door to the back room touched the highest point of the composition), by the dividing line between the canvases, and by the receding, although skewed, dual perspective of the work as a whole. Both vanishing points recede into this empty space, which is itself subdivided into empty frames of various sizes (the open lefthand flap of the double door, the French windows of the righthand door, the coffered ceiling).

One is struck by the contrast between the walls of the shop itself, which are covered with "full" frames (filled with paintings, all of which depict human subjects: there are no landscapes or still-lifes), and the cobbled street and back room, which are empty frames, devoid of all representation or art. One's gaze is drawn from the sidewalk, to the shop itself, and finally to the back room; from outside the shop, to inside, and behind (if not beyond) it. Surely this contrast is significant, and perhaps even more significant is the *sequence* in which the contrast is inscribed.

On the cobblestone pavement that extends across the entire bottom of the painting, there is only a sheaf of hay, a flea-ridden dog, and the weightless rear foot of the lady in pink, who has already begun to step up into the shop itself: this space contains no art objects (although the dog alludes to an art object) and no people (insofar as the distinction can be made here), either. In contrast, as we have noted, the shop itself is full of people, all of whom are so absorbed in looking at art that we cannot make eye contact with any of them. We may look at them, but they will never look at us. By dint of their absorption, the viewer is excluded from consideration.[68] Indeed, the objects in which these people are absorbed contribute to the beholder's sense of exclusion. For example, although the Great Monarch does look out of his frame, he seems to be looking at no one, which is why his glance looks "dead." Likewise, on the right, clients contemplate an enigmatic object. They can see the front of this object, but the viewer can see only the blank reverse. For this reason, to us (and to us only) the object looks spectacularly empty: we presume it is a mirror, but we may have just as much reason to believe that it is a small portrait. The viewer's imagination may "fill" this sign with any artistic content whatsoever: let us call it a "zero degree" art sign.[69] Finally, in the rear plane, the back of the shop is empty.

Could this pattern of absences also be emblematic of *L'Enseigne* itself? Although the shop sign's iconography has been viewed negatively (for example, in terms of *vanitas*), one can also take this emptiness affirmatively. From that perspective, an image like the king's lifeless portrait or (what appears to be) a mirror that one cannot see becomes an affirmation of artifice, of play, or maybe even of the market, before or beyond which there is nothing. From this perspective, one can see that art works have lost their sacred "aura," that they have become simply commodities, and (pace Walter Benjamin) one can celebrate that fact. Like the Great Monarch, like the Holy Child, all art works would then simply have become the subjects of paintings that are offered for sale, in a world that has lost all transcendence. From this perspective, the sacred sphere would have been emptied, leaving behind a space inhabited solely by commodities and the relationships they entail—by art works, art merchants, and art lovers.

In that case, the *Enseigne* would resemble Watteau's *Gilles* (1718?), the extraordinary life-size image of a moronic clown from the *commedia dell'arte*. For *Gilles* may also have been an urban shopsign, and only inappropriately Romantic values could make us believe that there is anything melancholy or sad about the image.[70] After Romanticism, it may be strange to see the sale of art presented affirmatively, without sadness, nostalgia, or any sense of a conflict between art and commerce. Nevertheless, it is possible that Watteau imagined the ending of the patronage system (emblematized by the crating of Louis XIV's portrait) and the opening of a space for art market relations (in Gersaint's shop), as a kind of liberation. He may have imagined Gersaint's shop as a glorious opportunity—for merchants, artists, and refined art lovers alike—to imitate the lady in pink, by going beyond the absolutist past, into the space of elite market relations. Watteau's shop sign may therefore be a utopian image, the sign of a mercantile fête galante, a stage where beautifully costumed lovers of fine art might see themselves reflected in the mirror of commodities.[71]

Watteau's "specular vision" of art entails various levels of unresolved ambiguity: the inconsistencies of perspective; the hesitation between a "realist" aesthetics of the sign (which ultimately stands for something outside itself) and a more "modernist" aesthetics of the self-referential "token"; and especially the way in which *L'Enseigne de Gersaint* seems simultaneously to invite its beholders to enter its beautiful world and to exclude them from it. Under the absolutist system, everyone had theoretically been subjected to the image of the Sun King, just as all political and cultural representations had been addressed to his royal patronage. But in Watteau's last shop sign, Au Grand Monarque no longer refers to the patron or ultimate addressee of all representation (to "the Great Monarch"), but simply states the name of an art dealer's shop ("at the sign of the Great Monarch"): the king's insignia has become *L'Enseigne de Gersaint*.

Love and Speculation

Marivaux

Love on Credit: *Le Jeu de l'amour et du hasard*

When it is a question of the king, the portrait is in some way and in some fashion the person it represents. — LOUIS MARIN, *Portrait of the King*

ACCORDING TO ABSOLUTIST DOCTRINE, a portrait of Louis XIV embodied the king himself, just as Counter-Reformation theology emphasized the real presence of Christ in the eucharist. In similar fashion, the presence in coins of a certain quantity of precious metal guaranteed their value and ensured that a louis d'or, for example, was worth its weight in gold. In the patriarchal hierarchy of absolutist society, human value was a treasure, continually on public display and transmitted by blood. Rank, in turn, was distributed by the Sun King, just as currency was measured in silver and gold; like currency, rank was also subject to rapid and unpredictable turns of fortune, to the sudden devaluation or revaluation that classical theater represented as a *coup de théâtre*.[1]

In contrast, post-absolutist culture was marked by an "increasing disembodiment of the status of value."[2] To a considerable extent, as we have seen in the cases of Saint-Simon and Voltaire, the value of individuals came to be measured in terms more abstract and intangible than blood, such as performance and respect for the law. In similar fashion, although John Law's bank ultimately failed, his monetary experiment relied upon paper notes, rather than precious metals, upon signs that lacked inherent value, but supposedly *represented* something valuable. One of the many investors who lost his fortune in the wake of John Law's bankruptcy was Pierre Carlet de Chamblain, better known by his pen name, Marivaux. Born (on February 4, 1688) into the luxurious milieu of the financial bourgeoisie, Marivaux spent his early childhood in Paris. His father, as director of the Royal Mint at Riom from 1698 on, produced gold and silver currency (just as John Law's father was a goldsmith). As in the monetary theory of Law, Marivaux's theater relied upon credit and speculation, devices that had not been acceptable in the absolutist ("classical") theater of Molière.

Arlequin actionnaire ("Harlequin the Stockholder," engraving). Photo: Roger-Viollet.

Credit

At the beginning of act III of Molière's *Le Misanthrope*, the two *petits marquis*, Acaste and Clitandre, argue about which of them has more reason to be satisfied with himself generally, and in particular to believe that the coquettish Célimène loves him. Acaste declares: "Mais les gens de mon air, marquis, ne sont pas faits / Pour *aimer à crédit* et faire tous les frais" ("For men like me, however, it makes no sense / To love on trust, and foot the whole expense.")[3]

According to Furetière's *Dictionnaire universel* (1690), the word *crédit* refers to the measure of a person's status within a given community, as in its first definition: "Belief, esteem, that one acquires *in the public* through one's virtue, one's probity."[4] *Crédit* is a value that one acquires in relationship to a certain public; it must be openly, publicly known. Individuals or groups acquire this sort of credit through action in the public arena. Although his first definition stresses moral values (virtue, probity), Furetière's first example ("The Greeks gave themselves *credit* with their sciences") suggests that the meaning of the term is not limited to the moral sphere. *Crédit* also refers more generally to what is publicly believed, or credited, about a person or group. In this sense, credit is the result of previous actions, but it is not itself active; it is the measure ("estime") of what a person or group is believed capable of doing.

Furetière's second definition of *crédit*, however, has a more active sense, which is retained in modern French: "CREDIT also refers to the power of the authority, of the riches, that one acquires by means of the reputation one has acquired. This minister has acquired great *credit* at court in the mind of the Prince."[5] According to the second definition, *crédit* is the publicly recognized value or reputation that a community grants a person, on the basis of his or her previous actions, and which allows that person to exert power over the other members of that same community. This sort of credit leads others to pay attention to one's opinions, or to entrust one with money or goods ("richesses"). Since it makes the past actions of a person or group even more valuable within the community, it is active, or productive, credit. In both the virtual and active senses recorded by Furetière, *crédit* refers to an interaction between the value or worth of an individual and the beliefs that are publicly held about that person. Credit, in other words, is based upon an economy of public belief.

The third meaning registered by Furetière locates this credit economy within a specifically commercial context. In business, credit is "the natural *loan* that is made in money and merchandise, on the reputation and solvency of a merchant."[6] Credit, in this sense, is a loan *(prest)* and therefore

never actually belongs to anyone. In business—but perhaps also in all
forms of human commerce—credit is always borrowed and can therefore
always be recalled by the lending community. The beliefs on which one's
credit is predicated are always subject to revision. "This banker has good
credit on the market," writes Furetière, "his bankruptcy has barely diminished his credit."[7] As this ominous example shows, long before the collapse
of Law's bank, usage linked credit with bankruptcy.

Another value of *à crédit* has survived in modern French (and English):
namely, "without paying cash." Furetière associates this meaning of the
expression with financial ruin: "One says, Extend *credit*, sell *on credit*, buy
on credit to say, to buy without paying cash. The *credit* that Merchants
give to great lords has ruined their fortune, their business."[8] Like Molière's
Acaste, Furetière does not approve of this sort of credit, though for somewhat different reasons. From his bourgeois perspective, Furetière implicitly condemns buying or selling "on credit," since the practice works to
the sole advantage of the great noblemen to whom credit is given, while
condemning their creditors (such as M. Dimanche in Molière's *Dom Juan*)
to ultimate ruin. When dealing with one of his peers, a nobleman like
Acaste has only disdain for loving "à crédit," for reasons that will soon
become clear. However, Furetière suggests another relevant sense of the
phrase, to mean "fruitlessly": "ON CREDIT is often used to mean, gratu-
itously, fruitlessly, without foundation. This man ruined himself *on credit*,
without displaying his expenditure."[9] In this example, one can still hear the
archaic conception of conspicuous, public expenditure ("dépense qui
parût") as the measure of a noble's worth. From that perspective, it is
useless ("sans utilité") to expend one's resources, unless it is done publicly,
in the eyes of the community whose recognition determines an individual's
value.[10]

Molière's Acaste goes on to explain why gentlemen of his rank cannot
possibly love "on credit":

> *Mais les gens de mon air, marquis, ne sont pas faits*
> *Pour aimer à crédit et faire tous les frais.*
> Quelque rare que soit le mérite des belles,
> Je pense, Dieu merci, qu'*on vaut son prix* comme elles,
> Que, pour se faire honneur d'un coeur comme le mien,
> Ce n'est pas la raison qu'*il ne leur coûte rien,*
> Et qu'au moins, *à tout mettre dans de justes balances,*
> Il faut qu'*à frais communs* se fassent les avances.
> (III, 1, 815–22; emphasis added)

For men like me, however, it makes no sense
To love on trust and foot the whole expense.
Whatever any lady's merits be,
I think, thank God, that I'm as choice as she;
That if my heart is kind enough to burn
For her, she owes me something in return;
And that in any proper love affair
The partner must invest an equal share.

In Acaste's social group (the upper court nobility), "loving" *(aimer)*
refers to a form of coded public display and certainly not to one's feelings
about another person. According to the conventions of *politesse*, love (like
friendship) is ritualized behavior that is conventionally performed in a
certain public situation. In this social context, *aimer* designates behavior
elicited by specific social relations. It has nothing to do with romantic love,
the kind of love in which one "falls," by chance. For example, in the
presence of an attractive young widow like Célimène, any gentleman who
wants to maintain his hierarchical position ("[qui] vaut son prix") simply
must "make love" to her, for the same reason that she must courteously
allow those advances to be made. According to the constraints of this
code, which would arouse Rousseau's indignation in his famously brilliant
misreading of *Le Misanthrope*, a concern with feelings (whether one's own
or those of other persons) is not only irrelevant but vulgar.[11] The *petit
marquis* declares "his" love conventionally (and so does Célimène, for that
matter),[12] in terms that are completely unacceptable to a spokesman for
sincerity, such as Alceste, Marivaux, or Rousseau. Acaste's words are not
supposed to convey an interior state, but to imitate (and derive their value
from) a traditional model.

What Acaste calls *aimer* is social behavior elicited by an aristocratic
form of self-esteem *(amour-propre)*.[13] This behavior is based, first of all,
upon an estimation of one's position (or net worth) in a hierarchy of
values: rank, wealth, and courage (insofar as the king allows a courtier
to display it). Jean-Marie Apostolidès has suggested that by relinquish-
ing their decision-making power to the king, courtiers like Acaste and
Clitandre obtain "honorability capital" in exchange:

Each courtier is provided with a supply of *honorability capital*, which is granted
to him in exchange for his decision-making power, which is placed in the
monarch's hands, and which varies according to his position in the hierarchy.
The protagonists of the play—Oronte, Clitandre, Acaste—never miss an op-

portunity to recall on what terms they are with the prince, that is, to specify the importance of their capital, whose yield they increase by serving the State well, and on which they profit in their social relations.[14]

"Loving" also depends upon an awareness of one's audience and requires that one possess various social graces, all of which are supposedly inherited (rather than acquired) and give effortless expression to a nobleman's social identity. When Acaste and Clitandre "make love" to a lady, they expect prompt recognition of their socially recognized worth, and therefore they have only contempt for "loving on credit" *(aimer à crédit)*. They know that a gentleman cannot court a lady without declaring his affections and without spending, not just money, but also other symbols of Love.

Regardless of his true feelings, in such situations a nobleman must make considerable symbolic expenditures, to which Acaste refers ("faire tous les frais," "à frais communs") in his speech. Making love has its costs; it requires investing in representations of Love and thereby diminishing, if only temporarily, one's recognized worth. Since loving Célimène entails offering tokens of Love to her without rapid repayment in kind, loving on credit (that is, without the lady's quickly signifying that she loves him too) is a risky investment. The more Acaste spends without being paid back, the more his worth is visibly diminished in the eyes of his peers. Since that necessary reevaluation cannot be postponed without a gentleman's devaluation, for him love on credit amounts to love discredited. As a matter of fact, at the end of this scene Acaste and Clitandre decide to force Célimène into a public declaration of her preference; this demand will precipitate her eventual downfall (her "bankruptcy," as Apostolidès calls it).[15]

Whereas in Molière one's worth must always be shown, publicly and theatrically displayed, in order to be effective—a situation that precludes the granting of credit—characters (at least, upper-class characters) in Marivaux will hesitate to take anyone, especially themselves, at face value, in terms of a public image. These post-absolutist characters therefore must commit themselves to the risks and pleasures of love on credit. In the utopian experiment performed in *Le Jeu de l'amour et du hasard*, credit is granted to "instruments" that are themselves worthless, but whose face value and yield are guaranteed, if the pun can be avoided, by Law.[16] In that utopian form, value is no longer fixed in the hierarchical order of the ancien régime, but seems rather to have been produced through the interplay of credit and speculation. (In fact, as we shall see, the results of the game can always be shown to have been predictable.) The result of this *jeu* (interplay, gambling) is a new order, supposedly based on individual performance rather than blood or "honorability capital."

Voltaire was pleased to note that during the "century of Louis XIV" the (noble) code of *politesse* had spread to all sectors of society: "Today one can observe, even in the back of a shop, that *politeness has spread to every social rank.*"[17] But during Voltaire's lifetime *politesse* was being replaced by a new code of sincerity. Whereas *politesse* implied an aristocratic subordination of the individual's true thoughts and feelings to the smooth functioning of the social group, the code of sincerity (as we shall see in Marivaux) required a constant effort to express and impose subjective truth. In a world governed by sincerity, "forms" would become synonymous with lack of real meaning, whereas they had previously been consubstantial with meaning. Forms, and signs in general, would ultimately be perceived as empty or "rhetorical," irrelevant (if not fundamentally opposed) to the expression of full, interior truth. Hence the preference for prose, rather than verse. With this semiotic shift, the status of social behavior and signs would become analogous to that of banknotes in Law's first System, insubstantial as paper money, yet guaranteed by the promise of something solid and reliable: land, gold, or the human heart. This "gold-language [langage-or]," observes Jean-Joseph Goux, "is also the language that expresses the truth of the speaking subject."[18] In France, this new code of sincerity first found expression in the exquisite linguistic practice that has come to be known as *marivaudage*.

A Specular Moment

Marivaux used this code of sincerity to wage war on inflated *amour-propre*, which, as Michel Deguy has pointed out, is related to the tendency of modern cities to "solipsize" their individual inhabitants: "Indeed Marivaux's enemy is the exaggeration of self-esteem *[amour-propre]*, as a psychological form of modern subjectivity, which grows with the urban mode of existence that solipsizes the man of the crowds. In Marivaux there is an ancestor of Baudelaire's *promeneur,* a solitary walker who is happy."[19] Deguy argues that Marivaux registers the emergence of the modern form of *amour-propre*—which differs from, for example, the *amour-propre* of Molière's aristocrats—forged by the historically new experience of the anonymous urban crowd. Although this experience would make Rousseau's "solitary walker [promeneur solitaire]" feel miserably alone, and would eventually cause Baudelaire's *flâneur* to withdraw into his garret (into a state of paralyzing "spleen"), at the beginning of the eighteenth century

Marivaux's anonymous "spectator" walked the crowded streets of Paris in a state of apparent self-satisfaction. All these solitary figures in the urban crowd underwent what Walter Benjamin called "a change in the structure of their experience" that made them think of themselves as superior to everyone around them.[20] In Deguy's view, "this historical-social circumstance" is what led Marivaux to see *amour-propre* as the typical romantic obstacle of his generation and to create a linguistic strategy *(marivaudage)* for removing that obstacle.[21] His theatrical characters use this strategy to make each other subdue their *amour-propre*—to surmount their tendency to value their own image more than anything else. On stage, they play out at a feverish pace this unpredictable, dizzying and exhausting *jeu* of self-image and language, which Deguy calls "breakneck speculation [spéculation étourdissante]": "In the theater, and thanks to the unpredictiblity of the game [jeu] . . . no one comes out unscathed. All of imagery is in crisis, and conjured away in a sense by the resolution of the crisis. Which one? The self-image that one expects the other to reflect back to one . . . the breakneck speculation . . . soon called *marivaudage*."[22] The unpredictability and speculative interplay of Marivaux's theatrical world (not to mention his disastrous experience of Law's System) also brings to mind the Enlightenment's obsession with gambling and chance, which has been analyzed by Thomas Kavanagh.[23] Whereas Kavanagh has studied the status of chance (or *le hasard*) in the Enlightenment (and particularly in the novel), here I shall focus on the workings of *amour-propre*, speculation (mirroring, risk-taking), and credit in Marivaux's plays.

Le Jeu de l'amour et du hasard, first performed in 1730, opens with a scene in which Silvia, the heroine, expresses her apprehensions about the marriage that her father has arranged for her. Like other leading ladies in Marivaux's *comédies d'amour*, Silvia suffers from inflated *amour-propre*. She believes that she and her ideals are unconventional, different from what one might expect to find in young ladies of her social position. She believes, or more precisely, she feels herself different from what she appears at face value. Behind her conventional appearance, she feels unique, singular, maybe even *originale* (that is, "odd": the word still retains a pejorative value in 1730).[24] Silvia feels that her values are unique, that they cannot be represented or reproduced, and therefore fears that the conventionally attractive young man her father has chosen for her may not turn out to be her type—that he may not be unique, like her.

In contrast, Lisette sees Dorante (Silvia's future husband) from the perspective of public opinion, according to which he is an ideal match: "They say that your future husband is one of the most eligible [honnêtes] men

alive, that he is charming, attractive [aimable], handsome [de bonne mine].
No man, they say, has more wit, no man has a better character. What
more do you want?" (I, 1).[25] At a time when *politesse* was being replaced
by sincerity, to call a man *honnête* was not necessarily (or exclusively)
to underline his conformity with certain social norms.[26] *Honnête* already
conveyed some of the meaning that it has in modern French ("straightfor-
ward, fair, sincere"), and it also implied possession of that curious form
of cultural capital that in England is called "breeding." Certainly for a man
to be *honnête*, he no longer needed to be of noble birth or to participate in
court life, where his precise worth was determined by the king. No young
lady, adds Lisette, would think twice about marrying this young man, for
not only is he attractive ("Aimable, bien fait, voilà de quoi vivre pour
l'amour" ["He's handsome and charming—there's fire to kindle love"]),
but also he has all the requisite social graces ("sociable et spirituel, voilà
pour l'entretien de la société" ["He's witty and good company—what
better companion could you have?" (I, 1)]).

Silvia, however, is more concerned with inner worth, or *bon caractère*,
than with appearances. She is particularly worried about the habit men
seem to have of putting on a public face that is very different from their
real selves: "Oui, fiez-vous à cette physionomie si douce, si prévenante,
qui disparaît un quart d'heure après pour faire place à un visage sombre,
brutal, farouche, qui devient l'effroi de toute une maison. Ergaste s'est
marié; sa femme, ses enfants, son domestique, ne lui connaissent encore
que ce visage-là, pendant qu'il promène partout ailleurs cette physionomie
si aimable que nous lui voyons, et qui n'est qu'un masque qu'il prend au
sortir de chez lui" ("Well, you can believe in this sweet, gentle, trustworthy face, but it disappears in private. A quarter of an hour later, in
his own home, Ergaste has a brooding, brutal face which is the terror of
his whole house. Ergaste has married. His wife, his children and his servants only see this second face while we, in public, are treated to the sweet
face we know so well. It's a mask he puts on when he leaves home" [I,
1; translation modified]).[27]

Of course, it turns out that Dorante has the same apprehensions about
Silvia, the same *amour-propre* and sense of his own uniqueness. In order
to negotiate this discrepancy between face value and real worth, between
public façade and domestic reality, Silvia and Dorante independently de-
vise (spontaneously, they think) a theatrical strategy as unique (or conventional) as themselves. With the complicity of Silvia's family and servants,
she and Dorante will trade places with their servants, in order better to
observe the other party, before making any rash commitments. The perfect

symmetry of their desires, duplicated by the apparently symmetrical desires of the chambermaid and valet, underlines the fact that Silvia and
Dorante are meant for each other. Paradoxically, by attempting to hide
behind the mask of a servant's identity, Silvia and Dorante make themselves vulnerable to a development that they fear even more than marriage—love.

Marivaux's well-bred characters like to see themselves as expert observ-
ers of the progress of love in others. However, their observations have
nothing "psychological" about them, insofar as psychology implies indi-
viduality or depth. As Deguy remarks, Marivaux's lovers exist only as
roles, as terms that repeatedly illustrate the same theatrical laws: "There
is none of the psychology that might singularize and identify the two (or
four) terms of the love relation. The protagonists of the amorous game
. . . whom their proper, functional name locates *qua* role, do not exist.
What is happening is a replay . . . of a law and its rules, which also
represent the very rule of theater."[28] Of course, the more often Silvia,
Dorante, and their like posit themselves as "spectators" (as in Marivaux's
Spectateur français),[29] endlessly describing the progress of love as if it did
not concern them personally, the more surely they reveal themselves as
characters who are themselves falling in love. What they take for an objective, almost "experimental" detachment from amorous phenomena always
betrays their own subjection to completely impersonal laws.[30]

Marivaux's well-born protagonists observe one of these laws by regularly falling in love when they first lay eyes upon each other and exchange
glances. Normally this exchange is prepared by a situation of reciprocal
vulnerability, such I have just described. At the beginning of *Le Jeu de
l'amour et du hasard*, neither Silvia nor Dorante imagines that the other
could remotely resemble her or him. Each therefore appears momentarily
to take the other at face value, as the valet Arlequin and the chambermaid Lisette, respectively—that is, as beings so clearly unlike their masters, so obviously unworthy of their love, that they need not be feared,
either. For a moment, Silvia and Dorante appear, to themselves if not to
the audience, to have suspended their prejudices against both love and the
servant class, long enough for the damage to be done.

Yet what happens at this moment has less to do with psychological (that
is, individual) vulnerability, than with an impersonal, economic process:
rhetorically, it is a "speculative" moment.[31] A speculative moment is, in
the first place, the moment when each character sees his or her image (that
is, the object of his or her *amour-propre*) in the other: when he or she sees
in the other the mirror *(speculum)* image of a unique and superior being,

who will not take others at face value. At the speculative moment, the
hero and heroine see in each other a mirror of their own imaginary uniqueness (their "ideal ego"). To Silvia and Dorante, falling in love is also
"speculative" because it seems so risky (that is, "speculative" in the economic sense). When they fall in love, Silvia and Dorante display confidence in the value behind an image and a subsequent willingness to invest
in that image (and to be invested by it). At that moment, investor confidence and credit are sufficient to create enough value for two exchange
units to be added to the the symbolic money supply: two "bank notes,"
with the images of Dorante and Silvia, have been placed into circulation.

At that speculative moment (of reciprocal mirroring of one's ideal self),
Silvia and Dorante have the impression of putting their unique identities
at risk. But their speculation will ultimately have involved no risk: the
masters will never really have had anything to lose, nor the servants anything to gain. The value Silvia and Dorante have at the end of the *Jeu*—
their redemption value, so to speak—will always have been guaranteed
(by their fathers, as we shall see). Thus Silvia's brother Mario argues
against letting his sister know that Dorante will also be disguised as his
servant, because Mario is confident that the two of them will sense what
they are worth anyhow: "Voyons si leurs coeurs ne les avertiraient pas
de ce qu'ils valent" ("Let us see if their hearts tell them what the other
is really worth" [I, 4]). A few moments later, the protagonists find themselves alone together for the first time, each pretending to be a servant,
and the first thing that the false Arlequin says to the false Lisette is: "[T]a
maîtresse te vaut-elle?" ("Is your mistress worthy of you?" [I, 7]). The
question already contains its own answer: No, the "mistress" is not as
"worthy"—that is, she is not worth as much as the false Lisette—no,
neither of them should be taken at face value. The question already implies
what Dorante feels in his heart but doesn't yet consciously know: namely,
that this chambermaid is really worth more than her mistress, because she
actually is the mistress.

From this speculative moment on, the *Jeu* plays itself out in symmetrical
patterns, visibly, in a stylized, Italianate performance style, as if to underscore the resemblance of the players to pieces on a game board and to
undermine the self-deceptively psychological terms in which the characters
interpret their destiny. The characters mirror each other's moves through
various coded stages of amorous development, until a conclusion that was
inevitable even before the first exchange of glances. But if the *Jeu* is a
game, the ground rules of the game were not written by the young lovers,
even though they lay claim to this privilege at the outset.[32] Before the

action of the play began, the rules of the game were laid down by M. Orgon and Dorante's (unnamed) father, when they arranged the marriage between Silvia and Dorante. In a sort of interior duplication, or *mise en abyme*, the two fathers stand for the abstract, impersonal social forces (such as social class) that post-absolutist culture cannot represent, and to which it gives names such as "general will" or (the game of) "chance." Impersonal forces determine the important choices that "individual" characters would like to believe they are freely and spontaneously making, and as Thomas Kavanagh has shown, these forces ultimately cannot be represented, except in abstract or statistical form: "Everything that might once have been framed in the context of the single individual finds itself redefined by the presupposition that any true understanding of that singularity necessitates the individual's being absorbed within the group, the large number, the ambient community."[33] These same forces also delude the fathers themselves, who think of themselves as liberal—that is, as gentlemen who give their children the freedom to choose a partner for themselves ("In this world we must be a little too good to be good enough," remarks M. Orgon [I, 2]).

The children will ultimately choose someone just like themselves, the same person that their fathers had intended for them. In contrast, young lovers in Molière always found themselves in conflict with male authority figures, whether fathers (Argan, the Orgon of *Tartuffe*, and so forth) or a guardian like Arnolphe, who want to marry the poor girl to someone (like themselves) whom she isn't suited for (because he is too old, too vulgar, or both), someone whom she couldn't possibly love. Curiously enough, when the stock figure of the father who conventionally opposes his children's desires is transformed into a father with a heart of gold (who has only his child's interest at heart, and so on), the audience can finally notice that (like the name of Dorante) even his name, "Orgon" (a conventional name for a father in French comedy), has gold (*or*) in it. The name of the father had lost its value through usage, but in Marivaux the play of speculation reinvests "Orgon" with gold and thereby reaffirms the paternal gold standard.

In Marivaux the obstacle, but also the means, to the realization of the father's desire (the Father's Law) is not another, more appropriate man, but *amour-propre:* the "solipsizing" tendency to value one's own image above everything else. As we have seen, Marivaux's theater exploits the specularity of *amour-propre*, the fact that falling in love requires looking at one's mirror *(speculum)* image; it is also "speculative" in the more modern sense that falling in love requires one to make a (seemingly) risky investment. To fall in love is to gamble and to invest in one's mirror image. In the *Jeu* the well-born heroine does not require any help from the servants in overcoming her father's tyrannical desire, since her father is enlightened and good; he and she ultimately desire the same thing. The strategic objective of the game is to ratify the father's judgment (the "gold standard," speaking anachronistically), to teach the daughter (and the audience) that father (even Marivaux's father, the director of the royal mint) knows best.[34]

In its speculative form, then, love is less an obstacle to realization of the father's desire than the ideal means of fulfilling it. As a speculative investment, love is ideal in Marivaux, since it guarantees a profit to the masters. M. Orgon acquires a worthy son-in-law, while enjoying the pleasure of staging the *Jeu*, a pleasure that for Mario can even be sadistic ("I must be there when they first meet—to annoy them both [les agacer tous deux]," says Mario [I, 4]). Silvia and Dorante will not only gain each other, but also, by overcoming their prejudices, they will prove themselves worthy of their fathers and transform their trial (*épreuve*, a favorite word in Marivaux)[35] into retrospective pleasure. "Perhaps," suggests Mario, "Dorante will take a fancy to my sister, even though she is a maid, and that would be delightful [charmant] for her" (I, 4). Mario doesn't mean to suggest that his sister will enjoy believing that she has fallen in love with a servant, but that when she learns the truth she will find her error quite *charmante*. At the end of the play, Silvia will look back at herself, and in a final speculative gesture, she will savor the nobility of her real character—the self that she has revealed to herself.

Dorante, too, has a final moment to savor his image in a mirror. In the very last scene, after having finally become conscious of Silvia's true identity, he exclaims: "[C]e qui m'enchante le plus, ce sont les preuves que je vous ai données de ma tendresse" ("[W]hat is most enchanting is the proof I have given you of my love" [III, 9]). One could say that what Dorante finds most delightful in the end is not the girl he loves, but the "proof," the image of an ideal ego, that he has produced by overcoming social prejudice and proposing marriage to a woman he apparently thought was a chambermaid.

For Silvia and Dorante the yield on this speculative investment in love, this *jeu de l'amour et du hasard*, is high self-esteem, based on a knowledge of their personal worth that they could only feel, or "credit," at the beginning of the play, but which now has acquired full-blown, objective reality. Their initial gesture of investor confidence in speculation has paid off, in self-esteem and pleasure. The initial sense of each other's worth ("ce qu'ils

valent") has now been confirmed by their own performance, in several
senses of the word, and retrospectively it has been a delightful experience.
Of course the experience, or experiment, was also meant to be *charmante*
(and profitable as well) for Mario and his father, the masters of ceremonies.
It would perhaps be more accurate to speak of them as the assistants in
a test or *épreuve* called *Le Jeu de l'amour et du hasard,* which they perform
for a hypothetical audience that, like M. Orgon, preferred to think of itself
as fundamentally good. This audience could enjoy the pleasure of seeing
on stage an idealized image of its own liberal self.[36] The importance of
these tests or *épreuves* in Marivaux has led critics to emphasize the "scientific" dimension of his theater, its way of constituting the audience as a
detached observer of the human heart.[37] But like Silvia and Dorante, the
audience sees only its ideal self in the experiment, the intellectual and
sentimental proofs of its worth. For at moments of "scientific" detachment
from the fiction on stage, there always remain unrepresentable (social,
economic) forces to which the spectators also are subject.[38]

In this play, the masters no longer see their value as a treasure (as in
Molière), determined or guaranteed by the reality of its public representation; it depends instead upon a "reality" that is hidden from public view
(money depends on land holdings, personal worth on the heart). And
whereas value in the ancien régime depended upon a systematic expenditure of resources whose emblem was the Sun, in the utopian economic
order of the *Jeu,* the granting of credit ensures a play of speculation, in
which the face value at risk is not only realized at the end, but even increased. In this theatrical facsmile of Law's System, planning and gambling
work together toward the same end.

Servants, however, do not see things this way, and they do not profit
from the *Jeu* in the same way, either. Arlequin and Lisette actually believe
in the credibility of their disguises, and think that they really can increase
their value in a spectacular way, by marrying the master or mistress. In
Marivaux, only servants can really believe that the person with whom they
have fallen in love (and who has fallen in love with them) is the master
or the mistress, and capable of taking her or him for their equal. Precisely
because they credit these appearances, the servants have no apprehensions
about love and marriage. For Lisette and Arlequin, it is as if nothing, no
regulation or law, determined their value, or that of paper money—nothing except the willingness of investors to credit it. For them it is as if
the paternal gold standard—all the implicit paternal controls over money,
persons, language, and love—had magically been abolished, simply by
their trading roles with their master and mistress. Yet the symmetry be-

tween masters and servants is only apparent, as Deguy points out: "This cross-dressing [travestissement] that confuses social differences with appearances can only prepare the triumph of truth, of the suitability of hearts and social positions."[39] Indeed, at the end of the *Jeu* Lisette and Arlequin are worth no more than they were at the beginning. Speculation and *marivaudage* do not concern them, although their labors do make these higher activities possible. Love on credit does not work to the servants' advantage.

Despite the existence of this double standard, both masters and servants in *Le Jeu de l'amour et du hasard* ultimately repudiate the value of appearances; they all refuse to credit face value or "forms." Either they believe that value is guaranteed by something more substantial than forms, or they believe that it is a pure convention, grounded in nothing more than public belief. In Marivaux's play, all the characters willingly commit themselves to a credit economy that could have been prescribed by John Law. In contrast, lovers in *Le Misanthrope* (not just Acaste and Clitandre, but also Alceste and Célimène, Philinte and Éliante) refuse to credit anything beyond appearances and therefore remain alone at the end, fatally in love with their own images. In the credit economy of *Le Jeu de l'amour et du hasard*, love and chance are allowed to interact through speculation, that combination of self-mirroring, planning, and gambling without risk. Thanks to this speculative investment, Silvia and Dorante are saved from the emotional bankruptcy of Molière's Alceste and Célimène.

Production of Value: *Les Fausses confidences*

One can also observe the workings of a post-absolutist "credit economy" in *Les Fausses confidences*, first performed in 1737 and the only Marivaux play that has been performed more often than *Le Jeu de l'amour et du hasard*.[40] In this product of Marivaux's artistic maturity, the main characters are the crafty servant Dubois, his impoverished former master Dorante, and Dubois's present employer, the rich young widow Araminte. These characters are older than those in *Le Jeu* and their social context more realistic, while their conversation is practically devoid of the brilliant *marivaudage* that characterized the earlier plays.[41] Despite these important differences, however, there are similarities: not only do the male leads of both plays have the same unrealistic, theatrical name (Dorante), but the *fausses confidences* of the title are part of the same economy of speculation and credit as in *Le Jeu de l'amour et du hasard*. As we shall see, the *fausses*

confidences ("false admissions" or perhaps "deceptive secrets") are speculative investments. To beguile Araminte into falling in love with Dorante,
the servant Dubois puts these *fausses confidences* into circulation at strategic
moments in the action.

Face Value: Une Bonne Mine

The problem that sets the plot in motion is "economic," in the most literal
sense (from Greek *oikonomia*, "management of a household"). To help
settle a property dispute with Count Dorimont, Araminte needs an *intendant*. During the ancien régime, *intendants* were administrators, either in
the state bureaucracy (public business, town or provincial affairs) or in
households, usually noble ones.[42] (The role of *intendant* thus resembles
that of the ancient Greek *oikonomos*, or "manager of a household.") Dubois's first objective is to convince Araminte that she should take on Dorante as her *intendant*. Dorante's uncle, M. Rémy, who is Araminte's barris-
ter (or *procureur*), recommends his young nephew for the position, thereby
making himself an unwitting accomplice in Dubois's plot. Araminte's
mother, Mme. Argante, would like her to employ someone recommended
by the count, since that person would doubtless urge Araminte to settle
her dispute out of court by marrying the nobleman. Dorante has no cre-
dentials for the job, other than his uncle's recommendation and his own
good looks *(bonne mine)*. Therefore, when he enters Araminte's household, preceded by the artful Dubois, it is solely on credit. It has taken but
a single glance to make Dorante fall passionately in love with Araminte:

DUBOIS: "You've seen her and you love her?"
DORANTE: "I love her passionately . . ."

(I, 2)[43]

Thus he at least has a moral justification for seducing the rich young
widow (as Deguy points out, were it not for Dorante's pure intention, he
would be acting like an immoral Don Juan).[44] Yet despite the purity of
his intentions, Dorante still worries that Dubois's plot may not succeed.
He wonders why Araminte should fall in love with, much less marry, a
man who (on face value) is worthless: "Cette femme-ci a un rang dans
le monde; elle est liée avec tout ce qu'il y a de mieux, veuve d'un mari
qui avait une grande charge dans les finances; et tu crois qu'elle fera
quelque attention à moi, que je l'épouserai, *moi qui ne suis rien, moi qui
n'ai point de bien?*" ("This woman is highly placed in the world, she sees

only the best people, she's the widow of a very wealthy banker, and you still think that she'll pay attention to me. That I'll marry her, *when I am nothing, and have nothing?*" [I, 2; emphasis added]). When Dorante looks in the mirror, he sees a man who "[is] nothing" (that is, has no title) and "[has] nothing" (that is, lacks a fortune); he sees only a handsome face, an appearance, as worthless as the paper on which a bank note is printed. But where Dorante sees "nothing," Dubois sees a gold mine, "a Peru": "Nothing? Your *looks are a gold mine* [votre *bonne mine est un Pérou*]" (I, 2; emphasis added). Because of its legendary gold mines, Peru had become the idiomatic equivalent of wealth in popular speech.[45] Marivaux plays upon both values of the French word *mine:* "appearance" or "looks," and "deposit" or "mine," just as Dubois will invest the *fausses confidences* to exploit Dorante's face value and make those good looks into a gold mine. To Dubois, Dorante's *bonne mine* is a source of tremendous potential wealth, if not yet an immediately marketable commodity. After insinuating himself into Araminte's household, Dubois can introduce his former master into the domestic economy. He knows that once Araminte has taken a look at Dorante's *bonne mine*, she will fall in love with him and find herself in need of reasons for giving him unlimited credit. Later in the play, even Count Dorimont (Dorante's rival) is struck by the value of Dorante's face, his *mine:*

COMTE: Did [Dorante] just go out?
MARTON: Yes.
COMTE: His appearance is indeed very pleasing [Il a *bonne mine*, en effet].
He doesn't much look the steward [et *il n'a pas trop l'air de ce qu'il est*].
(II, 4; emphasis added)

At the end of the play, Dorante will confess to Araminte that "[Dubois] voulait *me faire valoir* auprès de vous" ("[Dubois] wanted to make me worthy in your eyes" [III, 12; translation modified]). Dubois's task will have been to make Araminte *realize* (make real, understand, obtain) Dorante's worth and (therefore) fall in love with him.

Labor Theory of Value: The Faire Valoir

This ability of characters to realize value (or fail to realize it) was crucial to Marivaux's poetics. D'Alembert would recall Marivaux's conviction that his actors should behave as if they did not grasp the implications of their own words: "As Marivaux expressed it so well himself, the actors *must*

never seem to sense the meaning [valeur] of what they're saying, and at the
same time the audience must sense and sort it out through the sort of cloud
in which the author has had to wrap their speech."[46] Marivaux wanted his
performers to convey two levels of a character's meaning: a conscious
level (what they apparently think their words mean), and a level I shall
call "preconscious" (since the character is *almost* aware of it, while it is
so unambiguously clear to everyone else). The preconscious meaning is
what everyone else immediately understands, but which the performer
seems not to notice. Everyone (the character speaking, the other characters, the audience) understands what the character thinks he or she is saying, but only he or she must seem to imagine that the meaning stops there.

Marivaux did not think that his audience would identify the "value" of
what his characters say ("la valeur de ce qu'ils disent") with the preconscious meaning; rather, they would derive it from the interplay (or *jeu*)
between the two levels. For example, when Araminte makes her first en-
trance in *Les Fausses confidences,* after having seen Dorante for the first
time, she asks her companion *(suivante)* Marton a revealing question:
"Marton, who's that man who bowed to me so gracefully. Has he come
to talk to you [Est-ce à vous qu'il en veut]?" (I, 6). To deliver this line
properly, an actress has to persuade us that Araminte thinks she's asking the question out of idle curiosity. When Araminte falls in love with
Dorante at first glance (mirroring his own previous "specular" moment),
the audience has to credit her self-delusive sincerity. At the same time,
the audience grasps Araminte's preconscious meaning: that the man who
has greeted her so "graciously" must have a character that matches his
handsome face and must have come to see her, not Marton.[47] But to sense
the "value" of what she is saying, the audience has not only to understand
its preconscious meaning, but (realizing that asking this question is painful
to her *amour-propre*) to appreciate, in the *jeu* of these two levels, *how much
it costs her* to ask the question. One is not meant to take Araminte's question at face value, or to reduce its meaning to a barely hidden, preconscious
level, but to juxtapose both levels and then (as D'Alembert put it) work
to sort out *(démêler)* its true "value" through the rhetorical clouds. Just
as the value of a master like Dorante has to be realized by the labor of
a Dubois, so the "value" of a master's words is not a given (like the
amount of precious metal in a coin), but has to be produced, through the
combined efforts of the character (whose *amour-propre* has to "pay" for
it) and the audience (who must labor to interpret it).

It is remarkable for Araminte to see Dorante as her equal, since everyone else (including Dorante himself) sees him as her inferior. The rudeness

of Mme. Argante, Araminte's mother, toward M. Rémy probably suggests (as Charles Dédéyan has argued)[48] that Araminte has the same social origins (in the legal profession, or *robe*) as Dorante and Marton (and indeed Marivaux himself). Nonetheless Araminte has since acquired a considerably higher rank, thanks both to her marriage into the financial bourgeoisie and to her nobility of character: "This woman is highly placed in the world, she sees only the best people, she's the widow of a wealthy banker" (I, 2). Indeed, Mme. Argante now urgently wants Araminte to consolidate her gains and completely escape her origins, by marrying Count Dorimont. Dorante and Marton, on the other hand, are *déclassés:* due to financial reversals, both have fallen down a step on the social ladder. One may even infer (as Roland Morisse suggests) that Dorante, who was ruined only six months earlier, lost his money (like Marivaux) in the wake of Law's System.[49] In any case, the resemblances between Dorante and Marton are so striking that, to M. Remy, the two seem made for each other:

> [S]he comes from a very good family. Her father was a solicitor and I took over his practice when he died. He was also a good friend of your father's. Unfortunately, he was a little careless, went into debt, and his daughter has been left unprovided for. The lady here took her into the house as a companion, but she treats her more as a friend than as a servant. She has promised to do something for her when she gets married. There's also an old asthmatic relation who's well off and Marton stands to inherit from her. Since you'll both be living in the same house, I think you should marry her. (I, 3)

Yet despite the differences of fortune and rank that are obvious to everyone else, Araminte instinctively credits Dorante with a value equivalent to her own:

MARTON: I know he's generally well thought of *[estimé]*.
ARAMINTE: Yes, I can believe that: he certainly seems to deserve it *[il a tout l'air de le mériter]*. But Marton, he is so handsome *[il a si bonne mine pour un intendant]* that I have some qualms about taking him on. Might people not talk?

(I, 6; translation modified)

When Araminte sees Dorante, before she has said a single word to him, she immediately credits his demeanor, looks, and reputation. It then remains for Dubois to exploit this credit, which is where his *fausses confidences* come in.

The first *fausse confidence* was actually made by M. Rémy, when (not realizing that his nephew really loved Araminte) he told Marton (in I, 4) that Dorante was secretly in love with her. This first confidence (the "secret" it reveals) is false. Dubois then "confides" to Araminte that Dorante has fallen in love with *her:* but this (like all of Dubois's subsequent *confidences*) is true. According to Dubois (I, 14), when Dorante fell in love with Araminte, he took such leave of his senses that Dubois could not remain in his service. Although what Dubois confides to Araminte is true, everything else he says (his reason for having left Dorante's service and for now wanting to leave Araminte's) is false and meant to manipulate Araminte.

Throughout the play, all the *fausses confidences* conform to this pattern: whatever information Dubois confides is true, although its circumstances (or frame) are false, whereas whatever others confide is false, even when they believe they are telling the truth. For example, in Araminte's presence, the good M. Rémy tells Dorante that a rich, pretty, and rather well-born widow wants to marry Dorante—or so he has been told—and that therefore Dorante must leave Araminte's service (II, 2). This *fausse confidence* (presumably arranged by Dubois) forces Dorante to reject the advantageous offer and reveal that he already loves someone else ("J'ai le coeur pris; j'aime ailleurs" ["My heart is engaged elsewhere" (II, 2)]). Marton is then moved to thank Dorante, believing that it is for love of her that he is sacrificing riches, but Dorante responds to the expression of her gratitude in deliberately (and suspiciously) ambiguous terms:

MARTON: . . . I, Dorante, will always feel such gratitude.
DORANTE: No, no, you mustn't. I'm the only one concerned in this. I've only consulted my feelings, and you have nothing to thank me for. I don't deserve your gratitude.

(II, 3)

Araminte does not even believe she is telling the truth, when (in II, 13) she pays Dorante back for the previous *fausses confidences* by dictating to him a letter, in which she tells the count that she wants to marry him; her message (that she loves the count) is not true, either.

However, when Dubois stages a *fausse confidence*, its message (Dorante loves Araminte) is always true, despite the deceptive circumstances in which it is framed. In the first scene of act III, for example, we learn that Dubois has instructed Dorante to write another letter. In this letter, Dorante tells a friend that he desperately loves Araminte and is sure she will dismiss him when she finds out, indeed that he has resolved in that case to join his friend on a sea voyage. Of course, this "friend" does not exist; he has been invented by Dubois, who manages to have the letter intercepted by Marton, so that the "confidential" information it contains may be read aloud by the count, in the presence of Araminte, Mme. Argante, Marton, and M. Remy. At the end, in order to "deserve" Araminte's love, Dorante confesses the truth about the *confidences:* that with his consent, Dubois has invented them all "pour me faire valoir auprès de vous" (III, 12). Overwhelmed by his present sincerity, Araminte pardons Dorante for his past deceits, and announces to the count and her mother her decision to marry her *intendant.* (Two of Dubois's deceptively framed *fausses confidences* will, in fact, be conveyed by portraits, which I shall discuss below in the context of Dubois's "investment strategy.")

It can be said that, like all Dubois's other *fausses confidences,* the letter addressed to Dorante's fictional friend (in Lacan's famous words) "always reaches its destination."[50] However, in Marivaux's speculative economy, the letter (like any other investment vehicle, such as a portrait) always reaches its address indirectly. What is deceptive about each *confidence* is its mask of confidentiality: the assumption that this information was meant to remain confidential. Taken at face value, each *confidence* contains information that Araminte just "happens" to learn. Dubois leads Araminte to assume that she was not meant to discover that Dorante loves her, when in fact this message was meant only for her. To make Araminte credit this message, Dubois has to ensure that she will take it at face value. What is false or deceptive in Dubois's *fausses confidences* is not the explicit message (that Dorante loves Araminte), but its underlying frame of address. That indirect frame enables the vehicle (portrait, letter) to storm the citadel of Araminte's ego (to "invest" it).

The Widow's Estate

An additional obstacle to Dubois's objectives lies in what Frédéric Deloffre has called the "antinomy" of a widow's legal status in the ancien régime. On the one hand, widows were the only women not considered as minors by civil law, and consequently they enjoyed a considerable degree of autonomy (especially when rich, like Araminte). On the other hand, they had no legal protection from male abuse:

> The practical consequence of this fact was that a man could not only abandon [a widow] after having seduced her, but could dishonor her with impunity,

even if he had promised her marriage and left her with child by him! Let us suppose a very young woman, reduced to widowhood (there was no lack of such cases)—beautiful and predisposed to love, but rich and all the more attached to remaining her own master—exposed, at the slightest weakness, to the pitiless mockery of public opinion: this was a touching character indeed, who could not fail to attract a writer's attention.[51]

Among the writers who had already turned their attention to the case of the beautiful young widow, Deloffre mentions Pierre Corneille *(La Veuve)*, Madame de Lafayette (the end of *La Princesse de Clèves*), and Robert Challe (*Les Illustres Françaises*, seventh story).

But Deloffre could also have mentioned the most famous beautiful young widow in French classical theater, Célimène in *Le Misanthrope*. A brief comparison of Célimène and Araminte will provide another example of the difference between absolutist and post-absolutist poetics. Of course, Célimène belongs to the upper nobility, and Araminte (by marriage) to the financial bourgeoisie, but both these young widows suffer from an inability to make their words say what they mean (to control the value of their words). Indeed, Jacques Guicharnaud has argued that what keeps Célimène happy, at least until her almost "tragic" downfall, is the illusion that it is natural to respond favorably to *all* one's suitors, but in varying degrees.[52] Guicharnaud contends that Célimène believes in a hierarchy of feelings, rather than in their exclusiveness ("Célimène lives in a universe where exclusiveness is replaced by hierarchy").[53] Thus, when her letters to the various suitors are read aloud (act V, scene 4), Célimène continues to maintain her innocence, since there are nuances of expression in her language that only she notices, whereas everyone else construes these letters as incontrovertible evidence of her duplicity.[54] In other words, what Célimène takes for a universal code is really only her idiolect. She does not appreciate the conventional meaning of her words, outside her own subjectivity. Everyone (except Célimène) sees her words and behavior as those of a conventional social (and literary) type, the coquette. In contrast, what Araminte really means (the "value" of her words) is not objective, but hidden in the depths of her subjectivity. Like mineral ore, that hidden value is potential; for it to become real, her meaning needs to be extracted, labor has be performed on it. Like Dorante's face, the value of Araminte's words comes from a *bonne mine*, in the sense that it must be drawn out. While revelation of messages that were not meant for publication leads to Célimène's rejection by her suitors, feigned indiscretion leads Araminte to love and marriage.

Of course, Dubois realizes full well that this investment strategy would never succeed if his master were not already deeply worthy of Araminte. She is not going to fall in love with just any *bonne mine,* just as not all paper bank notes are credit worthy, good investments. Like the surface of a good Peruvian mine, Dorante's face is the sign of something precious hidden beneath the surface. To Araminte, this face is the surface manifestation of a sensitive character, so much like her own that she is immediately attracted to Dorante. As in *Le Jeu de l'amour et du hasard,* like attracts like, and the devoted labor of servants is primarily used to accredit the masters' value. In the *Jeu,* servants actualize the value of their masters through their own incapacity to act like masters, while in *Les Fausses confidences* the servant Dubois, by making Araminte realize what Dorante has always been worth, masterfully takes charge of the action.

Critics have observed that Dubois has the talents of a dramatist, that he orchestrates the plot and functions as a sort of dramatist within the play.[55] The Dubois character also represents perhaps the first appearance of the servant (and hence, of the dramatist) as investment adviser. The traditional function of the servant in theater (that of taking responsibility for actions, such as lying or stealing, that it would not be seemly for the master to initiate) is carried on in Marivaux, but with an important difference: the actions of servants in Marivaux help to establish, and even increase, a value that their masters do not automatically possess.[56] While the servant had traditionally served as a foil for her (or usually his) master, in Marivaux he or she becomes literally a *faire-valoir:* a character who *makes* (the master) *valuable.* Dubois's labors turn "a Peru"—that is, an accredited, face value—into real, marketable wealth. Thanks to Dubois's investment strategy, a man who thinks he is nothing ("I who am nothing") because he has nothing ("I who have nothing") will turn into the finest of gentlemen (in Araminte's words, "le plus honnête homme du monde" [III, 12]). We recall Dorante's final apology: "[Dubois] believed he could show me off to advantage here [*me faire valoir* auprès de vous]" (III, 12; emphasis added). Thanks to his servant's labor, Dorante will become "somebody," a man who is worth, according to Dubois's estimate (I, 2) at least 60,000 livres annually.

Indirect Investment

As long as Dorante is "nothing," other people have to tell Araminte that he loves her. His love can only be formulated in the third person ("he loves you"), in what the linguist Émile Benveniste has called the pronoun

of the "non-person."[57] Only when Dorante finally achieves social recognition as a "person," when he finally becomes a "somebody," can he use
the first-person pronoun to say, "I love you." Although his message is
truthful, at the beginning of the play Dorante himself cannot deliver it:
first, because he is not authorized to do so; second, because Araminte's
self-esteem (her *amour-propre*) forbids anyone to court her directly. As
Deguy aptly remarks: "With Marivaux, comedy displays a new figure,
the figure of self-sufficiency: the infernal torment of self-esteem [amour-
propre], and the heart gagged [baîllonné] by the knots of language."[58]
Dubois therefore invents a way of turning both obstacles—Araminte's
amour-propre and the fact that Dorante is not authorized to speak of love—
to Dorante's advantage, but indirectly.

First, Dubois "confides" in Araminte that Dorante loves her. Then he
pulls out that shopworn literary device, the portrait. There was a long
literary tradition behind the tactical use of a portrait in a lover's strategy.
Dubois, however, uses this device in a nontraditional way, as one can see
by contrasting the use of Araminte's portrait in *Les Fausses confidences*
with how portraits are used in Madame de Lafayette's *La Princesse de
Clèves* (1678). In *Salomé and the Dance of Writing*, Françoise Meltzer has
shown how portraits are used in *La Princesse de Clèves* to demonstrate
the hierarchical "economy of representation as absolute power."[59] While
Mme. de Clèves is conversing with the Princesse Dauphine (wife of the
heir to the throne) in the latter's ceremonial bedroom, she notices the duc
de Nemours stealing her own portrait. As a respectable married woman,
Mme. de Clèves cannot ask him to put the portrait back, without publiciz-
ing the fact that she is the object of Nemours's attentions; nor will she ever
be able to broach the topic in private, without tacitly allowing Nemours to
make a declaration of love.[60] Later in the novel, a painting is once again
the vehicle for an unwitting declaration of love, when Nemours (from
his hiding place in the darkness outside a pavilion of the park at Cou-
lommiers), who himself is being observed, surprises the princess gazing
upon paintings in which he is represented. In both these "absolutist" examples, what Deguy calls the "portrait trick" ("coup du portrait")[61] reveals
feelings of love that already exist, but which have been hidden from view.
Likewise, as Meltzer has pointed out, the portraits in *La Princesse de Clèves*
serve to represent "a specific position in the noble hierarchy, and a distinct
position in relation to the source of power in that hierarchy, the king."[62]

In Marivaux's play, however, two portraits of Araminte do not reveal
true love or affirm preexisting hierarchy, so much as they enable love
and value to develop. They are *fausses confidences*—that is, "investment"

vehicles. In act II, the son of a craftsman who has been commissioned to make a box for a portrait, arrives to deliver the box to its owner, whom he does not know. Count Dorimont and Marton agree that the box must belong to Dorante, although Dorimont jealously assumes that it contains a portrait of Araminte, while Marton expects to find her own portrait inside. Marton finally opens the box, in the presence of the count and Araminte: it contains Araminte's portrait. Blinded by her own love for Dorante, Marton insists (II, 9) that the portrait must really belong to the count. In the next scene, Dubois puts another *fausse confidence* into play, using yet another image of Araminte. In front of Araminte and Mme. Argante, he stages a quarrel with Arlequin, Dorante's servant. Arlequin naively defends Dorante's right to continue gazing with pleasure upon a painting of Araminte that was hanging in the *intendant*'s room, to which Dubois retorts that his duty to Araminte required him to take the painting down. As for the first image of Araminte, the portrait in the box, we (and Araminte) learn that it indeed belongs to Dorante and that he has painted it himself. In both cases, Dubois manages to publish supposedly confidential information about Dorante's fascination with Araminte's image. Yet, although it is true that Dorante loves Araminte, the assumption that this information was meant to be confidential is false: in fact, this "secret" was meant to be made public in Araminte's presence. Now everyone knows the socially unacceptable truth that Dorante loves Araminte, and no one knows what she will do about it. The whole point of the investment has been to put both portraits into circulation, and thereby both realize Dorante's face value and overcome Araminte's *amour-propre*.

In both the absolutist and post-absolutist examples, the gentleman's attachment to the lady's portrait (and thus, to the lady herself) is revealed before witnesses (that is, staged), thereby placing constraints on the lady's reaction. Marivaux, through Dubois, has Araminte discover that Dorante has had a portrait made of her, that he is (like her) in love with her image. In this way, Dorante does not have to say anything, until Araminte allows him to do so. Eventually Dorante will be required by social convention to declare himself directly to Araminte, but he still tries to do it indirectly, by "silently" referring to the woman he loves: "Me préserve le ciel d'oser concevoir la plus légère espérance! Etre aimé, moi! non, Madame. Son état est bien au-dessus du mien. *Mon respect me condamne au silence;* et je mourrai du moins sans avoir eu le malheur de lui déplaire" ("Heaven forbid I should ever conceive the smallest hope that she should love me! Me! No, no, she's too far above me, *respect will keep me silent,* always" (II, 14 [scene 15 in French editions]; emphasis added). Dorante confesses,

"I love her," because he knows that Araminte knows who "she" is. Believing that she has now extracted a confession from him, Araminte tries
to drive Dorante into a corner, where no more indirect address seems
possible, but it is she, in fact, who will finally have no choice but to hear
Dorante say that he loves her:

ARAMINTE: *(Aside)* I must push him all the way. *(Aloud)* Show me this
    portrait.
DORANTE: Please don't ask such a thing of me. I may be without hope, but
    I still owe her secrecy.
ARAMINTE: I found a portrait here *by chance. (Showing the box)*. Perhaps
    this is it?
DORANTE: It couldn't be.
ARAMINTE: *(Opening the box.)* Yes, that would be quite extraordinary. Look
    carefully.
DORANTE: Please remember I would have died a thousand deaths rather
    than admit to you *what chance has just revealed.* How can I atone for
    . . . *(He falls to his knees.)*
                    (II, 14 [French, II, 15]; emphasis added in dialogue)

Of course, it is not "by chance" *(par hasard)* that the box and portrait
have fallen into Araminte's hands. Despite all appearances, in this play
(or *jeu*), nothing about love *(l'amour)* is left to chance *(le hasard)*.

The Value of Titles

The fact that Dorante has finally been authorized to say "I love you" does
not mean that he somehow has become a unique individual. Quite to the
contrary, Dorante achieves validity as a speaker by making Araminte realize his self, his *mine,* as precisely equivalent to hers, just as the face on
a bank note or coin makes that unit exchangeable for any other with the
same face value. Like bank notes, titles do not in themselves guarantee
real worth. By themselves, titles have no more real value than a pretty
face, unless they are guaranteed by character (as bank notes are guaranteed
by precious metal).

In the society that Marivaux puts on stage, character or breeding (values
that lie below the surface of a person) is worth more than a title. If Araminte married the count, she would gain a title, but titles in Marivaux are
empty. In fact, Count Dorimont also happens to have character, and plenty
of wealth, too: but the *a priori* value of the count, the worth that Mme.

Argante automatically grants him by virtue of his title ("It's an illustrious name" [I, 10]) is based on no more than her vanity and social ambitions ("I'm delighted by the notion of becoming the mother of the Comtesse Dorimont, or perhaps something even better" [I, 10]). In fact, both Count Dorimont and Dorante have gold *(or)* in their names, like Silvia's father Orgon (and the other Dorante) in *Le Jeu de l'amour et du hasard*. In each case the title (or signifier) *or* happens to announce the golden character that the man possesses. But in this economy, a title and a pretty face are each devoid of value, until they can be admitted, exploited, and shown to stand for something real. Araminte approvingly refers (I, 7) to Dorante as one of the "gentlemen [honnêtes gens] without a fortune," and she likewise could have called the count a "gentleman with a fortune."

At first glance, Count Dorimont seems to have everything: title, money, and character. Yet Araminte does not want to marry him, even though by doing so, she would also avoid a lawsuit. Long before setting eyes upon Dorante, Araminte was reluctant to marry Dorimont, and not just because she failed to share her bourgeois mother's fascination with noble titles. Her reluctance stems from the fact that, precisely because the count has a title and she does not, Araminte cannot possibly see in him the object of her self-esteem *(amour-propre):* a person who is noble by virtue of values more genuine than a mere title. But in the mirror of Dorante's face, Araminte finally sees her *mine idéale*, the beauty and virtue of her ideal self-image. In a word, she "loves" him; just as Dorante, ever since he first saw her face, has loved Araminte. Insofar as *amour-propre* is the primary obstacle to Araminte's falling in love, *fausses confidences* enable her to succumb without entirely giving up her investment in herself.

Thanks to speculative interplay, the *fausses confidences* can be revealed as guileless and ultimately true. They turn out to have been based upon the true equivalency of two self-images, upon the fact that Dorante is really "worthy" of Araminte and she of him. In the end, Dorante's *mine* is worth Araminte's, and perfectly interchangeable with it. It is in the context of this specular economy that one must interpret Dorante's ultimate declaration and self-justification (III, 12).[63] Had it not been for his true love, Dorante would be a scoundrel, an empty opportunist.[64] Likewise, bank notes would be worthless, were they not backed by gold, land, or some other transcendent value. True love is Dorante's excuse for the whole staged performance, in which only he and Dubois knowingly participated, a performance without which neither Dorante nor Araminte would have been able to *realize* (recognize, actualize) what they are worth to each other.

Absolutist value was a treasure ("archetypal," in Goux's vocabulary), continually on public display and transmitted by blood, and was therefore incompatible with credit institutions. Post-absolutism discredited birth, titles, and other external signs of value, while placing a high value on inner worth and relying more on credit and speculation. These Marivaux plays suggest that, in the actual workings of the post-absolutist semiotic order, the play (or *jeu*) of credit and speculation was never free (as in the last form of Law's System), but implicitly regulated by a patriarchal class order. In this liberal society, one is not meant to fall in love or marry outside one's social class.

In the vocabulary of Jean-Joseph Goux, a transition is taking place between a logic of value as ideal or "archetype" (originating in the semi-divine, miraculously full presence of the Sun King in his representations, and emanating from him to his subjects) and a logic of value as "sign" (a term that conventionally stands for another that is more "real," such as a bank note for a certain quantity of precious metal, a *bonne mine* for a noble heart). Unlike the bank notes of Law's System (in its last, "mad" form), the *fausses confidences* of Marivaux's play are therefore revealed as fundamentally sound investment vehicles, truly worthy of investor confidence.

Drawing Kings

Casanova and Voltaire

Part I: Royal *Jouissances*

IN THE PREFACE TO *Histoire de ma vie,* Casanova begs his respectable readers to pardon him the sin of "painting too much" about his love life: "Those who think that I lay on too much color [auxquels je paraîtrai *trop peindre*] when I describe certain amorous adventures in detail will be wrong, unless, that is, they consider me a bad painter altogether. I beg them to forgive me if, in my old age, my soul is reduced to feeling no joys but those of memory *[ne pouvoir plus jouir que par réminiscence]*."[1] Surely, Casanova pleads, the reader will not deny a poor old man such innocent pleasures as remain to him. Of course, he knows that, were it not for these details (which today might be called too "graphic," that is, too vividly "written"), he would not have kept notes on his adventures, and he would certainly not have expanded on those notes in his old age.[2] Moreover, although Casanova's memoirs have been available almost exclusively in expurgated editions, they have become famous mainly because of these intimate revelations. In fact, if *Histoire de ma vie* did not contain the details of those adventures, the Casanova myth would not exist, and the reader would probably not have picked up the book.[3] This old libertine wrote his life story for the same reason that most people read it: to savor the graphic descriptions of his erotic adventures, thus satisfying a desire either for knowledge (of women, libertinage, or some aspect of human sexuality) or for vicarious erotic pleasures.

But what does Casanova mean when he speaks of "ne pouvoir plus jouir que par réminiscence"? The French words *jouir* (when used intransitively) and *jouissance* are notoriously difficult to translate. *Jouissance* refers to an intense (usually sexual) pleasure, often accompanied by a sense of fear.[4] In all likelihood, Casanova means to use *jouir* positively, even euphorically, to designate the blissful experience of the present moment. In this sense, *jouir par réminiscence* can mean "retrieving [the past] as a presence so intense that it recreates the past as present."[5] As Thomas Kavanagh puts it: "It is this goal of being able to 'jouir par réminiscence,' to achieve a 'bliss' which is as much metaphysical as physical, that drives Casanova's act of writing."[6] The episode entitled "The Beautiful O-Morphi" provides a particularly striking example of post-absolutist poetics, as Casanova explores the relationship between erotic portrait-painting and vicarious *jouissance*, subjects and kings.[7]

The title of this episode could make Casanova's reader suspect that it will contain a vivid account of how the great lover seduced a beautiful woman named "O-Morphi." However, in this episode Casanova does not emphasize his role as a seducer, nor does he "consummate" (at least in the conventional sense) his relationship with the woman. Instead Casanova portrays himself as a mediator, first in the pleasures of a friend, and then in the pleasures of the king. In fact, the story of "La Belle O-Morphi" is not about sexual seduction, but about the status and sexual, political power of portraits—portraits of the king, and of his subjects. It concerns the nature of the *jouissances* that portraits (if not representations in general) make available to the post-absolutist king and to his subjects.

The scene is Paris, in the fall of 1752.[8] Casanova's friend Patu (an advocate at the Paris Parlement) invites him to join him for a late supper at the home of an "actress" at the Opéra-Comique, named Victorine Murphy.[9] Although Victorine and her sister Louison were probably Irish, Casanova initially calls them both Flemish. As he recalls it, he himself was not interested in the girl (whose name he also spells "Morphi," "O'Morphy" and "Morphise"), but went along for his friend's sake: "La Morphy did not tempt me; but that did not matter—a friend's pleasure is motive enough."[10] Victorine's fee for the pleasure of her company is 2 louis (a gold coin worth 24 francs at the time, or about 1,200 French francs in 1996).[11] After supper, his friend wants to sleep with her, but Casanova would rather just sleep. He asks for a couch, and Miss Murphy's thirteen-year-old sister offers to rent him her bed for the night. The price, "a half écu [un petit écu]," a silver coin worth 3 francs.[12]

Casanova is about to give her the coin, when he discovers that what

Louison Murphy calls a "bed" is a straw mattress on a few boards. Such accommodations will hardly do, and he tells her so:

— Do you call that a bed?
— It's my bed.
— I don't want it, and *you shan't have the half écu [tu n'auras pas le petit écu]*.

(1:620 [vol. 3, chap. 11], emphasis added)

However, when he learns that the girl is accustomed to sleeping naked on this rough bed, Casanova imagines a more satisfying way of spending his money. He offers to pay little Miss Murphy 1 petit écu, just for the privilege of seeing her in her makeshift bed:

— Very well, go to bed yourself and *you shall have the half écu [tu auras le petit écu]*.
— All right, but you mustn't do anything to me.
— Not a thing.

(ibid., translation modified, emphasis added)

She undresses, lies down on the straw mattress, and covers herself with an old curtain. In a parody of "Enlightened" philosophical inquiry, Casanova recalls how, having shed all his prejudices, he then discovered her "perfect beauty" and proceeded (for an additional fee) to "examine" her more carefully: "I send every prejudice packing; I see her neither slovenly nor in rags, I find her a perfect beauty. I make to examine her completely, she refuses, she laughs, she resists; but a whole écu [un écu de 6 francs] makes her as mild as a lamb, and since her only fault is being dirty I wash her all over with my hands" (1:621). Conveniently enough, for this price the girl allows him to satisfy his philosophical curiosity in every way, except "what [he] did not want to do." The context makes clear that what Casanova allegedly did not want to do was to deflower Miss Murphy. In fact, the girl's older sister had warned her not to part with her virginity for less than 25 louis. But Casanova claims never to have cared about this precious commodity, to have been perfectly satisfied without it. The rest of the O-Morphi story will corroborate this impression that the girl's virginity interested him only for its potential as investment capital.

For Casanova, the Murphy sisters are originally Flemish, but they are also "Greek." As a "little Helen" (1:621), the younger Murphy is aesthetically Greek; Casanova identifies her older sister with two economic myths

about Greeks: the unscrupulous merchant, and the gamblers' myth of the
Grec, or "card cheat."[13] "[J]'ai enfin fait un accord que je lui donnerais
toujours douze francs, jusqu'à ce que je me déterminasse à payer les six
cents. L'usure était forte, *mais la Morfi* [the older sister] *était de race grecque
et elle n'avait sur cela aucun scrupule*" ("I finally came to an agreement to
keep giving her twelve hundred francs each time until I decided to pay
the six hundred. The rate of interest was usurious, *but La Morphy was a
Greek by nature, and she had no scruples in the matter*" [1:621, emphasis
added]).

Over the course of the next two months, Casanova paid regular visits
to Miss Murphy, always subject to the same limitations, and never asked
to deflower her, much to the older sister's surprise: "La grande Morfi me
croyait le plus grand des dupes, puisqu'en deux mois j'avais dépensé trois
cents francs pour rien. Elle attribuait cela à mon avarice. Quelle avarice!"
("The elder Morphy thought me the greatest of dupes, since in two months
I had spent three hundred francs for nothing. She attributed it to my stinginess. Stinginess indeed!" [1:621–22]). Due to this Enlightened investment
policy, Louison Murphy's virginity will eventually be sold to Louis XV:
thus, by virtue of an illusion (or a miracle) that he never bothers to explain,
Casanova eventually profits from "la belle O-Morphi," both erotically and
monetarily. Somehow he will manage to negotiate the imaginary barrier
that separates the pleasure of subjects from the *jouissance* of a king. In the
O-Morphi episode, the "medium" through which this illusion, or miracle,
operates is a painting.

Casanova got the idea of capitalizing upon "[his] little treasure" (1:621)
by having her painted in the nude. He paid a "German" painter to provide him with the means for mnemonic *jouissance*. It is not known for certain who painted this portrait of the girl, although Casanova's description
of it could very well refer to the portrait of Miss Murphy by François
Boucher.[14] He even makes her name into a Greek word for beauty. There
is no doubt that, whether in Casanova's description or in the Boucher
painting, the erotic and aesthetic ideal incarnated by Miss Murphy is that
of the Vénus Callipyge. Although his response to O-Morphi (both the
"live" model and the portrait) is erotic, rather than aesthetic, Casanova
portrays and sells her as aesthetic perfection incarnate—that is, archetypi-
cal Greek beauty.

At first, however, Casanova meant to use the portrait profanely, as an
erotic stimulant, and he describes it in those terms: "Elle était couchée sur
son ventre, s'appuyant de ses bras et de sa gorge sur un oreiller, et tenant
sa tête comme si elle était couchée sur son dos. L'habile artiste avait dessiné

ses jambes et ses cuisses de façon que l'oeil ne pouvait pas désirer de voir davantage. J'y ai fait écrire dessous: *O-Morphi*. Mot qui n'est pas ho-mérique, mais qui n'est pas moins grec. Il signifie *Belle*." ("She was lying on her stomach, resting her arms and her bosom on a pillow and holding her head as if she were lying on her back. The skillful artist had drawn her legs and thighs in such a way that the eye could not wish to see more. I had him write under it *O-Morphi*. The word is not Homeric, but it is Greek none the less. It means *'Beautiful'*" [1:622, translation modified, emphasis in original].)[15] Although he gave the portrait a title that was meant to be the Greek word for "beauty" (it should be *e morphe*), Casano-va's pleasure was clearly not disinterested, or "aesthetic," in Kantian terms. As his words imply ("the eye could not wish to see more"), he conceived of this portrait as pornography. When Jean Laforgue rewrote the passage in the nineteenth century, he "corrected" Casanova's prurient interest, along with the grammar and diction: "Elle était couchée sur *le* ventre, s'appuyant *des* bras et *du* sein sur un oreiller et tenant *la tête tournéé comme si elle avait été couchée aux trois quarts sur le dos. L'artiste habile et plein de goût avait dessiné sa partie inférieure avec tant d'art et de vérité qu'on ne pouvait rien désirer de plus beau*" ("With skill and considerable taste, the artist had drawn her lower part with so much art and truth that one could not desire anything more beautiful.")[16] Although Casanova himself did not disguise his symbolic voyeurism, Laforgue has him justify the portrait in terms of "taste," "truth," and "beauty." In fact, by retouching Casano-va's portrait of O-Morphi, Laforgue implies that what Casanova, in his preface to *Histoire de ma vie*, had called "laying on too much color" ("trop peindre") was actually an unwillingness to cover up the objects of his own erotic interest.

However, Casanova claims never to have imagined, when he had a copy made of the O-Morphi portrait, that either the painting or the model would ever make its way to Versailles. He allegedly had it made only to satisfy his friend Patu ("Can one refuse such a thing to a friend?"), for the same reason that he had agreed to spend that first night at Victorine Murphy's house ("a friend's pleasure is motive enough"). But Casanova was a great believer in the inscrutable workings of destiny; thus he ex-claims, "[W]hat are not the paths of all-powerful destiny" (1:622). As he tells the story, it was destiny that made everything work out so profitably and pleasurably for everyone.

Soon a copy of this portrait is shown at Versailles and comes to the attention of the king. Upon beholding this image of feminine beauty, Louis XV, like Casanova before him, does not mask the compellingly "inter-

François Boucher, *Nude (Miss O'Morphy?)*
(oil painting, Musée des Beaux-Arts, Reims) Photo: Roger-Viollet

ested" pleasure it arouses in him. According to Casanova's account, the king asks that the girl be brought to Versailles, so that he might judge whether the "original" (that is, not the original portrait, but little Miss Murphy herself, in the flesh) is as beautiful as the copy: "[T]he king . . . became curious to know if the portrait of the "Greek Girl" was a true likeness. If it was, the monarch claimed the right to sentence the original to quench the fire which it had kindled in his heart" (1:622). A few days later, the Murphy sisters are taken to Versailles, where the following scene reportedly takes place in a pavilion of the Parc-aux-Cerfs, while the "German" painter, outside, awaits the result of the negotiation:

> [T]he king came, alone, asked [Victorine Murphy] if she was Greek, drew the portrait from his pocket, looked carefully at her younger sister and said:
> — *I have never seen a better likeness.*
> He sat down, took her on his knees, caressed her here and there, and *after*

his royal hand had assured him that she was a virgin [emphasis added here], gave her a kiss. O-Morphi looked at him and laughed.

"What are you laughing at?"

"Because you are as like a six-franc piece as two peas [vous ressemblez à un écu de six francs comme deux gouttes d'eau]." (1:622)

At the conclusion of this episode, the painter receives 50 louis (25 of which—the original asking price for her virginity—goes to Casanova), while Miss Murphy settles into an apartment of the Parc-aux-Cerfs (where she remains until her disgrace, three years later) and is paid 1,000 louis.

One has the sense of an ending, the impression that something here has come full circle: Murphy laughs at the resemblance between the king and the coin that bears his name and image, just as the king is struck by the perfect resemblance between her and the portrait. Both the representation of theoretically perfect or absolute power on a coin and the image of perfect beauty perfectly resemble their models. Various tokens of value (monetary, erotic, aesthetic) have circulated between a modest Parisian apartment and Versailles, between little Miss Murphy and the king, but in the process they have taken on a less ideal or perfect appearance.

The various archetypes or ideals in this text (beauty, *jouissance,* the king) function like coins, as currency in an exchange transaction, rather than as ideal repositories of value. Rather than remaining inaccessible to all forms of sensuous appearance, the *eidos* (of power, pleasure, and beauty) circulates in this episode of Casanova's text like a coin, like a common bearer of general exchange-value. The process is all the more curious since, in *Histoire de ma vie,* Louis XV does not usually appear in this way, stripped of all transcendental illusion. In fact, Casanova placed Louis XV, the "Bien-Aimé," above all other kings, at the very top of the hierarchical order he admired. In the O-Morphi episode, Louis XV is momentarily deprived of his aura, and he becomes merely ironized, devaluated currency: the king is made into a coin, a louis. Yet in retrospect Casanova's belief in the transcendent grace of kings, and of Louis XV in particular, appears not to have been diminished in the slightest—perhaps, as Chantal Thomas explains, because that illusion was fundamental to his psychic economy: "With the death of kings, what collapses for Casanova is not so much a political system as his own economy of desire. In the first case, an adventurer like him could overcome the catastrophe; in the second, the catastrophe strikes him in a place where no modifications can be tolerated. It may be the fixed point of *an insuperable exteriority.*"[17] In Casanova's imagination, being loved by Louis XV would have been a sign of divine election, of grace, a gesture that lifted him, and him alone, above the ontological barrier that separated the king from common mortals. Yet instead of miraculously rising above that insuperable barrier, being elevated to the status of a demigod by the king's desire, Casanova here found himself in the position of a vulgar procurer, and thus unwittingly brought the king down to the level of an ordinary mortal.

The O-Morphi episode also suggests that the king, unlike his subjects, could afford to cherish a different illusion: namely, that theoretically inaccessible archetypes can be bought, sold, or somehow appropriated. By virtue of his semidivine position, and in order to demonstrate that position to himself and to others, the king cannot suffer any limitation upon his powers: he owes it to himself, or to his self-image, to have, not just a beautiful mistress, but Beauty itself as mistress. There is a mimetic economy in this episode, in which art and artists, representations and their makers, mediate among power, pleasure, and *jouissance*. Casanova's role in this story raises the question of vicarious power and vicarious *jouissance*, of how representatives and representations (writers, texts, readers) participate in pleasure and power. More specifically, this episode concerns the historical and theoretical limits of absolute power, and of absolute pleasure (that is, *jouissance*) as well.

Sets of recurrent signifiers facilitate this textual economy, like shifters among the various levels of representation (erotic, aesthetic, monetary) and of representation effects (power, pleasure, *jouissance*). To some extent, the text functions as representation (thematically) and as representation effect (rhetorically), thanks to the circulation of this material. The first set of signifiers:

MURPHY—MORPHÉE—O-MORPHI—E MORPHE

contains variants on two foreign words, an Irish patronym (Murphy) and a Greek noun (*e morphe*). The latter term is implicitly related to the name of the Greek god of dreams, Morpheus (French, Morphée). The second set of signifiers around the word *écu* underlines the commonplace identification of sex with money or, more precisely, with the female body as commodity. At the beginning of the episode, Casanova says to the girl, "You shan't have the half écu [le petit écu]." The etymological meaning of *écu* (from Latin *scutum*, "shield") further motivates the figural substitution of *écu* or *petit écu* for a woman's virginity, as well as the implication that virginity is meant to be purchased. Casanova's text reinforces this connection when, just after Louis XV has checked Miss Murphy's virginity, she begins to laugh at his resemblance to an *écu de six francs*. In this context, it is all the more striking that (whatever his intentions may have been) not only does Casanova use his *petits écus* to buy *everything but* Miss Murphy's virginity, he also makes it possible for her virginity to be used as investment capital, on which he takes a commission.

Louis XV perfectly resembles the coin that first aroused Miss Murphy's desire, just as she bears a perfect resemblance to the portrait that awakened the desire of the king. The king, his subject, and their representations perfectly mirror each other. To Louis belongs the *jouissance*—that is, the possession and enjoyment of O-Morphi, meaning both Miss Murphy and *e morphe* (archetypal Beauty). Such are royal *jouissances:* in principle, they belong to the only being who can have currency struck in his own image. Only the absolute monarch, to whom everyone and everything is theoretically subject, has the right and the means, if not the obligation, to obtain complete satisfaction of his desires. However, the "absolute monarch" is not so far removed from mortal contingency that he can enjoy his privileges without money: he cannot command the obedience of his subjects without paying them off in kind—that is, with monetary portraits of himself.

What makes Louis's *jouissances* royal is that they ostensibly derive from the possession of a model—that is, not just from "having" the empirical model for a work of art, but from taking possession of the model or archetype of Beauty itself. His subject Casanova expresses the desire to have Miss Murphy in a painting—that is, vicariously—but the king must have her as *eidos*—that is, as ideal (or transcendental signified)—and yet he can do so only with the mediation of his own images. Meanwhile Miss Murphy, she who miraculously incarnates that ideal, cares not a sou for the empirical royal person (for the father of the people and model of French currency), or for the model or archetype of political power that he supposedly is or has: all she wants is money, monetary portraits or copies of that model. Using the effigies of his person that he alone has the right to strike, the king must pay for the royal privilege (which is in fact the royal illusion) of "having" Beauty itself (Helen, Praxiteles' statue, and so forth) subject to his *jouissance*. The model serves here to buy monetary portraits of another model, just as these latter portraits pay for the model. In exchange for these metallic images of the king, Miss Murphy gives Louis the "only thing" that his subject Casanova had left intact, her *petit écu*. Casanova will have used the interplay of these mirror images to turn "la belle O-Morphi" into a very profitable speculative vehicle.

Thus the copy of Miss Murphy's portrait moves up the social hierarchy, and portraits of the king trickle down. O-MORPHI—that is, both a specific individual and archetypal Beauty—has been exchanged for 50 LOUIS—in

other words, for images of someone who is both absolutely unique and
absolutely general. Louis is unique, both as an individual who resembles
his image and as the archetypal king. But this image, due to the empirical
and ontological uniqueness of its model, is also absolutely general; it is
the general equivalent: money, a louis. A louis is *only* the present king of
France and *only* money. For a specific quantity of the coins that no one
else has the right to strike, Louis XV buys both figure and letter, the part
(or *petit écu*) and the whole of Beauty.

The transaction testifies to the king's desire to move from portrait to
model. In contrast, Miss Murphy uses one model *(e morphe)* to obtain
monetary copies—that is, portraits of another model. In other words, the
conflictual relationship that these portraits mediate between the king and
his subjects, and between men and women, is not nearly so simple as it
might appear. Whether we consider the king, Miss Murphy, Casanova, or
our own position as reader, it is not easy to decide who is being manipu-
lated and who has the last laugh, or the last transcendental illusion.

The Louis

"I'm laughing because *you are as like a six-franc piece as two peas in a pod*
[comme deux gouttes d'eau]" (emphasis added). Here Louison Murphy
claims that what makes her laugh is the amazing resemblance between
Louis XV and the silver coin bearing his effigy: Louis (the One, the
unique) resembles a louis (mechanically reproducible to infinity) "like
two peas [comme deux gouttes d'eau]." To tell Louis how much he resembles his currency, Miss Murphy uses a cliché ("comme deux gouttes
d'eau")—appropriately enough, since Louis's monetary effigy is also a
cliché. Like a louis, every occurrence/copy of a cliché is invariable. The
cliché "comme deux gouttes d'eau" posits a resemblance between two resemblances—that is, it posits an analogy, not a comparison. According
to this cliché, the king and his image on a coin are like two drops of water;
the king's perfect resemblance to his effigy on a 6-franc écu is like the
resemblance of one drop of water to another.

When Murphy says that His Majesty resembles his currency, she is
talking about similarity, not identity. Her analogy states that just as any
two drops of water look perfectly alike, but still are not the same drop
of water, so Louis looks exactly like his effigy on a louis, without "being"
the image itself. In official doctrine, the king may be incomparably noble
and unique, but nothing is more common than this perfect similarity. The
official mark of Louis's ontological superiority to everyone else must also
exist in a potentially infinite number of copies; just as there is only one

Louis XV, so his portraits in currency are potentially infinite. No one comes close to resembling the king, but every louis that has been struck in his image resembles him "comme deux gouttes d'eau," to coin a phrase. The king and his effigy resemble each other, not like a model and a portrait, but like two perfectly similar, "identical" members of an infinite series. In Murphy's language, the king may be exchanged for any one of his effigies without the slightest loss of force or form. At this historical moment, the king and his écus look like interchangeable coins, mirror images, which can be substituted droplet for droplet, coin for coin, Louis for louis. In principle, it is possible to exchange a sufficient number of louis for anything in the world. As in Watteau's *L'Enseigne de Gersaint*, the king's image has entered a market system.

For Louison Murphy, it is as if a miracle had taken place. Doubtless that fact helps to explain her laughter.[18] She says that what makes her laugh is the resemblance between the king and his monetary image. But Miss Murphy may also be laughing at the miraculous chain of events that has put her humble self in the presence of the model for all resemblance, in a position to verify the resemblance between Louis and a louis. This miracle has placed her in the king's presence and has made her the object of royal desire: she, her *petit écu*, is now the object that is about to be exchanged for a certain number of louis. She laughs at the amazing discovery that, in the eyes of the king, she is "O-Morphi"—that is, Beauty itself.

In absolutist culture, only a miracle could have abolished the distance that separated "the king" (not his empirical body, but his eucharistic representation) from his subjects. For the king and his subjects occupied radically different positions in the political economy of absolutist representation. As a result, the king and his subjects had radically different views of their portraits, and of representations in general. "C'est Louis le Grand," an utterance implicit in the portrait of Louis XIV, identifies the portrait of the absolute monarch with the essence of royalty: "The king is only truly king . . . in images. They are his *real presence*."[19] As absolute monarch, Louis XIV was, for himself and for his subjects, a representational effect: the king's portrait produced him as absolute monarch. As the model for an entire political, aesthetic, and monetary system, the king was condemned to dissatisfaction with anything less than other models. Louis XV behaves as if he (like the Sun King, and unlike a Casanova or a Murphy) could require nothing less than absolute, unmediated *jouissance:* politically, erotically, and aesthetically. Like Louis XIV, he could not pursue the goal of nonvicarious *jouissance* without delegating his power to a legion of representatives and representations. Unlike Louis XIV, however, Louis XV could no longer convincingly behave as if his pleasures were sovereign, according to the rule of "Car tel est notre bon plaisir." For one thing, the O-Morphi episode testifies to the fact that in post-absolutist culture neither the king's representation nor his person (the model) retained the power (to which Louis XIV lays claim in the Rigaud portrait) of making his subjects avert their gaze: in fact, Louison Murphy inspects the king from head to foot, before she breaks out laughing. Miss Murphy cannot "have" the king, nor does she want him, but she would like to have as many mirror images as possible of the king's portrait in currency.

Casanova has Murphy's portrait painted in order to possess her vicariously. In fact, the great seducer's curious lack of interest in her virginity testifies to an implicit recognition that *jouissance* of the model or *eidos* is not meant for a subject—as if Casanova somehow knew that O-Morphi was a *morceau de roi*. Furthermore, however perfectly Miss Murphy may incarnate perfect Greek beauty—or rather because her beauty is only conceivable in terms of a model—she and her portrait cannot really "be" Beauty, at least not in the same way that the king and his portrait "are" one. Unlike Murphy, the king has no other model than himself: he and his portrait are subject to none.[20]

Like the painter of Miss Murphy's portrait, Casanova is a procurer of *jouissances,* for himself and for his readers. Yet what he describes as his personal dilemma ("ne savoir plus jouir que par réminiscence") may in fact correspond to a more general historical situation. That situation is the paradoxical one in which the value of individual experience (whose most intense, most valuable form is *jouissance*) at once depends upon the untranslatability of experience and can only assert itself in translation. Casanova's need to translate his experience into the lingua franca of European Enlightenment (into French, *la lingua francese*) may be seen as a metaphor for a historical situation in which individual experience (my life, my body) appears precisely as re-inscription (*réminiscence*), in a lingua franca—that is, in general-equivalent terms.

Part II: Casanova *aux Délices*

> They are monarchs in the republic of Letters, these characters who last like Voltaire
> or M. de Chauteaubriand. They obtain, they usurp a kind of scepter.
> — SAINTE-BEUVE, *Chateaubriand et son groupe littéraire*

Casanova passionately believed in the ontological superiority of kings, and of Louis XV in particular. Yet when he actually encountered "le Bien-

Giacomo Casanova (engraving). Photo: Roger-Viollet.

Aimé," Casanova treated him simply as a man, and not as a demigod.
Likewise when Casanova finally met the first man of letters to be called
a king, he found only a man—one who was wittier, smarter, and more
learned than himself—but a man nonetheless, not a godlike being inhab-
iting a higher sphere of existence. Adding insult to narcissistic injury, Voltaire would then treat Casanova like an Italian buffoon ("une espèce de
plaisant"), instead of singling him out for royal favor. As we shall see, to
the master who held court at Les Délices, Casanova was merely an object
of ridicule—certainly not a "worthy subject of laughter" for "good society," not the entertaining but worthy interlocutor that Casanova always
aspired to become. Despite the deep monarchist convictions of Casanova
and Voltaire, the king had lost his awesome symbolic force, making it
impossible for either contestant to take anyone—except himself, that is—
for a superior being. In fact, these two monarchists could not have ascribed

a noble value to themselves without also implicitly devaluing the symbolic order of royal absolutism.

Eight years after the O-Morphi episode, in the summer of 1760, Casanova paid several visits to Voltaire at Les Délices. Although these encounters probably took place over a period of two months, in his memoirs Casanova condenses them into three successive afternoons, during which he and Voltaire engage in a three-round oratorical contest.[21]

Like most of the stories in Casanova's autobiography, the account of this contest is interrupted by parts of several other stories. Two of these interwoven narratives are thematically related to the Voltaire story and resonate with it in curious ways. One story is about a miracle of conception, while the other concerns a miracle of contraception. The first begins at Lausanne, before Casanova's visits to Les Délices, during his dinner with a learned young lady and her family. At table, Casanova has a theological argument with this young woman (whom he later calls "Hedwige") about the belief, attributed to St. Augustine by a certain French tradition, that the Virgin Mary had conceived Jesus through her ears, by virtue of what might be called the "illocutionary force" of the Annunciation.[22] At the beginning of this story, Casanova's interlocutor is herself a virgin, but several chapters after the Voltaire encounters, Casanova will finally seduce and deflower her.[23] In contrast, the second miracle narrative is about contraception. During the nights that precede and follow his daytime conversations with Voltaire, Casanova participates in orgies with a group of three young women.[24] Casanova recalls having been careful to ensure that— this being Calvinist Geneva—none of the ladies would get pregnant. For this reason, before beginning the second night's festivities, he offers each of the ladies a golden ball with allegedly miraculous contraceptive virtues. The syndic of Geneva, who has introduced Casanova to the young ladies, plays the role of impotent spectator to these orgies, while occasionally lending a hand.[25] We shall see how the meaning of Casanova's Voltaire narrative is implicitly affected by this interpolated context.

Voltaire and Casanova, the philosophe and the libertine, had a surprising number of things in common. Both had first become famous, in large part, for having done time in prison, in both cases for having expressed themselves too freely.[26] After their release from prison, both Arouet de Voltaire and Casanova de Seingalt had forged a noble title for themselves.[27] Both were also confirmed monarchists: Voltaire, the uncrowned king of Enlightened Europe, enjoyed holding court at Les Délices, as he would later at Ferney, while Casanova, a fervent admirer of Voltaire (whom he repeatedly calls "the great man"), could imagine nothing more delightful than becoming the king's favorite.[28] Voltaire and Casanova might conceivably have been perfect complements to each other, with Voltaire playing the king to the passive, yet magically privileged favorite that Casanova dreamed of becoming. But in the summer of 1760, when Casanova finally spent several afternoons in conversation with "[his] master" at Les Délices, he and Voltaire annoyed each other prodigiously.[29]

Later in that year, the perpetually mobile Casanova once again found himself near Geneva, and he was more than once invited to pay Voltaire a visit in the philosophe's new residence at Ferney. Yet he evaded these invitations. Although he was a man of insatiable curiosity, who had always professed the greatest admiration for Voltaire, and for *l'esprit français* in general,[30] Casanova later confessed in his memoirs that his subsequent public criticism of Voltaire had been motivated by a wounded ego (although he may also have criticized Voltaire simply to please the Venetian inquisitors): "But I was left with a grudge against him which for ten years made me criticize everything I read, old or new, which the great man had given or was giving the public."[31] As for Voltaire, in a letter to his friend Thieriot, written on July 7, 1760, while Casanova was visiting Les Délices, he makes an amused but disdainful allusion to the "espèce de plaisant" who was visiting him at the time: "We have here a sort of fool [une espèce de plaisant], who would be quite capable of making a kind of *Secchia rapita*, and of painting the enemies of reason in all the excess of their impertinence. Perhaps my fool will make a gay and amusing poem, on a subject that doesn't really look that way."[32] An intersection of references leaves little doubt that the person to whom Voltaire disparagingly refers in this letter was indeed Casanova. In Casanova's detailed account, he and Voltaire had a brief exchange about the lighthearted epic to which Voltaire refers in his letter, Tassoni's *Secchia rapita*. He claims to have noticed a copy of the book on a large table in Voltaire's bedroom, next to the *Summa theologica* of St. Thomas Aquinas(!).

As a result of that discussion, writes Casanova, he made Voltaire a present of Folengo's macaronic classic *Il Baldus*, but Voltaire does not seem to have appreciated Folengo's poem any more than he did Casanova himself. Casanova recalls that "[Voltaire] began at table by saying that he thanked me for my present of Merlin Cocai [i.e., Folengo], certainly made with good intentions, but that he did not thank me for the praise I had bestowed on the poem, since I had been the cause of his wasting four hours reading nonsense [des bêtises]" (2:419 [vol. 6, chap. 10]). In this remark, Voltaire links Casanova to the low poetic register, which for him was a complete waste of time—whether he encountered it in Folengo, in

Rabelais, or in Shakespeare. For Voltaire, only the high, the noble, and
the serious were worthy of full attention. Casanova, in contrast, never
considered anyone or anything a waste of his time. By staging his autobiography as a kind of theatrical performance, Casanova was seeking to
have laughter, and therefore himself, taken seriously—or as he puts it in
the preface, "donner un noble sujet de rire à la bonne compagnie" ("to
provide a most worthy subject of laughter to my well-bred audience").
Although Voltaire was a chronic insomniac, it is no wonder that after
spending half the night trying to read Folengo's "bêtises," he was in a
bad mood the next day. Casanova, who (as Henri de Régnier remarks)[33]
rarely had any trouble falling asleep, somewhat disingenuously notes that
"the great man was pleased on that day to indulge in raillery, ill-humored
jests, and sarcasm" (2:419). It is not surprising that after such an inauspi-
cious beginning, the meeting between Casanova and Voltaire immediately
developed into a contest and ultimately degenerated into a nasty political
argument.[34]

An Athletic Contest

Casanova claims to have left Les Délices quite pleased with himself, as
usual: "I left rather well pleased that on this last day I had reduced *the
gladiator* [cet athlète] to reason" (2:424, emphasis added). The reference
to Voltaire as a gladiator raises, among other points, the issue of performance in the life of Casanova.

Casanova recalls his conversations with Voltaire as a sort of oratorical duel in several rounds.[35] In *Casanova: Un Voyage libertin*, Thomas distinguishes between two registers of performance in Casanova, the heroic
and the erotic. She cites the encounter with Voltaire as an example of the
former: "addressed to a powerful interlocutor, who is noble, rich, and
male, before whom Casanova is in the position of a courtier, and therefore
in a relationship based upon humility that he must above all avoid turning
into humiliation."[36] However, this "heroic" performance, like the orgies
that frame it, also takes place in front of an audience—that is, the ladies
and gentlemen whom he and Voltaire were trying to seduce, figuratively
speaking. In addition, considering that the account of Casanova's performance at Les Délices is interrupted by that of his orgies, framed by the
erotic-theological story of "Hedwige," the learned virgin, the story of his
daytime performances takes on both a heroic and an erotic aspect.

In chapter 2, I referred to the essentially theatrical mode in which Voltaire presented himself to the world. Likewise (as Thomas notes), Casa-

nova always imagined his seductive powers theatrically, "essentially as the art of catching and maintaining attention."[37] When he had the attention of an audience, in bed or in a salon, Casanova had the fullest sense of his own existence. At these moments, what he saw in the mirror of the audience's captivated desire was the image he admired above all others: that of an irresistibly charming and handsome man, detached, euphoric, and always master of the situation. Casanova just loved to imagine himself on center stage, turning in a magnificent performance. Thus he portrays himself emerging victorious from a final day of dialectical engagement with Voltaire: "I left rather well pleased that on this last day I had reduced the gladiator to reason."

There is something suspicious about the way Casanova announces this triumph to the world—something odd about applying the word *athlete* to the chronically moribund Voltaire (except perhaps in the etymological sense of a "contestant"), and about claiming to have made Voltaire, of all people, submit to reason. The irony of the words "cet athlète" is made explicit in the next sentence ("I was left with a grudge against him . . ."). By speaking of Voltaire ironically, as an "athlete," Casanova could present himself as Voltaire's superior, physically (especially in the context of his evening athleticism) if not morally. The epithet recalls the physical differences between the handsome Italian adventurer, then an astonishingly vigorous man of thirty-five, and the perpetually hypochondriacal and sickly Voltaire, sixty-six years old at the time. Although Voltaire was never much of a physical specimen (and not much of a sexual performer either: one recalls Mme. du Châtelet's reference to him as "un amant de neige"), he clearly had won the contest of wit. As we shall see, over the course of a verbal duel that lasted several days, the "great man" was able to score repeatedly, almost at will, against his Venetian opponent. From the point of view of the audience at Les Délices, Voltaire was obviously the winner, and still champion. On the other hand, Casanova was never one to belittle the judgment of an audience; for this inveterate performer, the audience was always right. Hence his attempt, in writing his memoirs (during his final performance), to seduce an audience that was not already won over to Voltaire's point of view.

Casanova's ironic bravado suggests that the meeting with Voltaire also forced upon him the unpleasant realization that he could not always coincide with his euphoric, idealized self-image. This ideal image was, as Thomas Kavanagh has shown, the systematically discontinuous self of the gambler, living solely and entirely within the present moment.[38] Kavanagh distinguishes between the "utterly solipsistic present" of Casanova's gambling self (independent of any past and future, totally determined by the present throw of the dice) and the more traditional autobiographical self, which is the relatively coherent nexus of interaction with a fairly coherent world. Casanova's ironic portrayal of Voltaire suggests that, however much he wanted to see himself as a detached spectator on the stage of life,[39] Casanova always also wanted—perhaps even more strongly—to see himself as a consummate performer. Consequently, even when he portrayed himself as a euphoric gambler, who had magically overcome all concern with everything outside the present moment, he always implicitly moved beyond the present time and place, toward an audience.

In other words, when Casanova speaks of having "mis cet athlète à la raison," he is not really recalling a victory, but trying to overcome what he hopes will have been a momentary setback. Writing these words enables Casanova to win an imaginary final round of the contest of wits he implicitly admits to having lost. By telling the story of his life, he could hope finally to triumph over Voltaire ("on this last day [ce dernier jour]"— that is, on the day of final reckoning). What he could not obtain with wit *(esprit)* in 1760, perhaps he could win, toward the end of his own life, with the retrospective phantasm of triumphant wit *(esprit d'escalier)*. In the end, this irony enabled this consummate magician and charlatan to imagine having put even Voltaire in his place, reducing him "to reason."

As Thomas remarks, the fact that Casanova immediately transcribed his conversations with Voltaire suggests that his displeasure at being treated like an Italian buffoon and humiliated in front of the ladies had been mixed with the pleasure of performing in front of an audience.[40] By first transcribing his performance, just after it took place, and then rewriting it many years later, he could transmute into solitary *jouissance* the mixture of pleasure and pain (already inscribed in his ambivalent relationship to the French language)[41] that had marked his exchanges with Voltaire. Rewriting the "experience" ultimately allowed him to "jouir par réminiscence" and in so doing to deliver another performance, as heroic as it was erotic, before an audience that was inaccessible, and therefore ideal—like the kings of his dreams.

Opening Gambit: The King and His Fool

Casanova emphasizes the "solemn" circumstances of his first entry on Voltaire's stage, suggesting that the outcome of his ensuing joust with Voltaire had been determined by unfavorable circumstances, and not by the valor of the contestants: "We went to Monsieur de Voltaire's, who was just getting up from table. He was surrounded by gentlemen and ladies, so my presentation became a solemn occasion. This solemnity was very far from predisposing Voltaire and the company in my favor" (2:400–401 [vol. 6, chap. 9]). As I mentioned, both Voltaire (François-Marie Arouet de Voltaire) and Casanova (Giacamo Girolamo Casanova de Seingalt) had already given noble titles to themselves. Nonetheless, Casanova implies here that the solemnity of his introduction to Voltaire made him look like a buffoon. "M. de Voltaire," he suggests, encountered Casanova in such courtly circumstances ("surrounded by gentlemen and ladies") that the former had to play a serious, noble role, putting his Venetian guest in the ignoble, comic role that Voltaire would later call that of the "plaisant." The only serious roles in French classical theater were, of course, noble. Surrounded by a court of admirers, "the great man" obviously had to play the king. In fact, when Laforgue edited and partially rewrote Casanova's memoirs, he made Voltaire's royal solemnity even more explicit, by turning Les Délices into a "court," where Voltaire was king. In Laforgue's version, the phrase "Il était environné de seigneurs et de dames" ("He was surrounded by gentlemen and ladies") is transformed into "Il était *comme au milieu d'une cour* de seigneurs et de dames" ("He was *as if in the midst of a court* of gentlemen and ladies").[42] As a gambler and a great believer in the powers of chance,[43] Casanova concluded that he had just been unlucky: that when fate dealt the cards, Voltaire had drawn the king (the serious role), leaving Casanova to play the knave, if not the fool (or foil). The scene had to be played out, in his view, even though its outcome was rigorously determined by (post-absolutist) circumstances that not even the future "king of Ferney" could really control.

Casanova opens with a respectful bow before his "master"—that is, with what his readers will recognize as the usual humility gambit. But Voltaire does not take this humility seriously and keeps putting him in his place: *à la raison*, so to speak. Time and again, the master refuses to take his self-styled disciple seriously, turning a rhetorical pirouette around each token of Casanova's humility. To Voltaire, everything the Venetian visitor says becomes material for wit, and at Casanova's expense:

"This," I said to him, "is the happiest moment of my life. At last I see my master; it is twenty years, Monsieur, since I became your pupil."

"Honor me with another twenty, and then promise to bring me my wages."

"I promise; but, on your side, promise to wait for me."

"I give you my word for it, and only death—not I—will break my word [et je manquerai de la vie plutôt que d'y manquer]."

> A general laugh greeted this first Voltairean sally [cette première pointe voltairienne]. (2:401 [vol. 6, chap. 10])

With this first "pointe," Voltaire easily wins the first round of the contest.

Casanova does not mind being the occasional butt of Voltaire's wit, and he harbors no resentment, either against those who laugh at him or against the master who makes them laugh: "It was in the nature of things. The function of such laughter is to encourage one disputant, always at the expense of the others; and he to whom the laughers give their suffrage is always sure to win; they constitute a claque which operates in good society [en bonne compagnie], too. I expected as much, but I hoped that my turn would come to let fly at him [de lui livrer chance]" (2:401). He does not mind playing the buffoon, as long as he can believe that the reason why he has lost the first skirmish is structural (built into the dynamics of tendentious wit) and not personal (not a judgment of his real worth). Unlike Rousseau, Casanova had nothing against the cruel impersonality of upper-class wit, and he adored its theatricality. Indeed, he willingly assumed the values of "la bonne compagnie," that noble elite of European society to whom his memoirs are addressed.[44]

Voltaire then stands up (Casanova notes this detail) to greet the two Englishmen who have just entered the room. He (the "great man" who had remained seated in Casanova's presence) declares—in a rhetorical formula that Casanova finds irritating—that he envies these gentlemen . . . simply because they are English: "*Ces Messieurs sont Anglais, je voudrais bien l'être*" (emphasis in original). From the perspective of a self-styled "man of honor," Casanova parenthetically takes Voltaire to task for this compliment: "A poor compliment, for it forced them to answer that they wished they were French, and perhaps they did not want to lie, or they should be ashamed to tell the truth. A man of honor, I think, has the right to put his own country above all others" (2:401–2). As soon as the Englishmen have politely returned the compliment and moved on, Voltaire again turns his attention to Casanova (who has remained standing in front of him), this time in terms of the latter's own "nation." But before addressing his visitor "as a Venetian," the philosophe sits down again. To address Casanova "as a Venetian," the great man now assumes a different, less reverent, tone of voice: "No sooner has he sat down again than he returns to me, saying to me *in a very polite but cheerful tone [d'un ton très poli, mais toujours riant]*, that as a Venetian I must certainly know Count Algarotti" (translation modified, emphasis added). This tone, "very polite, but cheerful [riant]," is that of urbane, sophisticated wit, and it conveys a light and resolutely superficial way of addressing oneself to an interlocutor.

Round Two: Giacomo Furioso

Voltaire's stage movements having clearly demonstrated that he cannot take Casanova seriously, the latter now suggests that they play a different game. In a preeminently French battle of wits, Casanova ("en qualité de Vénitien") has no chance of beating Voltaire. For him it is hopeless to engage the world champion, on his home field, in that most superficial (and, in a sense, noblest) of games. So Casanova descends to a more serious (less noble) form of competition, the contest of knowledge, and he chooses the topic: Italian language and literature. He tries to show the audience that, at least in this category, he knows more than Voltaire. Thus when Voltaire refers to the "forty-six" cantos of Ariosto's *Orlando furioso*, Casanova objects that the poem really has fifty-one. Moving to the attack, he then chastises Voltaire for having (in the *Essai sur la poésie épique* [1726]) expressed a preference for Tasso over Ariosto. But rather than defend that position, Voltaire willingly concedes that he had taken it through prejudice and simple ignorance. He then proves his admiration for Ariosto, astonishing Casanova in the process, by faultlessly declaiming long excerpts of the *Orlando furioso*:

> It was then that Voltaire astonished me. He recited by heart the two great passages in the thirty-fourth and thirty-fifth cantos of the divine poet in which he tells of Astolpho's conversation with St. John the Apostle, never skipping a line, never pronouncing a word except in accordance with strict prosody; he pointed out their beauties to me, with reflections which only a truly great man could make. One could have expected nothing more from the most sublime Italian commentators. I listened to him without breathing, without once blinking my eyes, *hoping in vain to catch him in a mistake;* turning to the company, I said that I was overwhelmed [excédé] with astonishment, and that I would inform all Italy of my wonder and the reason for it. (2:405, translation modified, emphasis added)

Everyone present applauds Voltaire, although Casanova remarks that none of them understands Italian. Nevertheless, Casanova takes up the implicit challenge by delivering (what he recalls as) an even more astonishing performance, of an even greater passage from Ariosto: the thirty-six stanzas that describe how Orlando, upon realizing that his beloved Angelica had slept with Medoro, went mad with jealousy.

Like Voltaire, Casanova probably memorized verse for the pleasure of declaiming it (or imagining himself doing so) before an audience. Since the passage he declaimed before Voltaire and company is one of the most famous in Ariosto, it is understandable that Casanova should have committed it to memory.[45] Still one may wonder whether, in the context of his competition with Voltaire for the favor of the audience, Casanova had once again found himself playing a role (the jealous Orlando) that he would not willingly have chosen. In any case, so convincingly does he recite these verses that when he reaches the passage where Orlando, thinking himself alone, gives vent to his sorrow with a river of tears, Casanova bursts out in tears, and the audience does so as well. At that point, he recalls:

> [M]y tears burst from my eyes so impetuously and abundantly that everyone present shed tears, too, Madame Denis shuddered, and Voltaire ran to embrace me; but he could not interrupt me, for Orlando, to go completely mad, had to discover that he was in the same bed as that in which Angelica had lately lain stark naked in the arms of the too fortunate Medoro, which happened in the following stanza. My plaintive and mournful tone gave place to the tone of terror inspired by the madness whose prodigious force drove him to ravages such as only an earthquake or lightning could cause. At the end of my recitation I somberly received the congratulations of the entire company. Voltaire exclaimed:
>
> "It is what I have always said: to draw tears, one must weep oneself; but to weep, one must feel, and then the tears come from the soul." (2:407–8, translation modified)

Finally Casanova had managed to upstage Voltaire and seduce his rival's audience: in Casanova's imagination, at least, Orlando had momentarily won back the favors of Angelica.

A few days earlier, in Lausannne, Casanova had learned of Voltaire's own conviction (which the poet had tried to impose upon amateur actors there)[46] that to convey pathos effectively, an actor must shed real tears. At Les Délices he conforms perfectly to this desire of his "master" and portrays himself receiving the compliments of the audience in a state of post-performance sadness: "I somberly [tristement] received the congratulations of the entire company." He recalls that he was still "in" his role (like Diderot's inconsistent *comédien sensible*), still caught up in the pathetic state to which he had moved himself. In other words, Casanova won this victory by giving up his *libertin* image: the image of himself as detached, lighthearted, and always in control of the situation.

But Casanova would not have held a grudge against Voltaire simply for having been forced to play the role of a spurned lover, obliged to present a different image from that of a euphoric and irresistible charmer. For Casanova never invested himself in any particular role (sexual or otherwise). What he wanted most was to occupy center stage and to be taken seriously in whatever role he happened to be playing. And despite what Casanova suggests, this is precisely what Voltaire would not allow him to do. Indeed, after applauding Casanova's moving reenactment of Orlando's jealousy, Voltaire promised to deliver the same stanzas on the next day, and to make the audience cry as well.

And so he did, for Casanova notes: "Il m'a tenu parole." As this tellingly elliptical summary implies, Voltaire had decisively won the competition—not only with his wit and erudition, or by showing that he could also make an audience cry by reciting Ariosto from memory, but also by making Casanova subject himself to the weight of powerful emotions (terror, anger, jealousy), emotions unbecoming to a *libertin* of any stripe. In Casanova's memoirs, at the very moment when he sensed that he had finally won over Voltaire's audience, when he reincarnated Orlando's terror, his jealousy, his furor—at the moment when a *libertin* might have been able to savor his own successful seduction of the audience—Casanova could only feel the jealousy of Orlando, in the very bed where Princess Angelica had slept with the poor shepherd Medoro. At the decisive moment of his seduction, when he portrays himself *aux délices* at having moved Voltaire's audience to tears, the *libertin-séducteur* also shows himself having been humiliated, at the hands of an aging but intellectually vigorous athlete.

Future of an Illusion

"[A]nd even if you did, pray tell me with what you would fill its place." Of all the words that Casanova claims to have addressed to Voltaire, these are the most frequently quoted. The remark comes from Casanova's response to Voltaire's expressed desire to destroy superstition. The *libertin* was convinced that superstition was absolutely necessary to keep the people in their place, just as Voltaire believed (in words even more famous, which Casanova may unwittingly have paraphrased when he later wrote his memoirs) that "if God did not exist, it would be necessary to invent him."[47] Casanova vehemently despised the people, since he had spent his life trying to raise himself above his own popular origins (he was the son of two poor actors, his mother a shoemaker's daughter). He could therefore not view the people with the haughty, "aristocratic" contempt of Voltaire, who was born into privilege.[48] In his final years, he would fulminate about how even the French Revolution ("the people as king") depended upon fooling the people, but what he saw as the illusion of democracy was incompatible with his own desire to imagine himself as the privileged interlocutor of superior beings.[49] Casanova could only imagine himself happy in the hierarchical order of monarchy, and that required using superstition to make the people obey: "La superstition est . . . nécessaire," he tells Voltaire, "puisque sans elle le peuple n'obéira jamais au monarque" ("Superstition is . . . necessary, since without it the people will never obey the monarch" [2:422]).[50] In one of the stories interwoven with the Voltaire narrative, we observe Casanova blithely deluding his three sexual partners into believing that a golden ball can keep them from getting pregnant. In that story, he plays upon the imaginary powers of gold just as cynically as he had capitalized upon the image of O-Morphi: to Casanova, nothing in the world has any value, except insofar as his own happiness can be enhanced by the willingness of others to credit that value.

In marked contrast, Voltaire passionately believed in "virtue"—that is, in the value of fundamentally altruistic, disinterested actions. For Voltaire (especially from the 1760s on), nothing mattered more than to serve all humanity—and not just his own pleasure—by combatting superstition. In the *Dictionnaire philosophique*, he decried the manipulation of superstitious people by knaves: "The superstitious man is to the knave what the slave is to the tyrant."[51] To combat superstition, Voltaire was convinced of the importance of writing "for everyone" and of not being satisfied with just a few, elite readers. Casanova's well-known retort emerges from their argument on this point:

> [Casanova:] "You do not write *contentus paucis lectoribus* [satisfied with a few readers]."
>
> "If Horace had had to fight supersitition he would have written for everyone, as I do."
>
> "You might, it seems to me, spare yourself the trouble of fighting it, for you will never succeed in destroying it, and even if you did, pray tell me with what you would fill its place." (2:421 [vol. 6, chap. 10], emphasis in original)

To Voltaire, however, Casanova's cynical *trait d'esprit* defies common sense. Indeed, nothing better dramatizes the conflict between Voltaire the *libertin-philosophe* and Casanova the *libertin-séducteur* than the following brief exchange:

> "I like that. *When I deliver the human race from a ferocious beast which is devouring it, can I be asked what I will put in its place?*"
> "It is not devouring it; on the contrary, it is necessary to its existence."
> (translation modified, emphasis in original)

To the philosophe there is no question that the battle against superstition has to be fought, for his conception of reason is not only fundamentally critical and empirical, but also ethical. There is an ethics of reason, for insofar as reason requires meaning and coherence, it also serves to reduce the irrational power of "enthusiasm," extinguish divisive passions, and protect humankind from domination by those who would exploit these irrational forces: hence the motto, "Ecrasez l'Infâme." To reason ethically conceived, it makes no sense to replace one predator, one "ferocious beast," with another. But what matters to Casanova, the *libertin*, is to take advantage of everything that furthers his own liberty and happiness—even if it should be the illusion of liberty that makes his happiness possible.[52] To him, superstition was therefore necessary: first, to make the people tolerate (or even accept) their miserable existence, in the unenlightened monarchy on which his own liberty and happiness depended; and second, so that he could personally exploit the superstitions of his rich benefactors (early in his career, the Venetian Senator Bragadin; during his stay in Paris, Mme. d'Urfé).

To be *heureux* ("fortunate, happy"), both the philosophe and the libertine need to consider themselves free, but they think of liberty in markedly different ways:

> "Loving the human race, I should wish to see it happy as I am, free; and superstition cannot be combined with freedom. What makes you think that servitude can make a people happy?"
> "Then you would wish to see sovereignty in the people?"
> "God forbid! One alone must govern."
> "Then superstition is necessary, for without it the people will never obey the monarch." (2:421–22)

Neither man believes in full political liberty, and certainly not in democracy. They both believe that "the people" can only find happiness in obedience to a leader. However, the "liberty" that counts most for Voltaire is liberty of expression, whereas Casanova passionately needs to believe in his own metaphysical liberty, that he always depends only upon what the present moment may bring.

In Casanova's avowedly Hobbesian view, the people will never obey without superstition, but for Voltaire superstition is incompatible with liberty of expression and, more important, with the reign of a true (that is, enlightened) monarch:

> "I want him to command a free people, then he will be its leader, and he cannot be called a monarch, for he can never be arbitrary."
>
> "Addison tells you that such a monarch, such a leader, is not among possible beings. I am for Hobbes. Between two evils, one must choose the lesser. A people without superstition would be philosophical and philosophers never obey. The people can be happy only if they are cursed, downtrodden, kept in chains."
>
> "If you have read me you will have found the proofs by which I demonstrate that superstition is the enemy of kings."

Casanova retorts that he has indeed read Voltaire's works, and has read them so attentively that he understands them better than their author. In his view, Voltaire makes the mistake of loving humanity, not as it is, but as he would like it to be. In his eyes, this passion for humanity is nothing more than blind highmindedness, and it makes Voltaire look as ridiculous as Don Quixote:

> Your first passion is love of humanity. *Est ubi peccas* [And that is where you err (Horace, *Epistles*, II, 1, 63)]. That love blinds you. Love humanity, but you can only love it as it is. It is incapable of the benefits you would lavish upon it; and, giving them, you would only make it more unhappy and more wicked. Leave it to the beast which devours it; and the beast is dear to it. I have never laughed so much as when I saw Don Quixote having a very hard time defending himself from the galley slaves to whom he had just magnanimously given their freedom.

In the episode that Casanova claims to have found so hilarious, Quixote heaps so much abuse upon the galley slaves he has just freed from their guards that they hurl a shower of stones at him, making the Don fall from his horse, whereupon they proceed to give him a beating.[53] Casanova suggests that Voltaire's love of humanity has no basis in reality, it is unrequited, and therefore it will ultimately make him look silly. By recalling how much he had laughed at the spectacle of Quixote's beating, Casanova also takes a particularly nasty swipe at Voltaire, who had received a famous beating from the lackeys of the Chevalier de Rohan and "se serait avili s'entendant toujours appeler à rouer" (2:434 [vol. 6, chap. 10]). Whatever Casanova and Voltaire may actually have said to each other in 1759, when the old libertine wrote his memoirs (during the French Revolution) he may also have been making bitter fun of the liberal ideologues who had been masters before 1789, only to find themselves beaten, if not devoured, by the monster of Revolution.

Although both these self-styled nobles are monarchists, of sorts, the philosophe thinks that monarchy must become enlightened, whereas the libertin believes that enlightenment and monarchy are incompatible. The philosophe writes for humankind (le genre humain), whereas the libertin sees himself writing primarily for his own kind, "good society [la bonne compagnie]," with full awareness that this knowledge and pleasure depend upon a necessary stock of illusions. Indeed, he tells Voltaire that "possibly we are both mistaken" (2:423 [vol. 6, chap. 10]). For the philosophe Voltaire, one's degree of liberty depends upon political institutions ("The freedom we have is not as great as that which the English enjoy"), whereas for Casanova liberty is all in one's imagination ("[T]o be free, it is enough to believe that one is so").

One may also view the encounter of Voltaire and Casanova as a meeting of two forms of libertinage: the free-thinking, skeptical, philosophical libertinage of a Voltaire, who incarnated liberty from religion and from the State, and the sexual libertinage of Casanova, the compulsive seducer. When the men who embodied these two forms of libertinage met at Les Délices in 1760, the libertin-philosophe won a decisive victory over the libertin-séducteur.

Conclusion

The Coronation of Voltaire

IN 1719 FRANÇOIS-MARIE AROUET made himself into Arouet de Voltaire, upon publicly dedicating his first tragedy to one of the noblest ladies in France. Yet post-absolutist conditions, which made it possible for a bourgeois poet to give himself a title, also made it impossible for Voltaire's audiences to take *Œdipe* (or any other tragedy) seriously.[1] In the last year of his life (1778), when he attended a performance of the shoddy anticlerical drama *Irène,* the last of his tragedies that he would ever see staged, Voltaire himself reenacted this paradoxical situation. He had finally been allowed to return to Paris, the city of his birth, after decades of exile. On March 30, 1778, after being honored by the Académie Française, Voltaire personally attended the fourth performance of *Irène* at the Comédie-Française. The audience gave him a hero's welcome, amid endless applause, standing ovations, cheers, and general frenzy.[2] In Voltaire's loge, a crown was placed upon his head; on stage, another crown was placed on a bust of the poet and benefactor of humanity. At this theatrical moment of apotheosis, unfeigned tears of joy (real tears, the kind he had always thought most convincing)[3] streamed down the old man's cheeks.

At the crowning moment of his life, amid the audience's wild applause, Voltaire may well have felt that his lifelong dream had miraculously been fulfilled: that a heroic Voltaire had finally restored the "royal spectacle" to its legitimate place (just below epic) in the hierarchy of genres, that he had finally accomplished the herculean task of bringing back tragedy from the kingdom of the dead. Indeed, Voltaire never ceased com-

Coronation of Voltaire at the Théâtre Français
(engraving, Bibliothèque Nationale, Paris). Photo: Giraudon/Art Resource, New York.

posing tragedies, twenty-seven in all (plus a dozen comedies). Moreover, some of these works *(Zaïre, Alzire, Mérope)* had enjoyed such remarkable commercial success that they had largely kept the Comédie-Française in business throughout those sixty years.[4] Yet despite the substantial profits created by his plays, the poet acclaimed by Diderot (in *Le Neveu de Rameau*) as the genial "author of *Mérope*" had actually fought a desperate and hopeless battle against the historic decline of tragedy, the absolutist genre par excellence. In reality, the same post-absolutist conditions that had enabled Arouet de Voltaire to claim nobility on the basis of poetic achievement had also assured the success of Voltaire's often melodramatic attempts at tragedy, which bore implicit witness to the decline of the genre.

Legitimacy

The first of these post-absolutist conditions was a new standard of legitimacy. Absolutist culture had conceived of legitimacy in terms of blood. In fact, until the end of the ancien régime, the king derived his legiti-

macy from the particular qualities (generosity, honor, courage) allegedly
contained in his family's blood and transmitted only through male heirs;
according to the same logic, the privileges of the entire nobility were
grounded in blood. In addition, French kings had gradually acquired the
right to legitimize the superiority of a person's blood, by simply conferring
nobility upon him.

Post-absolutist culture redefined legitimacy in terms of law and performance. In his account of the 1718 *lit de justice*, Saint-Simon did so unwittingly, despite his reactionary aims. Arouet de Voltaire quite deliberately
rejected blood as a measure of human worth, in the 1719 dedication of
Œdipe. Philippe d'Orléans implicitly tolerated Voltaire's claim, although
other nobles were unwilling to humor the erstwhile commoner with similar
indulgence. Nevertheless, by the 1750s it had become a fairly simple matter
for a commoner to call himself noble, so that in 1759 even a Giacomo
Casanova could get away with calling himself Casanova de Seingalt (although he could not manage to convince the future "king of Ferney" to
take his nobility seriously).

On March 30, 1778, notes Henri Lagrave, "another play was being performed" outside the Comédie-Française, a representation whose implications Louis XVI and his court grasped no more fully than Voltaire had
understood the meaning of his own coronation: "The people acclaimed
'the defender of the Calas.' When he emerged from the theater, the crowd
accompanied Voltaire with undiminished enthusiasm to the hôtel de Vil-
lette, where he was staying. It was a civic demonstration, a 'national' demonstration before the term existed, which caused some disturbance at Versailles, but whose importance no one fathomed."[5] Like the dual coronation
of Voltaire inside the theater, this other play, this outdoor "national" demonstration, consecrated neither the absolute monarch nor his representation, but the philosophe, the defender of the Calas family, and his representations. The people of Paris honored Voltaire for having bravely defended
the principle that (*pace* Casanova) everyone, including the king, must be
made subject to the same law.

Value

Post-absolutist culture also produced a new standard of value. After the
Council of Trent, absolutist ideology had laid increasing emphasis upon
the eucharistic "real presence" of the king's semi-divine body in his image:
the measure of all value was ostensibly a treasure, really present in his
image, just as there really was a certain quantity of precious metal in the

Dual coronation of Voltaire and his image at the Théâtre Français
(engraving, Bibliothèque Nationale, Paris). Photo: Bibliothèque Nationale.

louis, the coin that bore the French monarch's name. In principle, therefore, all value emanated from the Sun King's presence in his image, so
that his subjects considered themselves worthy of esteem, not just by virtue
of birth, but also through public display of their proximity to the source
of all value, the Sun King. In contrast, post-absolutist culture considered
public displays as superficial, as mere indications of deeper reality. Value
was no longer conceived of as a treasure, but as a sign.

By concealing his heroism behind the mask of a courtier, and only
daring to reveal it in his posthumous memoirs, Saint-Simon unwittingly
retreated from the public displays of valor that had distinguished great
nobles in the age of Louis XIII. Likewise, in Marivaux's post-absolutist
comedy *Le Jeu de l'amour et du hasard* (1730) characters were skeptical
of everyone's face value, behaving instead as if real value were hidden
beneath worldly appearances: in this regard, Marivaux's characters represented themselves very differently from those in Molière's absolutist clas-
sics. In similar fashion, the famous rhetoric of sincerity *(marivaudage)* in
Marivaux's comedies formed part of a strategy for overcoming narcissistic
ego-inflation, in order to reveal one's real value, to oneself and to others. A

post-absolutist credit economy was also at work in Marivaux's *Les Fausses confidences,* where the "false admissions" were really speculative investments. The play demonstrates that a noble title is now worth no more than a pretty face or a paper bank note, unless it can be shown to stand for something beyond appearances.

In post-absolutist culture, the royal image no longer lays claim to a higher, truer register of being, as the semi-divine standard of a hierarchy of value. In *L'Enseigne de Gersaint,* the Rigaud portrait of Louis XIV (which also advertises the name of Gersaint's art shop, Au Grand Monarque) has become an expensive artistic commodity, like so many others within the frame of Watteau's shop sign. It has also become part of a rich, complex emblem, which displays the ambiguous status of art in the post-absolutist era. On the one hand, both the customers and the art works in Gersaint's shop represent a social and artistic world outside the sign itself, thus exemplifying the notion that value is measured by signs, which stand for a "reality" located elsewhere. On the other hand, the figures in this painting are emphatically stylized: as in the fêtes galantes, they refer more to art and artifice than to "life." Likewise, the paintings that line the walls of Gersaint's shop stand for various artistic traditions, rather than for any extra-artistic reality. On the basis of this latter evidence, *L'Enseigne de Gersaint* has also been interpreted in terms of modernist aesthetics, as a self-referential fiction or token, as the artistic equivalent of John Law's paper notes. Although the conception of the general-equivalent as a sign, rather than a token, ultimately prevailed in post-absolutist culture, the semiotic ambiguity remains, both in Watteau's painting and in its cultural context. Indeed, this conflict between two registers of the general-equivalent illustrates what I have called the "critical" nature of post-absolutist culture, the way in which that culture corresponds to a moment of semiotic experimentation and decision.

The poet Voltaire's symbolic coronation eloquently testified to the almost total disappearance of the king as a symbolic force, just as his dual coronation (in his loge, on the stage) demonstrated that the body of this "king" and his representation had to be crowned in two different places. More generally, this situation implied that, in Goux's terms, representation had become completely "disincarnated."[6] Nor did anyone avert his terrified gaze from either Voltaire's person or his statue: instead, all eyes respectfully rested upon first the man and then his graven image. Voltaire's Parisian audience placed a crown on the head of a "great man," not a superior being; they honored the benefactor of humanity, not the father of the people.

Subjectivity

Voltaire's "crowning" on the stage of the Théâtre Français can also be seen as an emblem of post-absolutist subjectivity. In the first place, the spectacle was characterized by the complete separation between actors and audience, which had been achieved through the elimination (in 1759) of onstage seats. Voltaire himself had long opposed this French tradition, arguing that the presence of spectators onstage distracted the rest of the audience and kept them from viewing the awe-inspiring "royal spectacle" of tragedy with suitable reverence. Seventeenth-century French theaters had also been conceived in terms of rational, Euclidean perspective, with a single focal point, the so-called "king's seat," the only place that allowed for a perfect view and for complete understanding of the action. As Jean-Marie Apostolidès has shown, under absolutism the entire theatrical space was organized around the king's solar gaze, a spectacle in which everyone was publicly and equally subjected to the transcendent will of God's representative on earth.[7] But absolutism also divided the king's subjects in two: between a public self (displayed in theater by "actors" and "audience" alike) subjected to the sovereign and a secretly free, private self.

As the spectacle of Voltaire's crowning shows, however, post-absolutist culture (like eighteenth-century royal theaters)[8] eliminates the explicitly transcendent, "royal" position; it makes everyone, including the king, publicly subject to the sovereign principle of law. Voltaire is crowned by the people, not by God, and he rules by popular mandate, not by divine right. At the same time, however, this post-absolutist culture implicitly reintroduces that transcendent position, within the culture (and for Voltaire, within the theater) itself. As the self-styled M. de Voltaire is crowned on the stage of the Théâtre Français, he realizes his secret, post-absolutist dream that anyone (regardless of birth) can overcome his or her subjection to the law of common mortals and achieve the godlike immortality of the absolute monarch's body. Similarly, Saint-Simon, unlike the aristocratic heroes with whom he identified himself, displays "the radiant splendor of [his] triumph" only in secret, behind the impenetrable mask of a courtier and in the pages of his memoirs. He thus unwittingly illustrates the structure of the post-absolutist subject: divided between a public self who modestly subjects himself to the law and a private self free to form his own opinions, and who proudly imagines himself as a god; split between a face value he displays in public and the real value he ascribes to himself, but which he keeps private.

During the French Revolution, nearly two centuries before images of

Voltaire were finally printed on real French bank notes, representatives of a grateful fatherland *(la patrie reconnaissante)* placed copies of his bust, along with busts of his arch-enemy Rousseau and other "great men," at strategic locations throughout the city of Paris. Although Voltaire imagined himself as the king of poets ("le poète Roy"), and Rousseau represented himself to the world as inimitable and unique, their revolutionary statues bore no crowns upon their heads and their images were common currency. In post-absolutist culture, nothing could have been more common than to take oneself for a superior being. In this book, I have spoken of "post-absolutist" (rather than "pre-revolutionary") culture; I have done so in order to emphasize that political history and cultural or semiotic history do not necessarily unfold at the same pace. This position implies that although political absolutism came to a violent end during the French Revolution, absolutist culture had died long before the Revolution. Long *after* the Revolution, post-absolutist values (such as semiotic realism, individual performance, and universal rule of law) seem to have remained vital in France: exactly how when and these values may themselves have declined remains to be seen.[9]

For the Revolution, Voltaire was a great man, but he was also (as Philoctète had put it, in *Œdipe*) an "ordinary" man: human blood flowed in his veins, and the value of his effigies derived from the actions of the man they represented, not from any miraculous powers or the inherent nobility of their materials. What conferred value and power upon post-absolutist subjects—upon Voltaire, Saint-Simon, Marivaux, Watteau, and Casanova—was not their essence but their performance, the greatness of what they put before the public, in the king's wake.

Value and Subjectivity

The main characters of Voltaire's *Œdipe* act in a way that patently contradicts the author's conscious emphasis upon individual performance, since their heroism and innocence is in direct proportion to their lack of responsibility for their actions. Our examination of "Voltaire's Oedipus" (that is, of the public declaration of nobility, in the dedication of *Œdipe;* the various "oedipal" investments in Voltaire's life; and finally the play itself) pointed to an apparently inescapable contradiction of post-absolutist agency. In the wake of the Sun King, new emphasis was placed upon both personal (character, performance) and impersonal (the law, chance, the market, heredity) factors as causes of human action.

From his supreme position in the absolutist patronage system, Louis
XIV had commissioned the famous ceremonial portrait of 1701 from Rigaud, whose work asserted both the Sun King's "real presence" and the
power of his sovereign glance to inspire awe in all his subjects. In principle,
the absolutist monarch always bore ultimate responsibility for the actions
of his subjects. In post-absolutist culture, as Watteau's last shop sign suggests, ultimate responsibility for human action was divided between two
ultimately contradictory authorities. *L'Enseigne de Gersaint* celebrates the
liberation of artists from the constraints of a patronage system, while subjecting them to the impersonal force of the market; it frees some royal
subjects to define themselves as members of the post-absolutist cultural
elite, by subjecting themselves to the market for refined luxury goods.

With his last shop sign, Watteau thus uses art to define a post-absolutist
relationship between value and subjectivity. *L'Enseigne de Gersaint* portrays a kind of mercantile fête galante, in which art depends upon the
demands of an anonymous, abstract market, rather than on the whims of
a royal patron. The work celebrates the liberation of art from the patronage system and consecrates the accession of art to commodity status, but
it does so with the ambiguity inherent to a work that is both art and a
commercial advertisement. Watteau's last great image implicitly defines a
post-absolutist hierarchy of being, in which certain persons possess the
gift for fashioning themselves into elegant consumers: the shop sign invites its beholders to imitate the customers (but not the workers or merchants) in Gersaint's shop, by stepping up into a higher level of being.
But *L'Enseigne de Gersaint* is not just an advertisement, it is also an art
work: none of the elegant figures in the richly decorated shop pays the
slightest attention to the beholder; contrasting with the wealth of luxury
goods and elegant customers in the shop itself, the rear of the shop is
empty; more disquieting still, the sunlight that illuminates the art works
and customers cannot possibly stream from the same source as the mysterious light that filters into the back of the shop. Watteau, with full knowledge of his imminent death, simultaneously celebrates the liberation of art
from subjection to royal patronage and recognizes that even his incomparable art will not enable either refined customers or great artists to transcend their own mortality. Whatever *L'Enseigne de Gersaint* may promise
as a shop sign, as a work of art it excludes beholders and artists alike from
any certainty of acceding to a state of grace.

Notes

Introduction

1. Leora Auslander points to the "paradoxical" tendency of absolutism to limit (and even undermine) itself: "The absolute king could never survive in pristine detachment above the actual exercise of power; he could authenticate its majesty only by engaging in testing its limits. Sustaining an absolutist regime required an endlessly careful, sometimes paradoxical, manipulation of power: *the crown's power had to be used to prove its existence, but some uses diminished while others augmented it; sometimes select exceptions to absolute control helped secure the illusion of total control*" (*Taste and Power: Furnishing Modern France* [Berkeley: University of California Press, 1996], 29 [emphasis added]). See Robert Mandrou, *L'Europe "Absolutiste": Raison et raison d'État, 1649–1775* (Paris: Fayard, 1976), for an extremely well-documented presentation of the theory and practice of absolutism, in its European context.

2. See Marin's discussion of the eucharistic utterance, in *La Critique du discours* (Paris: Minuit, 1975), as well as *Le Portrait du roi* ([Paris: Minuit, 1981]; translated into English as *Portrait of the King* [Minneapolis: University of Minnesota Press, 1988]). See also *La Parole mangée* (Paris: Méridiens, 1986), and *De la représentation* (Paris: Gallimard / Le Seuil, 1994). I discuss Marin's argument in chapters 4 and 5. Orest Ranum makes a similar point in "Courtesy, Absolutism, and the Rise of the French State, 1630–1660," *Journal of Modern History* 52 (September 1980): 433; see my chapter 1.

3. Now in the Louvre, this large portrait was formerly displayed in the Salon d'Apollon at Versailles.

4. "Le Corps glorieux du Roi et son portrait," *La Parole mangée*, 206. Marin argues that the royal portrait was responsible for the imaginary status of absolute power, while positing the king's body as that which ideally exists in the form of an image. The king came into himself, according to Marin, literally *became himself*, through his image. In this sense, the royal "portrait" literally

"draws forth" the king's royal being, and forcefully re-presents him, but to himself alone.

5. The Rigaud portrait implicitly asks how such a royal command performance is possible: how can the king be shown, pointing to himself and naming himself, for himself alone? See Marin, *Portrait of the King*, 200–202.

6. *Portrait of the King*, 12 (emphasis added).

7. In "Watteau's *L'Enseigne de Gersaint* and Baroque Emblematic Tradition," *Gazette des Beaux-Arts* 104 (November 1984): 153–64, Robert Neuman characterizes the crating of Louis XIV's portrait in this painting as a gesture of entombment. See my chapter 3, below.

8. Kenzaburo Oe testifies to a remarkably similar experience (although from a very different cultural perspective) in "The Day the Emperor Spoke in a Human Voice," *New York Times Magazine* (7 May 1995), 103–5.

9. The most detailed account of Law's "system" can be found in Edgar Faure, *La Banqueroute de Law: 17 juillet 1720* (Paris: Gallimard, 1977). Faure relies to a large extent on the work of Paul Harsin (ibid., 701–32). I am relying here upon Larry Neal's extremely lucid and useful explanation of Law's policies and their historical context, in *The Rise of Financial Capitalism: International Capital Markets in the Age of Reason* (Cambridge: Cambridge University Press, 1990). Neal emphasizes the linkages between the "Mississippi bubble" and the English "South Sea bubble."

According to the Littré dictionary, the word *millionaire* was coined to describe people whose fortunes, thanks to Law, numbered in the millions of francs.

10. Cited by Paul Harsin in *Les Doctrines monétaires et financières en France du XVIe au XVIIIe siècle* (Paris: F. Alcan, 1928), 146.

11. "By Concoction, I understand the reducing of all commodities, which are not presently consumed, but reserved for Nourishment in time to come, to some thing of equall value, and withall so portable, as not to hinder the motion of men from place to place; to the end a man may have in what place soever, such Nourishment as the place affordeth. And this is nothing else but Gold, and Silver, and Mony. For Gold and Silver, being (as it happens) almost in all Countries of the world highly valued, is a commodious measure of the value of all things else between Nations; and Mony . . . is a sufficient measure of the value of all things else, between the Subjects of a Common-Wealth. By the means of which measures, all commodities, Moveable, and Immoveable, are made to accompany a man, to all places of his resort, within and without the place of his ordinary residence; *and the same passeth from Man to Man, within the Common-Wealth; and goes round about, Nourishing (as it passeth) every part thereof; In so much as this concoction, is as it were the Sanguification of the Common-Wealth: For naturall Bloud is in like manner made of the fruits of the Earth; and circulating, nourisheth by the way, every Member of the Body of Man*" (Thomas Hobbes, *Leviathan*, edited with an introduction by C. B. MacPherson [Harmondsworth, Middlesex, England: Penguin, 1986], part 2, chap. 24, p. 300).

12. John Kenneth Galbraith, *Money: Whence it Came, Where it Went* (Boston: Houghton, Mifflin, 1975), 23–24.

13. See Faure, *La Banqueroute de Law*, 15.

14. "Il est de l'intérêt du Roi et de son peuple d'assurer la monnaie de banque et d'abolir la monnaie d'or" (Law, *Mémoire sur le discrédit*, quoted in ibid., 36).

15. Kindleberger, *A Financial History of Western Europe*, 60. According to Kindleberger, Law's experiment had such a traumatic effect upon the French imagination that "there was hesitation even in pronouncing the word 'bank' for 150 years thereafter" (98).

During the French Revolution, the experiment with *assignats* would prove even more disastrous. However, as Pierre Vilar emphasizes, *assignats* "were not a form of money, but an 'assignation' on the value of the expected sales [of ecclesiastical property], an interest-bearing acknowledgment of a debt. It is very important not to confuse the *assignat* (at least as it was originally conceived) with money guaranteed on the value of land in general such as was proposed in England in the late 17th century, and such as Law himself had for a time thought of it" (Vilar, *A History of Gold and Money: 1450–1920* [London: NLB, 1976], 303; first published as *Oro y Moneda en la Historia [1450–1920]* [Barcelona: Ediciones Ariel, 1969]). Vilar also shows how the *assignat* nevertheless came to be used as money (*A History of Gold and Money*, 303–6).

16. Law's notes were used primarily in payment of government expenses, and were declared legal for the payment of taxes. Since these notes could be exchanged only for certain goods and services (because they were not in what Marx called the "general-equivalent form"), they were not money, in the strict sense of the term. The first paper money was issued by the Massachusetts Bay Colony in 1690. See Galbraith, *Money: Whence it Came*, 51. Indeed, it has been argued that the notes issued by Law's bank lacked credibility because they were not really bank notes, not because they were printed on paper: "The overly severe judgment of the Swiss banker Rilliet is not without foundation: 'Law did not give you a bank, which is precisely the crime that he has committed against you; he insidiously and treacherously gave the name of bank notes to State notes'" (Marcel Courdurie, "Crédit, banques," in *Dictionnaire européen des Lumières*, ed. Michel Delon [Paris: Presses Universitaires de France, 1997], 286).

17. "If we leave it at that, with the initial plan, we can only bear the tribute of our admiration to this faultless structure.

"Was it however sufficient to turn around the public finance situation and sustain the life of the public economy?

"Although one would have to rewrite history, we can answer: yes. *Law could have left it at that, his first plan, with a reasonable chance of success*" (*La Banqueroute de Law*, 226, emphasis in original).

In *The Rise of Financial Capitalism*, Neal suggests that "these two 'plans' correspond, perhaps, to the 'rational' and 'irrational' bubbles discussed in finance literature today" (76). He defines a "rational" bubble as "a continuing rise in the price of an asset that is generated by market participants anticipating that rises in its price will continue to occur" (75). "Irrational bubbles," in contrast, "are those in which the relationship of an asset to its market fundamental simply breaks down because of overzealous trading or an unrealistic appraisal of the value of the stock" (76). Neal's subsequent examination of available empirical data (80–88) on the rationality of the Mississippi bubble yields inconclusive results. However, he finds considerable empirical justification for the view that a "rational" bubble in South Sea stock occurred, "but only during the period 23 February through 15 June [1720, using the "old" or Julian calendar], precisely the period . . . when foreign participation was most active" (77).

18. Faure, *La Banqueroute de Law*, 230.

19. Kavanagh's theoretical position (that the distinction between rational and irrational economic activity is itself somewhat specious) recalls Georges Bataille's argument (elaborated notably in *La Part maudite* [Paris: Minuit, 1967]) that rational activity ("limited operations" ["l'économie restreinte"]) always implicitly requires nonrational activity (gambling, play: "l'économie générale").

20. Thomas Kavanagh, *Enlightenment and the Shadows of Chance* (Baltimore: Johns Hopkins University Press, 1993), chap. 3 ("Law's System and the Gamble Refused"), p. 75. (See my review in *Substance* 24, no. 3 [November 1995]: 132–35.)

21. "The System's downfall came not as a result of any internal contradiction or personal malfeasance but because the universal and frenetic hopes for still further profits on which its rapid rise had been built were doomed to collapse once stock prices began to move in the opposite direction. As late as only a week before the turnaround, informed investors (whose money was streaming into Paris from all corners of Europe) could legitimately conclude that Compagnie des Indes stock still offered the best available investment opportunity. In that volatile climate, Law's enemies, the clique of wealthy financiers who had been cut out of the game by his successes on every front, were preparing to act. The Pâris brothers, earlier fined for malfeasance in royal tax farming, convinced both the duc de Bourbon and the prince de Conti to demand immediate repayment in gold for their considerable stock holdings" (Kavanagh, *Enlightenment and the Shadows of Chance*, 81).

22. "Businessmen have no confidence in a note guaranteed by a State that is burdened with debts. The problem is not the paper, but the origin of the guarantee" (Courdurie, "Crédit, banques," in *Dictionnaire européen des Lumières*, 286).

23. "The system of John Law contained such a great mixture of elements and controlled directly so many of the conceivable policy variables that it has remained a fascinating question whether or not it could have worked, either in part or with some minor modification" (Neal, *The Rise of Financial Capitalism*, 76).

24. Paul Hazard, *La Crise de la conscience européene: 1680–1715* (Paris: Fayard, 1961).

25. Jean-Joseph Goux, *The Coiners of Language* (Norman: University of Okla-

homa Press, 1994), 28 (emphasis in original); originally published as *Les Monnayeurs du langage* (Paris: Galilée, 1984).

26. Ibid., 29.

27. Ibid., 17 (emphasis in original).

28. Ibid., 30.

29. The methodological difficulties inherent in trying to criticize a text "historically" (particularly in the context of the United States) are discussed by Samuel Weber in the course of his comments on Stanley Fish and Fredric Jameson, in "Capitalizing History," in *Institution and Interpretation* (Minneapolis: University of Minnesota Press, 1987), 40–58.

Chapter One

1. "This reading of history, and especially private memoirs of recent times since François I, which I did by myself, instilled in me the desire to write the memoirs of what I would see in the desire and hope of bearing some responsibility and in order to know as best I could the affairs of my time" (*Mémoires: Additions au Journal de Dangeau*, 8 vols. [Paris: Gallimard/Pléiade, 1983–88], 1:20, translation mine). There is no published English translation of the complete text of Saint-Simon's memoirs, a complete version of which was not published even in French until 1829–30. The most complete and accurate (although often excessively literal) translation is that of Bayle St. John, *The Memoirs of the Duke of Saint-Simon on the Reign of Louis XIV and the Regency* (New York: Willey Book Company, 1936; originally published in England in 1876). For some passages from the *lit de justice* episode omitted from the St. John translation, I also rely on the selections translated and edited by Desmond Flower, *The Memoirs of Louis de Rouvroy, duc de Saint-Simon, Covering the Years 1691–1723* (New York: Heritage Press, 1959). Unless otherwise noted, the St. John translation will be used in this chapter, with some modifications. Citations of Saint-Simon's memoirs in the text and notes refer to the volume and page numbers of the Pléiade edition, ed. Yves Coirault, 8 vols. (Paris: Gallimard/Pléiade, 1983–88).

2. Saint-Simon, *Mémoires*, 7:1610.

3. Little is known about the successive stages by which the "espèces de Mémoires" that Saint-Simon began to write in 1694 were transformed into the text that was first published posthumously, in 1788, as the two-volume *Mémoires de M. le duc de Saint-Simon*.

4. Saint-Simon, *Mémoires*, 7:1609–11. Coirault has compared these two versions of the *lit de justice* in "'Un Morceau si curieux . . .': La Stylisation historique dans les *Mémoires* de Saint-Simon d'après les deux récits du 'lit de justice'," *Revue d'histoire littéraire de la France* (March–April 1971): 207–25.

5. Coirault writes in his "Notice" on the *lit de justice* (Saint-Simon, *Mémoires*, 7:1611, translation mine): "Here is the paradox and obvious specialty of our au-

thor: his jubilation triumphs, when all distances increase; his vengeance becomes delirious, when life becomes more literary, and the past more flamboyant. The task of his writing, so mad and so learned, is to set down the ecstasy of memory!"

6. Ibid., 6:665.

7. Jean-Baptiste Colbert, marquis de Torcy (1655−1748), was the nephew of Louis XIV's great minister of that name. Among his accomplishments as minister of foreign affairs under Louis XIV, Torcy was responsible in part for the Treaty of Utrecht (1715).

8. Saint-Simon, *Mémoires*, 1:li (translation mine, emphasis added).

9. Claude Lévi-Strauss, "Symbolic Efficacy," in *Structural Anthropology* (Garden City, N.Y.: Anchor Books, 1967). Marc Bloch has noted that popular belief in the miraculous power of the "royal touch" to cure scrofula persisted well into the eighteenth century, though in attenuated form: for example, the words accompanying the royal touch were no longer in the indicative mood ("Dieu te guérit") but in the subjunctive ("Dieu te guérisse"). See Bloch, *The Royal Touch: Sacred Monarchy and the Scrofula in England and France* (London: Routledge and Kegan Paul, 1973; original French edition, 1924), book 2, part 6. In what follows, I shall be concerned with the decline in the power of the king's *representations*, rather than with the power that the historical Louis XV or Louis XVI may have retained in the popular imagination.

10. Malina Stefanovska, "A Well-Staged *Coup de Théâtre:* The Royal *Lit de Justice* of 1718," *Substance* 80 (1996): 94; Philippe Erlanger, "Le Réveil du Débonnaire," in *Le Régent* (Paris: Gallimard/Folio, n.d.; originally published 1938), 225−37.

11. Sarah Hanley, *The "Lit de Justice" and the Kings of France: Constitutional Ideology in Legend, Ritual and Discourse* (Princeton: Princeton University Press, 1983), 340. According to Hanley, what made this particular *lit de justice* "bizarre" was not so much the secret preparations in which the duc de Saint-Simon collaborated, but the fact that by the early eighteenth century the assembly itself had become meaningless: "From the mid-seventeenth century the *Lit de justice* (which associated Parlement with the king in the Grand-chambre of the royal palace) eventually became institutionally defunct: the dynastic mysteries formerly elucidated through ceremony had become secular axioms, hereditary succession for officeholders was assured within dynastic officialdom, and a more ostentatious Bourbon cult of rulership was propagated through a wide variety of rituals staged by ceremonial masters. In the Inaugural *Lit de justice* of 1715, therefore, when the Parlement of Paris was allowed to act as legislative tutor of a minor king for the first time and pre-registration remonstrance was first legalized, the young Louis XV was displayed as dynastic successor but not as legislator. All the more incomprehensible was the Minority *Lit de justice* of 1718, which attempted to turn back the clock of ceremonial symbolism" (341). In this superbly documented study, Hanley demonstrates that the conventional image of the *lit de justice* as

an absolutist weapon, and as an ancient and integral part of the French Constitu-
tion, is based upon a historical fiction that was created in the Renaissance. Saint-
Simon idealized the reign of Louis XIII, which was (Hanley shows) the period
in which the *lit de justice* enjoyed the greatest vitality as an institution.

From Hanley's perspective (in terms of the history of the *lit de justice* as an
institution), there is no question that Saint-Simon completely misconstrues the
real situation. Likewise, from the standpoint of political history (in terms of the
power struggle between the Parlement and the crown), the Minority *lit de justice*
was merely a setback for the Parlement. Conflicts between the Parlement and
the king broke out repeatedly throughout the century—over Jansenism, fiscal
policy, and so forth—and most notably during the Maupeou affair in 1770 (paro-
died by Diderot in *Jacques le fataliste*).

12. Stefanovska, "A Well-Staged *Coup de Théâtre*," 93.

13. I am referring here to Louis Marin's notion of baroque political action,
to which I shall return below.

14. In "Etiquette and the Logic of Prestige," in *The Court Society* (New York:
Knopf, 1980), Norbert Elias shows the profound social and political logic of the
obsession with etiquette in court society. Elias's use of certain examples drawn
from Saint-Simon's memoirs has recently drawn criticism from the historian Emmanuel Le Roy Ladurie, who devotes "Annexe I" of *Saint-Simon, ou le système
de la cour* (Paris: Fayard, 1997), parts of which were written in collaboration with
Jean-François Fitou, to disparaging the "superficiality" and "teleological vision
of history" (516) that he believes characterize Elias's comments on Saint-Simon.
The main point of this polemical annex (515–20) on Elias is to explain why, in
the course of a long, ostensibly scholarly book on Saint-Simon, he and his collabo-
rator have "deliberately" (515) avoided discussing Elias's influential comments
on the duke. In support of his position, Le Roy Ladurie alludes favorably (although without actually citing his source) to Daniel Gordon's criticisms of Elias
in *Citizens without Sovereignty* (Princeton: Princeton University Press, 1994), 86.
In this context, I would simply observe that there is no foundation to Gordon's
claim that Elias, by adopting the methodological distinction between (French)
civilisation and (German) *Kultur*, betrays a "nationalist antipathy toward France"
(91). See Joan De Jean's historically nuanced discussion of the culture/civilization
distinction, in *Ancients against Moderns: Culture Wars and the Making of a Fin
de Siècle* (Chicago: University of Chicago Press, 1996, 124–39).

15. On the status of the king's body under French absolutism, see Robert
Descimon and Alain Guéry, "Justifications: La 'Monarchie royale'," in *Histoire
de la France*, edited by André Burguière and Jacques Revel, vol. 2: *L'Etat et les
pouvoirs* (Paris: Seuil, 1989–93), 209–40.

16. Ibid., 237.

17. Marin, *Portrait of the King*, 14 (translation modified).

18. "The spectacle of January 21, 1793, consummates the break between the

two bodies: the bourgeoisie takes the place of the sovereign, inscribing its incarnation within the geographical limits of a territory called France" (Jean-Marie Apostolidès, *Le Roi-machine* [Paris: Minuit, 1981], 13, translation mine).

19. See, for example, Malina Stefanovska, "Un 'Solipse' absolu: Le Portrait de Louis XIV par Saint-Simon," in *Actes de Lexington, Papers on Seventeenth-Century French Literature*, Biblio 17, vol. 87 (Paris: PFSCL, 1995), 121.

20. Ranum, "Courtesy, Absolutism, and the Rise of the French State," 433; quoted by Leora Auslander in *Taste and Power: Furnishing Modern France* (Berkeley: University of California Press, 1996), 35.

21. See Marin, *Portrait of the King*.

22. According to Marin, the absolute monarch's "secret" is that he is really not absolute (*Portrait of the King*, 237). Indeed, "this conjunction of portrait and secrecy, which is that of infinite representation and absolute power, signifies that the king in his portrait, *the absolute monarch, is an empty monument*, a cenotaph, *a tomb that contains no body but that is royal body in its very emptiness*" (238 [slightly modified]). Saint-Simon's account implies that long before September 1, 1717, this secret had been public knowledge.

23. In the semiotic vocabulary of Jean-Joseph Goux, the "rule of honors" requires that one believe in the king as an archetypal sign or ideal standard (to be honored in all its incarnations, living or dead). Under the rule of fashion, the king is a "token," a sign whose value is entirely arbitrary—neither inherently valuable (as "treasury") nor valuable as the representative of an ideal standard (or "archetype")—and contingent upon its subjects' willingness to credit it.

24. In a particularly eloquent fit of passion, Saint-Simon claimed that Louis XIV had made Paris into the European home, not only for bastards, but for "bastards of bastards"; he observed punningly that the Sun King's *goût* (taste) for illicit pleasures had turned Paris into an *égout* (sewer): "The taste, the example, and the favor of the late king had made of Paris the sewer of voluptuous pleasures of all Europe, and continued it long after him. In addition to the mistresses of the late king, his bastards, those of Charles IX—for I saw a widow and a daughter-in-law among them—those of Henri IV, those of M. the duc d'Orléans, to whom his regency made an immense fortune, the two branches of the two Bourbon brothers, Malauze and Busset, the Vertus bastards of the last duke of Brittany, the bastard daughters of the three last Condés, and including the Rothelins, *bastards of bastards* . . . , Rothelins, I say, who in recent years have dared to take themselves for something, and almost persuasively, through the audacity of the crown of a prince of the blood that they have worn since all crowns have fallen into the most surprising plunder. In addition to this people of French bastards, Paris has collected the mistresses of the kings of Bavaria and Sardinia, and two of the elector of Bavaria, and the numerous bastards of England, Bavaria, Savoy, Denmark, Saxony, and including those of Lorraine, all of whom have made rich, great, and rapid fortunes in Paris, where they have accumulated orders, ranks that are more than premature, an infinite number of favors and distinctions of

all kinds, several of the most distinguished ranks and honors, not one of which would even have been considered in any other country of Europe; finally, including the most infamous fruit of the most monstrous incests, those of a little Duc de Monbéliard, solemnly declared as such by the aulic council of Vienna, rejected as such by all the empire and the entire house of Würtemberg, who nonetheless had the audacity to act like princes, and in Paris obtained the support of other so-called princes who, through *usurpation* of rank and a legitimate, French birth, are no more princes than they are" (*Mémoires*, 6:143–44, translation mine, emphasis added). The entire passage reads like a grotesque parody of the sacred genealogy of kings in the Book of Genesis. In this degraded genealogy of illegitimacy, the goodness of God's orderly creation and of human procreation has turned into evil, and has gone diabolically out of control.

25. See Saint-Simon, *Mémoires*, 6:246: "Formation d'un parti aveugle"; 6:252; 6:601–2 (where Saint-Simon associates bastardy with women).

26. Among the many other examples of this conflict (all cited by Coirault in ibid., 7:116n.5), see 5:40, 86–90 (where the Parlement calls itself "the first body of the State"); 6:428 and n. 17; 6:586, 616 ("these so-called tutors of our minor kings, these alleged protectors of the kingdom and its peoples").

27. Kavanagh, *Enlightenment and the Shadows of Chance*, 68. Kavanagh also recalls that "Saint-Simon was happy to serve as Law's political godfather so long as he saw the Scotsman's rise as a way of humiliating the duc de Villeroy, the rival whom Philippe d'Orléans had chosen over him to head the Conseil des finances at the beginning of the Regency. Villeroy's early and vocal opposition to Law's plans made it a pleasure for Saint-Simon to defend him behind the scene" (99).

28. Ibid., 99.

29. On what Saint-Simon sees as the inevitably horrible disorder of a world governed only by money, see also *Mémoires*, 6:40, 7:648. For a discussion of the tensions in seventeenth-century France caused by aristocrats' need for money, see Jonathan Dewald, *Aristocratic Experience and the Origins of Modern Culture: France, 1570–1715* (Berkeley: University of California Press, 1993), chap. 5.

30. The allusion contains an implicit comparison between writing (*scripta*) and filth (*crasse*), symptomatic of the anal-sadistic investment in Saint-Simon's writing. The comparison brings to mind another "great hater" among Saint-Simon's contemporaries, Jonathan Swift. See Norman O. Brown, *Life against Death: The Psychoanalytical Meaning of History* (New York: Vintage Books, 1959), especially part 5, "Studies in Anality." Saint-Simon's memoirs remained in manuscript form until 1788, when excerpts from them were published. Voltaire, among others, managed to get his hands on the manuscript.

31. "M. le duc d'Orléans had by the actress Florence a bastard, whom he never recognized and who nonetheless made a great fortune in the Church. He had him called the abbé de Saint-Albin. Madame [the princesse Palatine], who was so hostile to bastards and all bastardy, had taken a liking to this one so

capriciously that on the occasion of a thesis he defended at the Sorbonne, she furnished *the most scandalous and newest display,* and in a place where a woman, however grand she might be, had never set foot, or had even imagined doing so. . . . All the court and town were invited to the thesis, to which they flocked. Conflans, the first gentleman of the chamber of M. le duc d'Orléans, did the honors to it, and in that respect it took place as if it had been M. le duc de Chartres [the regent's only legitimate son] who had defended the thesis. Madame attended with pomp, and was greeted and led to her portière by the cardinal de Noailles, with his cross going on before him. Madame sat down in an armchair, on a platform that had been made ready for her. The cardinals, bishops, and all the distinguished parties in attendance, sat in chairs with backs rather than arm-chairs. M. le duc d'Orléans and Mme. la duchesse d'Orléans were the only ones who did not go, and I did not go either. This singular scene was much spoken of in society; M. le duc d'Orléans and I never spoke of it" (*Mémoires,* 6:601–2, translation modified, emphasis added). In this scene one can observe Saint-Simon's unmistakable way of interpreting the slightest gestures of great figures at court as actions laden with cosmic theatrical import. Likewise his judgment on this "spectacle" as a scandal without precedent ("le plus scandaleux et le plus nouveau") typifies his tendency to consider all innovation as synonymous with scandal.

32. It is apparently for this reason that Saint-Simon (who normally represents himself as a firsthand, masked observer, and authorizes his observations in those terms) emphasizes the fact that he did not honor this charade with his presence ("I did not go," 7:602), and portrays it from the perspective of polite society ("This singular scene was much spoken of in society [dans le monde]"). Likewise, while the duke usually portrays himself as the regent's friend and confidant, in this case he explicitly states that "M. le duc d'Orléans and I never spoke of it" (7:602).

33. For an interpretation in terms of mimetic rivalry of the notion of *skandalon* in the Gospels, see René Girard, *Things Hidden since the Foundation of the World* (London: Athlone Press, 1987), book 3, chap. 5, "Beyond Scandal." In Girardian terms, the numerous similarities between Saint-Simon and Philippe d'Orléans (born five months earlier than Saint-Simon, on August 2, 1674) might lead one to think of the future regent as Saint-Simon's noble double, and of various members of the Parlement as his ignoble doubles.

34. Lucien Goldmann, *The Hidden God: A Study of Tragic Vision in the "Pensées" of Pascal and the Tragedies of Racine* (London: Routledge and Kegan Paul, 1964).

35. In the years that followed, seeing himself as powerless to do anything about the improprieties that surrounded him, Saint-Simon devoted himself to revising his memoirs, and to supplementing them with frenzied comments on the journal of the courtesan Dangeau. Writing would remain the only arena in which he could wage his private battle against the forces of illegitimacy. During most

of his life, the only way he could hope to act upon the world was with a pen. And even this private writing could not be lawfully published until long after it had ceased to pose a threat to anyone. The royal censors did not allow the revised manuscript of his journal (completed in 1752, three years before Saint-Simon's death) to be published until 1829–30, during the Restoration.

36. Erlanger, *Le Régent*, 153.

37. See my gloss on *jouissance* in chapter 5, note 4.

38. Saint-Simon, *Mémoires*, 7:238. See my comments on this passage, below.

39. "At the end of this first act, the second was announced by the keeper of the seals" (ibid., 7:261). "When he had closed the second act, the keeper of the seals went on to the third" (7:262). Whether or not Saint-Simon meant to use *acte* in a theatrical sense, in context the word has this connotation.

40. Louis Marin, "Pour une théorie baroque de l'action politique," preface to Gabriel Naudé, *Considérations politiques sur les coups d'État* (Paris: Éditions de Paris), 20; quoted in Stefanovska, "A Well-Staged *Coup de Théâtre*," 96.

41. "Nobody was more composed than the maréchal de Tallard, but he could not suppress an inner agitation that often peeped out. The maréchal d'Estrées had a stupefied air, as though he saw nothing but a mist before him. The maréchal de Bezons, enveloped more than ordinarily in his big wig, appeared deeply meditative, his look cast down and angry" (Saint-Simon, *Mémoires*, 7:233, translation modified).

42. "The suffocated monosyllable of the maréchal d'Huxelles tore off the rest of the mask" (ibid., 7:235, translation modified).

43. See Peter Szondi, "*Tableau* and *Coup de Théâtre:* On the Social Psychology of Diderot's Bourgeois Tragedy," in *On Textual Understanding and Other Essays* (Minneapolis: University of Minnesota Press, 1986), chap. 7.

44. The entire Regency Council meeting can be read as a play in five "acts," each one of which is marked by performative utterances or gestures, and the *lit de justice* as a second performance of those acts.

45. Saint-Simon, *Mémoires*, 7:232 (trans. Flower, modified).

46. "The eyes of all, occupied with the regent, had been removed from the door, so that the absence of the bastards was by no means generally remarked" (ibid., 7:229).

47. Ibid. (translation mine, emphasis added).

48. "Je ne répondais mot, en considérant la compagnie, qui était un vrai spectacle" (ibid., translation mine).

49. La Bruyère, *Characters* (Harmondsworth, Middlesex, England: Penguin, 1970), 129 ("De la cour," 2[1]).

50. "The prince de Conti, astonished, distracted, meditative, seemed *to see nothing* and to take part in nothing. . . . The duc de la Force hung his head, but examined on the sly the faces of us all. The maréchal de Villeroy and Maréchal Villars spoke to each other now and then; both had irritated eyes and long faces" (Saint-Simon, *Mémoires*, 7:232–33, emphasis added).

51. Consider Saint-Simon portraying his own composure, just after the decree eliminating the "intermediary" rank has been read: "I . . . tried to assume [je composai toute ma personne] an air of gravity, of modesty and of simple gratitude" (ibid., 7:240, trans. Flower).

52. The deep silence that follows the regent's speech allows Saint-Simon to savor its effect on the faces of his peers: "Many faces were clouded and somber. On those of the maréchaux de Villars and de Bezons, of Effiat and even of the maréchal d'Estrées, anger showed clearly. For a moment or two Tallard seemed to have taken leave of his sense, and the maréchal de Villeroy's face fell. I could not see the maréchal d'Huxelles's face, much to my regret, and it was only occasionally that I could catch a sidelong glimpse of the duc de Noailles" (ibid., 7: 237–38; trans. slightly modified).

53. "I had to take extra care to compose my own features, over which I had laid as it were an extra layer of gravity and modesty. I forced my eyes to move more slowly and never looked up" (ibid.).

54. "Contenu de la sorte, attentif à dévorer l'air de tous, présent à tout et à moi-même, immobile, collé sur mon siège, compassé de tout mon corps, pénétré de tout ce que la joie peut imprimer de plus sensible et de plus vif, du trouble le plus charmant, d'une jouissance la plus démésurément et la plus persévéramment souhaitée, je suais d'angoisse de la captivité de mon transport, et cette angoisse même était d'une volupté que je n'ai jamais ressentie ni devant ni depuis ce beau jour. Que les plaisirs des sens sont inférieurs à ceux de l'esprit, et qu'il est véritable que la proportion des maux est celle-là même des biens qui les finissent!" (ibid., 7:238, translation modified).

55. Mitchell Greenberg, *Canonical States, Canonical Stages: Oedipus, Othering, and Seventeenth-Century Drama* (Minneapolis: University of Minnesota Press, 1994), 92.

56. "I knew that nothing could serve to hold them in check as well as this sight of their own signatures" (Saint-Simon, *Mémoires*, 7:239; trans. Flower). See also 6:173.

57. Ibid., 7:239 (trans. Flower, modified; emphasis added).

58. Ibid., 7:241 (trans. Flower, slightly modified; emphasis added). Rather than conveying affection for the virtuous comte de Toulouse, this "involuntary reaction" betrays the existence on the Council of an illegitimate "party." With marvelous concision, Saint-Simon records the reactions of members of the enemy camp: "Villeroi confounded, Villars raging, Effiat rolling his eyes, Estrées rolling his eyes, Estrées beside himself with surprise, were the most marked. Tallard, with his head stretched forward, sucked in, so to speak, all the regent's words as they were proffered. . . . Noailles, inwardly distracted, could not hide his distraction. Huxelles, entirely occupied in smoothing himself, forgot to frown" (ibid., 7:241–42).

59. Son of the duc de Bourbon and the former "Mlle. de Nantes" (herself a legitimized daughter of Louis XIV and Mme. de Montespan). Monsieur le duc

asks to be entrusted with the duty of overseeing the education of the future Louis XV. He notes that when the late king gave this responsibility to the duc du Maine, Monsieur le duc was still a minor, and the duc du Maine was still eligible to succeed to the throne. The king's "legitimized" son, having been reduced to the rank of duke, is no longer eligible to become king. Monsieur le duc therefore claims that *he* should be entrusted with this noble responsibility. His last words are addressed to a member of the "illegitimate" party, the king's present tutor, the maréchal de Villeroi: "'I hope (and here he turned toward his left) that I shall profit from the instructions of the maréchal de Villeroy, learn to acquit myself under his guidance, and deserve his friendship.'

As the maréchal de Villeroy listened to this speech, and heard the words 'superintendence of the education,' he bowed himself almost to the ground, leaning his forehead on a stick, and remained thus for several minutes. It even seemed as if he heard no more of the speech at all. Villars, Bezons and Effiat bent their shoulders as though this were the final blow. . . . Estrées was the first to recover his wits; he shook himself, gave an odd kind of whinny, and looked upon the company like one who has come back from the other world" (ibid., 7:243-44, emphasis added).

60. In his footnote to the verb *devais* (which is rather odd in this context), Coirault writes: "It would not be impossible for the memorialist to have misread *disais* (misreadings are not uncommon when he corrects his own text while editing his marginal notes). But is it appropriate to attribute such a fortunate correction— which underlines the impression of a break, and the breathless rhythm of such thanksgiving—to so minor a cause? For what is at stake here is a theophany of the Ego (without which the 'radiant splendor' of the spectacle would not have dazzled him), one might as well say an egophany—a neologism is not inappropriate to describe such a deliciously voluptuous sensation, of self-glorification by oneself in supreme harmony *(secum ipse concors)*, of the sublime in vengeance (the sublime being, according to Longinus, or the pseudo-Longinus, 'the resonance of a great soul')" (ibid., 7:1137n.3, translation mine).

61. On this subject, see ibid., 5:54 and 5:1143n.2.

62. Ibid., 7:1138n.5.

63. In chapter 4 ("Montaigne and the Paradoxes of Individualism") of *System and Structure* (London: Tavistock, 1972), Anthony Wilden elaborates the paradoxes entailed by the construction of the "self": "[Montaigne] writes 'for himself'—but then he publishes his writings for others" (90). Before reformulating the problem in terms of the relationship between analog and digital communication, Wilden had previously reflected on Montaigne's "self" in "Par Divers Moyens On Arrive à Pareille Fin: A Reading of Montaigne," *Modern Language Notes* 83 (1968): 577-97. Both interpretations rely, as I do below, on René Girard's theory of triangular desire. On the meaning of writing in seventeenth-century aristocratic culture, see Dewald, *Aristocratic Experience*, chap. 6.

64. Reinhart Kosseleck, *Kritik und Krise: Eine Studie zur Pathogenese der*

bürgerlichen Welt, rev. ed. (Frankfurt: Suhrkamp, 1973), 29. (The words "in secret free" come from Hobbes's *Elements of Law*, II, 6, 3.) The French translation, *Le Règne de la critique* (Paris: Minuit, 1979), is based on the first German edition, published in 1959 (see p. 31).

65. Kosseleck, *Le Règne de la critique*, 16.

66. Descimon and Guéry, "Justifications: La 'Monarchie royale'," 231.

67. Here I am alluding to René Girard's classic analyses of "deviated transcendence" in *Deceit, Desire, and the Novel* (Baltimore: Johns Hopkins University Press, 1965).

Chapter Two

1. This letter, to the earl of Ashburnham, has been published in *Voltaire's Correspondence*, edited by Theodore Besterman, 51 vols. (Geneva: Institut et Musée Voltaire, 1953–77), 1:91, letter 62. This self-described "definitive" edition of the correspondence also contains many letters written *to* Voltaire. The Pléiade edition, 13 vols. (Paris: Gallimard, 1977–), where this letter can also be found (1:53, letter 38), is less exhaustive. In what follows, I shall follow the scholarly convention of referring to items in Voltaire's correspondence as *"D 62"* (for Besterman's edition), *"P 38"* (for the Pléiade edition), and so forth.

2. See René Pomeau, *D'Arouet à Voltaire: 1694–1734* (Oxford: Voltaire Foundation, Taylor Institution, 1988), 70–71, 126.

3. Ibid., 120.

4. In his 1764 edition of the plays of Corneille, Voltaire came to the following conclusion about *Œdipe:* "One must . . . conclude that *Oedipus* had to be treated in all its Greek simplicity. Why have we not done so? Because in the absence of choruses, our five-act plays cannot be drawn out to the final act, without the help of material that is extraneous to the subject" (*Théâtre de Pierre Corneille,* 7:129–30).

5. *Zaïre*, for example, is still available in a Classiques Larousse edition, but it has not been performed at the Comédie-Française since 1936.

6. The editor, Jacques Truchet, expresses his doubts about whether Voltaire's first play could be performed today: "Could *Œdipe* be staged today? One may have one's doubts" (*Théâtre du XVIIIe siècle*, 2 vols. [Paris: Gallimard, 1972], 1:1378).

7. Besterman, *Voltaire* (Chicago: University of Chicago Press, 1969), 79–80. Besterman and Pomeau (*D'Arouet à Voltaire*, 1:121) both speak of thirty first-run performances, although Truchet (*Théâtre du XVIIIe siècle*, 1374) mentions forty-five.

8. "Voltaire's share of the profits, over 3,000 francs, exceeded any previous figure" (Besterman, *Voltaire*, 79–80).

9. "Representing the king on one side and Milord the Duc d'Orléans on the other" (Pomeau, *D'Arouet à Voltaire*, 131). Richard Waller has shown that when

Œdipe appeared, Voltaire did not receive an annuity of 1,200 livres from the regent, as had been alleged by Longchamp and Wagnière. See "Voltaire and the Regent," *Studies on Voltaire and the Eighteenth Century* 127 (1974): 2–39; and "Voltaire's 'Pension from the Regent': Foulet Was Right," *Studies on Voltaire and the Eighteenth Century* 219 (1983): 59–62. See also *D* 178 and *P* 125.

10. For a discussion of *Œdipe* in the context of Voltaire's biography, see Pomeau, *D'Arouet à Voltaire*. Pomeau also has discussed the play in the context of literary history, in "Un Œdipe voltairien," *Studi di letteratura francese* 15 (1989): 69–77. In terms of the history of ideas, see Ronald S. Ridgway, "La Propagande philosophique dans les tragédies de Voltaire," *Studies in Voltaire and the Eighteenth Century* 15 (1961): 1–260; as well as P. C. Mitchell, "Voltaire's *Œdipe:* Propaganda versus Art," in *The Classical Tradition in French Literature* (London: Grant and Cutler, 1977), 167–77. José-Michel Moureaux has published a "psychocritical" interpretation of the play, entitled *L'Œdipe de Voltaire: Introduction à une psycholecture* (Paris: Les Lettres Modernes, 1973). For a Lacanian perspective on the play, see J.-M. Raymond, "Oedipe sans complexe," *L'Infini* 25 (1989): 109–18.

11. As Pomeau notes, Voltaire himself had little to say on this score, just a few words appended to the letter to Jean-Baptiste Rousseau. Scholarly debate on this topic has been largely concerned with the positivist question of assigning an *origin* (a similar place name or word, a psychological desire) to the name "Voltaire." In a classic article ("Voltaire's Name," *PMLA* 44 [1929]: 546–64) Ira O. Wade pointed to the thematic and psychological significance of the move. "Voltaire" may have been (according to one hypothesis) an acronym for "Arouet." According to another hypothesis, the name comes from a piece of land called "Veautaire," possibly bequeathed to Voltaire by his mother. In the seventeenth century it was not uncommon for bourgeois families with aristocratic ambitions to tack a particle and place name onto their family name. Molière makes fun of this practice in *L'Ecole des femmes*, act I, scene 1. Another possible derivation for the name is theatrical: in an obscure tragedy by Jobert, dating to 1651, there was a character named "Voltare" ("who, incestuous like Oedipus, poured out blasphemies against the gods" [Pomeau, *D'Arouet à Voltaire*, 116]). It has also been suggested that "Voltaire" was meant (through allusion to the Latin *volvere*) to suggest the rapid movements that in fencing are called *voltes*. The various etymologies that have been advanced for the choice of the pseudonym are summarized by Pomeau, *D'Arouet à Voltaire*, 116–18.

12. After the humiliation of "Arouet de Voltaire" at the hands of Rohan's lackeys (see below), Roy made fun of his quasi-homonym in a so-called *calotte*, to which Voltaire allegedly responded. For a summary of the other episodes in the rivalry between these two "enemy brothers" (to borrow a phrase from René Girard), see Didier Masseau's entry "Roy, Pierre Charles," in *Inventaire Voltaire*, edited by Masseau with Jean Goulemot and André Magnan (Paris: Gallimard, 1995).

13. Besterman begins his classic biography by stating categorically that "we do not know who was Voltaire's father" (*Voltaire*, 19). The second chapter of

Pomeau's more recent *D'Arouet à Voltaire* is entitled "Two Fathers? Two Baptisms?"

14. Moureaux, *L'Œdipe de Voltaire*, 89.

15. Besterman, *Voltaire*, 21n.13, 19–23.

16. Moureaux, *L'Oedipe de Voltaire;* and Pomeau, *D'Arouet à Voltaire*, 73, 132–33. In the Romantic perspective inherited by Freud, the Oedipus story is a tragedy of self-knowledge.

17. Besterman, *Voltaire*, 61.

18. The accusations contained in the poem had nothing new about them; as a matter of fact, by the time he became regent in 1715, Philippe d'Orléans had also been accused of trying to poison his wife.

19. Letter to Jean Aymar Nicolay, marquis de Gouissanville, 20 October 1716 (*D* 44; *P* 32).

20. See Besterman, *Voltaire*, 50–54. It was in this same building that Louis XVI and his family were imprisoned in 1792.

21. *Histoire de ma vie*, 3 vols. (Paris: Robert Laffont, 1993), 1:434 (vol. 2, chap. 10). See chapter 5, below, for a discussion of the meeting in 1760 between Voltaire and Casanova.

22. Rohan, supposedly a friend of Voltaire at court, apparently made fun of the poet's noble pretensions, to which Voltaire "made the obvious retort that Rohan dishonored his own lineage" (Besterman, *Voltaire*, 113). Shortly thereafter, when Voltaire was dining with the duc de Sully, Rohan had the poet called to the front door and beaten by his lackeys.

23. Ibid., 114. Rohan rewrote, or "corrected," this self-styled noble's name. At the same time, Voltaire received a message that he would never forget: that the basis of nobility under the ancien régime was nothing but brute force. Voltaire took fencing lessons and made it clear that he would accept nothing less than a duel with Rohan. Of course, the authorities would never allow their definition of a commoner to cross swords with a member of the nobility, and Voltaire ultimately had to leave for England. Just before his departure Voltaire wrote to the comte de Maurepas, "Since that time I have always sought to repair, not my honor, but his, which was too difficult" (*D* 271; *P* 186). In contrast, Casanova (3:453–74 [vol. 10, chap. 8]) claimed that a petty Polish nobleman, a certain Count Branicky, had personally challenged *him* to a duel. Casanova was wounded in the encounter, but doubtless derived from it some recognition of his self-styled nobility.

24. See Pomeau's discussion of the Arouet de Voltaire mask, in "Arouet de Voltaire, auteur d'*Œdipe*," chap. 8 of *D'Arouet à Voltaire*. The meeting at Les Délices between Voltaire and Casanova, discussed below, took place in 1760, when Voltaire was preparing to inhabit Ferney and had started calling himself "Messire François Marie Arouet de Voltaire, chevalier, gentilhomme ordinaire de la Chambre du Roi, comte de Tourney, Prégny et Chambésy, seigneur de

Ferney." For a thorough discussion of the years 1759–61, see René Pomeau et al., *Écraser l'infâme*, in *Voltaire en son temps*, edited by René Pomeau, 5 vols. (Oxford: Voltaire Foundation, Taylor Institution, 1994), 4:66–79.

25. Moland, for example, in a footnote to his edition of Voltaire's plays, asserts that the dedicatee of *Œdipe* was "Françoise-Marie de Bourbon, dite Mlle de Blois, fille de Louis XIV et de Mme de Montespan, épouse de Philippe, duc d'Orléans, régent" (Voltaire, *Théâtre*, 5 vols. [Paris: Garnier, n.d.], 1:8.) Erlanger repeats this claim in *Le Régent*, 240.

26. See Besterman's note to *D* 70; *P* 42. As evidence that *Œdipe* was dedicated to the princesse Palatine, the editor of the Voltaire entries in the Bibliothèque Nationale catalogue (presumably René Pomeau) cites the markings on a first edition of *Œdipe*. Having examined this volume, I can confirm that a seal identifies it as part of the princesse Palatine's library. However, this seal does not establish the dedicatee's identity.

27. See Erlanger, *Le Régent*, 240.

28. Louis Moland, ed., *Œuvres complètes de Voltaire*, 52 vols. (Paris: Garnier Frères, 1877–85), 10:247. According to a footnote (signed "M. D.") to Moland's "critical edition" of Voltaire's plays, Voltaire sent a copy of the play to the king of England and to the duke and duchess of Lorraine (Voltaire, *Théâtre*, 1:8n.2). Voltaire also claimed (in a letter to Jean-Baptiste Rousseau [*D* 72], probably written in March 1719) that he had sent a copy of *Œdipe* to Prince Eugene of Austria.

29. Pomeau, *D'Arouet à Voltaire*, 117–18.

30. At the beginning of the eighteenth century tragedy and epic were still the most prestigious poetic genres; they were the great, noble genres, in which aristocrats performed heroic feats (and endured trials) to which commoners could not aspire. To achieve recognition as a serious poet, Voltaire had to succeed in both tragedy and epic. Alluding to his noble achievement, Voltaire later wrote that "the author of the *Henriade* need care little what his grandfather was" (cited by Besterman, *Voltaire*, 23). It was a characteristically ambivalent assertion of his own identity. The sentence begins with an affirmation ([I am] "The author of the *Henriade* [that is, I am noble])," only to conclude with a reactive denial ("need care little what his grandfather was" [that is, I am not a bourgeois]). As the new identity achieved recognition, his name change lost much of its reactive element ("I am *not* [Arouet, Roy, *à rouer*]"), and the more affirmative value of the name ("I *am* [de Voltaire, the author of *Oedipe*, the author of the *Henriade*]") eventually prevailed.

When Arouet de Voltaire first appeared in public, his signature was what linguists call a performative utterance: it carried out an operation, by creating a new identity. At once performance, performative utterance, and the name of a performer, "Monsieur de Voltaire" produces a new theatrical persona. Over the years, however, the name Arouet de Voltaire became more a way of registering a fact than an act of defiance and self-creation. The performative sense of the signature ("I am calling myself Monsieur de Voltaire") was eventually supplanted by the constative sense ("Monsieur de Voltaire wrote this").

31. Pomeau, *D'Arouet à Voltaire*, 117.

32. Ibid., 129.

33. In this autobiographical work, *Commentaire historique sur les œuvres de l'auteur de la* Henriade (translated by Besterman as "Voltaire's Autobiography"), the young "author of *Oedipus*" utters the remarks quoted in the epigraph to this chapter, in conversation with the prince de Conti, an amateur poet. See Besterman, *Voltaire*, 625–26. Just as Voltaire was the first author whose correspondence was collected during his lifetime with a view to publication, he was also the first to write his own autobiography, and publish it during his lifetime.

34. Besterman, *Voltaire*, 86n.38.

35. Ibid., 625–26.

36. Pomeau, *D'Arouet à Voltaire*, 118.

37. In his introduction Greenberg points out that theater was "the privileged form of representation of the emerging absolutist states" (*Canonical States, Canonical Stages*, xxvii). During this period of historical transition, theater enjoyed a privileged status because it—more than any other form of representation—"engages individual myths—those narratives individuals construct and are constructed by, to explain and thus situate themselves within social and economic forces that preexist them—with collective narratives" (xxviii).

38. Ibid., xxviii.

39. Ibid., xxiv. Theatrical space and theatrical experience have their own inherent ambivalence: "As a social institution the theater figures the locus in which notions of individual and collective identity are impossible . . . to distinguish clearly. Paradoxically the theatrical locus is a space of identification, a term that presupposes a distinct subjectivity and, at the same time, by identification, a space of 'indifference': through the process of identification, the distinction self-other is abandoned" (ibid., xxvii).

40. Ibid., xxxi. "Certainly no myth was more pregnant with ambivalent meaning for a culture so invested in the relation to a newly emerging patriarchy with its concomitant family romance than the myth of Oedipus, a myth that an entire renascent tradition of classical scholarship had, in the fifteenth and sixteenth centuries, rehearsed and made ready for the seventeenth-century theater" (xxx). Greenberg here extends to the sociopolitical realm the Freudian notion of "family romance," which he had previously applied to theater in *Subjectivity and Subjugation in Seventeenth-Century Drama and Prose* (Cambridge: Cambridge University Press, 1992).

41. The poem at the origin of this scandal became known by its opening words, *Puero regnante*. In Besterman's translation (*Voltaire*, 73), it reads as follows: "A boy reigning, a man notorious for poisoning and incest ruling, with

ignorant and unstable councils and more unstable religion, an exhausted treasury, public confidence violated, in peril of an imminent general revolt, the fatherland sacrificed to an iniquitous and premature hope of the crown, France was about to perish."

42. Pomeau, *D'Arouet à Voltaire*, 121.

43. Erlanger, *Le Régent*, 240.

44. Ibid., 241.

45. "An audacious hand had crossed out the name of *Œdipe* on the poster, and written in its place that of *Philippe*" (Erlanger, *Le Régent*, 241).

46. Besterman, *Voltaire*, 83. At this time, of course, legal publication implied the granting of royal permission ("Avec Approbation, & Privilège du Roy," as it says on the title page of the 1719 edition).

47. Significantly enough, Voltaire did not dare compare himself to Racine, even though he eventually (while composing the *Commentaires sur Corneille*) came to believe that Racine had brought tragedy to an unparalleled degree of perfection. In "Spectres de Shakespeare," *Furor* (1994): 75–85, Pierre Saint-Amand has shown that Voltaire never ceased trying to conjure away the poetic and political "specter" of Shakespeare. Saint-Amand also notes that "to resolve his Oedipus, Voltaire substitutes other fathers, other adopted ancestors, for Shakespeare . . . Corneille, in particular, will play this role" (81).

48. For a concise discussion of the circumstances in which the *Commentaires* was written, see Henri Lagrave, "Commentaires sur Corneille," in the invaluable *Inventaire Voltaire*. The *Commentaires* was eventually incorporated in Voltaire's edition of Corneille, *Théâtre de Pierre Corneille, avec des commentaires, & &c &c.*, 12 volumes in-8 (n.p. [Geneva], 1764). Voltaire had the edition financed by subscription, and printed by the Cramer brothers of Geneva. In addition to composing his own prefaces and notes, and inserting many other documents (such as the *Examens* and various incidental verses) related to Corneille's plays, Voltaire also juxtaposed excerpts from Shakespeare and Lope de Vega for the sake of comparison. For example, in volume 2, Corneille's *Cinna* is followed by a translation of *Julius Caesar*, acts I–III. (I am grateful to Madeleine Joret-Meisel for having generously allowed me to consult her copy of these volumes.)

49. The practice of addressing oneself to an elite group of subscribers (as was also the case with Grimm's *Correspondance littéraire*) represents a transitional stage between the patronage system, in which artists addressed themselves to a specific person, and the market system, in which works are composed for an abstract public.

50. These events, and the lively reactions to Voltaire's comments, are summarized in chap. 7 of René Pomeau et al., *"Écraser l'infâme,"* 103–13. The reactions moved Voltaire to prepare a second edition of the *Commentaires*, in 1774.

51. After seven years spent in Rouen translating religious verse and meditating on the state of his soul, Corneille fell in love with Marquise du Parc, the beautiful young female lead in Molière's troupe, paid fruitless court to her, and addressed to her the famous "Sur le départ de Marquise." Corneille's *Oedipe*, and especially the role of Jocaste, was written for Marquise. See Corneille, *Théâtre complet*, edited by Maurice Rat, 3 vols. (Paris: Garnier, n.d.), 3:1–2.

52. Ibid., 3:6. According to Fontenelle (cited by Maurice Rat in a footnote to this passage), the first of the three subjects suggested by Fouquet was Oedipus (3:758n.4).

53. "Despite *Pertharite*, and despite several rather weak plays, and despite *Œdipe* itself" (Voltaire, ed., *Théâtre de Pierre Corneille*, 7:5).

54. At the end of the fourth "Lettre sur *Œdipe*," Voltaire adds, "Sophocles did not take the trouble to correct this fault; Corneille, by trying to repair it, did still worse than Sophocles; and I succeeded no better than they" (*Théâtre*, 1:35). In "Œdipe, sans complexe" Raynaud claims that the greatness of Voltaire's *Œdipe* has become unintelligible to modern readers because of what Raynaud calls its "subject" (132–33).

55. "This subject has never been treated properly in France, because of the unfortunate construction of our theaters, and because of our miserable habit of always introducing love, or rather gallantry, into subjects that exclude all love" (*Théâtre de Pierre Corneille*, 7:82).

56. Cited by Pomeau, *D'Arouet à Voltaire*, 84. These remarks are taken from the dedicatory epistle of *Oreste* (1750), addressed to the duchesse du Maine. In that text, Voltaire recalls his enthusiastic response to hearing Malézieu read translations of Sophocles and Euripides. In a similar vein, he criticizes a passage of his *Œdipe* for lacking "that manly and terrifying style, precise and pure, that characterizes Sophocles" (*Théâtre de Pierre Corneille*, 7:13–14). As Pomeau notes (120), the love interest (and probably the Philoctète character, as well) seems to have been part of the 1715–16 version of *Œdipe*. Voltaire claimed to have written "a tragedy almost without love." In a letter written in 1730 to Père Porée (his former instructor in rhetoric at Louis-le-Grand), he claimed that in the April 1730 edition of the play, "I took care to erase as much as possible the pale colors of a misplaced love story, which I had mixed despite myself with the manly and terrifying traits required by this subject" (D 392). See Pomeau's discussion of this question in *D'Arouet à Voltaire*, 120–21. Voltaire consistently speaks of tragedy as a strong, virile genre (and of love interest as weak, effeminate).

57. "The actress who played Dircé in Corneille's *Œdipe* said to the new author, 'I play the female love interest [l'amoureuse], and if I do not have a role, the play will not be performed.' At these words, 'I play the *amoureuse* in *Œdipe*,' two sensible foreigners broke out laughing; but the actors' demands had to be satisfied; one had to make oneself the slave of the most miserable abuse; and if the author, indignant at giving in to this abuse, had not put the absolute minimum of amorous conversations into his tragedy, if he had uttered the word 'love' in

the last three acts, the play would not deserve to be performed" (*Théâtre de Pierre Corneille*, 7:130–31).

58. See Jay Caplan, "1759, 23 April: Clearing the Stage," in *A New History of French Literature* (Cambridge, Mass.: Harvard University Press, 1989), 473: "What the theatergoing public of Voltaire's time found most attractive in the comedies of the previous century was no longer the spectacle of heroism and violence, but love. The most popular tragic actresses (Adrienne Lecouvreur, Mlle. Gaussin) carried off their greatest triumphs in the role of the tender victim (Ariadne, Racine's Bérénice, Voltaire's Zaïre) whose sufferings moved the audience to tears." In this article I discussed Voltaire's desire to have contemporary audiences again take tragedy seriously, and argued that his (and Diderot's) proposal to clear the French classical stage of seats meant that the conception of theatrical illusion and space was being transformed in the course of the eighteenth century. In the early 1660s, when Voltaire again raised the question of the performability of *Œdipe* in the *Commentaires sur Corneille*, the onstage seats had just been eliminated from the Théâtre Français. He therefore hoped that if the play were staged properly, a convincing performance of the play would finally be possible (see *Théâtre de Pierre Corneille*, 7:14–15). However, he still had his doubts: "I do not know if even today, when the stage is free and cleared of all that disfigured it, it would be possible to show Oedipus covered with blood, as he appeared in the theater of Athens" (*Théâtre de Pierre Corneille*, 7:13).

59. Already in the *Examination* of *Œdipe* Corneille had claimed that, in order to appease the delicate sensibilities of the ladies ("nos dames"), he had been forced to weaken the play by making the violence less graphic. In his view, modern audiences had become so soft and effeminate that they could no longer bear even a report of the quintessentially tragic moment when Oedipus loses his sight: "I realized that what had passed for marvelous in their time could seem horrible in ours; that the eloquent and serious description of how this unfortunate prince cuts out his eyes, which fills the entire fifth act, would offend *the delicacy of the ladies, whose disgust easily causes that of the rest of the audience*" (III, 8; emphasis added). The ladies in the audience, Corneille claimed, already had the power to determine the success of a tragedy. Following their lead, public opinion (*la voix publique*) had itself become effeminate, and dramatists in turn were required to cut all the virile violence in their tragedies. For this reason, "tragedy" could succeed only in an effeminate, mutilated, *castrated* form. Now an effeminate *voix publique* required dramatists to tell love stories, instead of representing real tragedies. Audiences required superficial "charms [agréments]" from the theater (III, 8). According to Corneille, *agréments* were superficial, contingent, deceptive— that is, feminine. In La Bruyère's classic formulation ("Des Femmes," in *Les Caractères*, 11 [iv]), "Charm is arbitrary, beauty is something more real." For Corneille, the scandal (or perhaps the irony) of the situation was obvious: on the one hand, women were so weak that they could not bear the sight of Oedipus cutting his eyes out; on the other hand, these delicate creatures had the strength

to determine public opinion. Fashion and charms were female, eloquence and seriousness were male. Authentically tragic actions (such as Oedipus' putting out his eyes), which earlier, more virile times had considered "eloquent and serious," now had to be removed from view; they had to be cut and replaced by love stories: "These considerations led me *to hide such a dangerous sight from the eyes,* and introduce the fortunate episode of Thésée and Dircé. I *cut* the number of oracles, which could be importune and make Oedipe too suspicious about his birth" (III, 8; emphasis added). In his discussion of this symbolic castration, Corneille thus made a connection between a part of the Oedipus story (seeing Oedipus cut out his eyes) that *could not be seen* (that *had to be cut*), and parts that an implicitly effeminate audience had forced him to add.

60. "In *Œdipe* there is a manual intended for kings" (Ridgway, "La Propagande philosophique"; quoted by Truchet, *Théâtre du XVIIIème siècle,* 1: 1377n.2). At a more general level Kosseleck, *Le Règne de la critique,* 85–87, has shown how philosophes turned the stage into a tribunal, where the state was judged from the perspective of reason.

61. In *D'Arouet à Voltaire,* 124–25, Pomeau lists the numerous allusions to the contemporary political situation found in *Œdipe.*

62. *D* 1968, quoted in ibid., 23.

63. Besterman, *Voltaire,* 82 (emphasis added).

64. *Œdipe,* II, 4 (Besterman translation, modified).

65. "The high priest, who has just denounced Œdipe's guilt, anticipating the results of the inquiry, has evinced very real 'knowledge'; he does not abuse the 'credulity' of a 'vain people.' But what does it matter!" (Pomeau, *D'Arouet à Voltaire,* 124).

66. *Œdipe,* V, 1.

67. Here is Besterman's summary of the action: "Jocaste and Philoctète, prince of Euboea, were in love, but Jocaste had been made to marry Laius, king of Thebes. Philoctète goes into exile, but returns after some years still loving Jocaste. The curtain rises as he meets his friend Dimas, from whom he learns that Laius died four years earlier, that Jocaste was now married to Oedipe, the new king, and that a plague was ravaging Thebes. The high priest (who is not named) declares that the pestilence can be averted only if the slayer of Laius be discovered. Oedipe is told by Jocaste that Phorbas, a follower of the dead king, is suspected of the crime and has been hidden by her because she thinks him innocent. Philoctète is then accused of the murder, but Jocaste, asserting his innocence, admits that he still has a place in her heart, that she never loved Laius, and that she has only affection for Oedipe. The high priest then accuses the king of the crime; Oedipe is indignant, but troubled by vague memories, and finally realizes his guilt when the details of the crime are reported by Jocaste and Phorbas. He asks to be executed, but Jocaste maintains that he was not guilty, since he was not aware of his victim's identity. Icare announces the death of Polybe, king of Cor-

inth, the reputed father of Oedipe. It now transpires from the confrontation of Icare and Phorbas that Oedipe was only his adopted son, that he was brought to Corinth from Thebes, and that he is in fact the son of Laius and Jocaste. The high priest, amidst thunder and lightning, announces the end of the pestilence. Jocaste stabs herself to death, reproaching the gods who forced her crime upon her." This helpful plot summary first appeared in *Voltaire's Correspondence*, 1:356; it was subsequently incorporated in *Voltaire*, 80–81. As an analytic tool, Moureaux's more detailed summary of the action in *Œdipe* (*L'Œdipe de Voltaire*, 7–16) is invaluable, and I shall refer to it below. See also Pomeau, "Un *Œdipe* voltairien," 71–75.

68. In the second 1719 edition, the play's opening lines were altered, so as to draw less attention to the problem of plausibility (*vraisemblance*): "Philoctète, est-ce vous? quel coup affreux du sort / Dans ces lieux empestés vous fait chercher la mort? / Venez-vous de nos dieux affronter la colère?" ("Philoctète, is it you? What hideous blow of fate / Makes you seek death in this plagued place? / Do you come to confront the wrath of our gods?"). In part because its revisions reflect initial audience reactions, the second 1719 edition is (as Truchet has noted [*Théâtre du XVIIIème siècle*, 1:1379]) among the most interesting published versions of the play.

69. Voltaire, *Théâtre*, edited by Moland, 1:36.

70. In a letter dated 6 December 1713 (*D* 14). For an account of the affair with Pimpette, see Besterman, *Voltaire*, 56–60; and Pomeau, *D'Arouet à Voltaire*, 60–64.

71. Decades later, in a similar mode, Voltaire would give his niece (and mistress) Mme. Denis the nickname "chère maman." It should be noted that such phrases as "mon aimable enfant," "cher enfant," and "chère maman" were banal tokens of affection in eighteenth-century France, and did not necessarily have the incestuous resonance they do today. (A similar problem arises in regard to Rousseau's habit of referring to Mme. de Warens as "Maman.")

72. Moureaux, *L'Œdipe de Voltaire*, 55.

73. Ibid., 62–63.

74. It has been alleged that during the discussions at Tilsitt in 1807, upon hearing this last line, concerning the gift of a great man's friendship, at a performance of *Œdipe*, Czar Alexander I shook Napoleon's hand and said to him: "Je ne l'ai jamais mieux senti" (see Voltaire, *Théâtre*, edited by Moland, 1:61n.1).

75. Moureaux, *L'Œdipe de Voltaire*, 75–80.

76. Ibid., 89.

77. In modern French, the common noun *laïus* means a speech, often a vague and bombastic one. According to the *Nouveau Petit Robert*, this meaning is derived from an essay topic proposed in 1804 at the École Polytechnique entry examination: "Laïus . . . n.m.; de *Laïus*, du père d'Œdipe, le sujet de composition

fr. *le discours de Laïus* ayant été proposé au concours d'entrée à Polytechnique, en 1804."

78. The resemblance to a criminal inquiry has been noted by Pomeau, "Un *Œdipe* voltairien," 72.

79. See the entry for *Œdipe* in *Dictionnaire Voltaire*, edited by Jacques Lemaire, Raymond Trousson and Jeroom Vercruysse (Brussels: Hachette Référence, 1994), 144.

80. Absolutist ideology provided the state with a theoretical justification for crushing all forms of internal disorder, by separating politics from conscience. However, once relative public stability had been achieved (foreign wars having generally replaced civil wars), the rational justification for the split between politics and morality was gradually forgotten. Indeed, Kosseleck has shown that it was thanks to the success of absolutist policies in achieving a climate of relative security that philosophes like Voltaire could call for an "enlightened" politics and demand that political actions finally become consistent with the demands of individual conscience. Thus in the Enlightenment the absolutist state was perceived in the end not as morally neutral, but as immorality itself. The logic of absolutist ideology would ultimately unfold into the demand that enlightened "criticism" itself take power, in the place of a morally corrupt absolutist state. See *Le Règne de la critique*, chap. 2, "The Conception That the Philosophers of Enlightenment Had of Themselves."

81. In this play, "the protagonists respond to predestination with the *but* of their innocence" (cited by Eric Van der Schueren, in *Dictionnaire Voltaire*, 144).

82. In "The Death of Tragedy," in *Against Interpretation* (New York: Delta, 1966), 136, Susan Sontag takes issue with Lionel Abel's claim (in *Metatheater*) that tragedy implies acceptance of "implacable values": "If the fate of Oedipus was represented and experienced as tragic, it is not because he, or his audience, believed in 'implacable values', but precisely because a crisis had overtaken those values. It is not the implacability of 'values' that is demonstrated by tragedy, but the implacability of the world. The story of Oedipus is tragic insofar as it exhibits the brute opaqueness of the world, the collision of subjective intention with objective fate. After all, in the deepest sense, Oedipus is innocent; he is wronged by the gods, as he himself says in *Oedipus at Colonus*. Tragedy is a vision of nihilism, a heroic or ennobling vision of nihilism." The author of the *Poème sur le désastre de Lisbonne* and *Candide* would not have agreed with Sontag that "tragedy says there are disasters that are not fully merited, that there is ultimate injustice in the world" (137). Sontag herself continues to affirm the liberal, skeptical, cosmopolitan values represented by Voltaire (one thinks, for example, of her participation in a production of *Waiting for Godot* in war-torn Sarajevo).

83. Jean-Marie Apostolidès, *Le Prince sacrifié* (Paris: Minuit, 1985).

84. Voltaire summarizes this "hope" in the famous concluding lines of the *Poème sur le désastre de Lisbonne:* "Un jour tout sera bien, voilà notre espérance / Tout est bien aujourd'hui, voilà l'illusion."

Chapter Three

1. Pierre Champion, *Notes critiques sur les vies anciennes d'Antoine Watteau* (Paris, 1921), 62. Gersaint's biographical notice on Watteau was written long after Watteau's death, in 1744. Julie Anne Plax has scrutinized these remarks by Gersaint in her dissertation, "Antoine Watteau's Paintings and Cultural Politics," University of Missouri, Columbia, 1989, 142–54, and later in "Gersaint's Biography of Antoine Watteau: Reading between the Lines," *Eighteenth Century Studies* 25, no. 4 (summer 1992): 545–60.

2. *"L'Enseigne de Gersaint," Bulletin du Laboratoire du Musée du Louvre* 9 (1964): 16.

3. Donald Posner, *Antoine Watteau* (Ithaca: Cornell University Press, 1984), 276. Plax discusses this issue in "The Meeting of High and Low Culture in *L'Enseigne de Gersaint*," chap. 4 of "Antoine Watteau's Paintings and Cultural Politics."

4. Mary Vidal, *Watteau's Painted Conversations: Art, Literature, and Talk in Seventeenth- and Eighteenth-Century France* (New Haven: Yale University Press, 1992), chap. 5 ("*L'Enseigne de Gersaint* and the Conversational Structure of the Artistic Sign"), 173–96.

5. According to Pierre Alfassa, *L'Enseigne de Gersaint* probably entered Frederick II's collection (along with *L'Embarquement pour Cythère*) between 1744 and 1747. See *"L'Enseigne de Gersaint," Bulletin de la Société de l'Histoire de l'Art Français* (1910): 147. At the end of World War II (between March 1945 and April 1946), Louis Aragon wrote a polemical essay entitled *L'Enseigne de Gersaint* (Neuchâtel: Ides et Calendes, 1946), in which he called for the repatriation of all French art works that were held in German collections. He conceived of this gesture as a way of making Germany pay back, not just food and machines, but some of France's "spiritual blood" (17). To Aragon, Watteau's last signboard was the most poignant example of "the French spirit" in exile. In *Ancients against Moderns* (152n.3), Joan De Jean proposes the *Enseigne* as an emblem of the modern notion of time.

6. These comments are based upon Plax's informative discussion of the semiotics of signboards in eighteenth-century Paris. Plax, *Antoine Watteau's Paintings and Cultural Politics*, 124–33.

7. On the "low" status of signboards and signboard painters in Watteau's culture, see ibid., 133–36. Plax also recalls (135–36) the art-historical myth ("canonized" by the Goncourt brothers) according to which Chardin achieved recognition thanks to the "discovery" of the signboard he had painted for a surgeon's shop. See also Martin Eidelberg, *Watteau's Drawings: Their Use and Significance* (New York: Garland Press, 1977), 232–52. See G. Lebel, "A Propos de deux esquisses d'enseignes du XVIIIe siècle," *Bulletin de la Société de l'Histoire de l'Art Français* (1921): 55–61).

8. On the basis of various scientific tests, Hélène Adhémar concludes that

once the sign was taken down from its original position above the entry to Ger-saint's shop, vertical strips were cut off the left and right sides of the painting. These strips were then rearranged horizontally on top of the painting, and some additional details were painted (also by Pater) to fill the rectangular space that had been created. See Hélène Adhémar, *Watteau, sa vie, son œuvre*, preceded by René Huyghe, *L'Univers de Watteau* (Paris: Editions Pierre Tisné, 1950), 10–11.

9. Posner, *Antoine Watteau*, 272.

10. Martin Sperlich, "Watteaus Ladenschild und die Perspektive," in *Forma und subtilitas: Festschrift für Wolfgang Schöne zum 75. Geburtstag* (Berlin: De Gruyter, 1986), 219–24.

11. As Sperlich observes, Pater himself does not seem to have noticed this discrepancy in the foreshortening, as one can see by examining the large landscape over the mirror on the left side of the shop. In the original *Enseigne*, which had the form of a flattened arch, Watteau painted only the lower right corner of this painting; in expanding the work to its present rectangular shape, Watteau's stu-dent enlarged this landscape to dimensions that, if projected onto the right wall, would be "friezelike." This deviation has the effect of accentuating the unreality of the wall with windows in the back room, and helps remove the entire shop from the realm of everyday life. "Through the most direct connection with a sensuously liveable reality, the overall appearance of the painting is artfully re-moved from measurable geometric structure and enters a numinous, unreal sphere, [and] is a real enchantment" (ibid., 222).

12. Through examination of various sources, Sperlich has been able to show that Watteau's representation of the shop at 35, Pont-Notre-Dame, is at least grounded in empirical reality. The appearance of the cobblestone pavement and the implied width of the shop are measurably realistic. Furthermore, the floorplan of this block shows that (since the three adjoining houses had been shortened) No. 35 would indeed have had two windows on the left side of the back room. Ibid., 220–21.

13. Note the resemblance between this portrait and Rigaud's half-length por-trait of Louis XIV in the Musée des Beaux-Arts, Dijon. Since Rigaud painted more than one portrait of Louis XIV, the royal portrait in *L'Enseigne* is not necessarily, as Vidal claims, a "fragment or partial copy of Rigaud's full-length state portrait" (Vidal, *Watteau's Painted Conversations*, 182).

14. The shops that covered the Pont-Notre-Dame were razed in 1786.

15. As Plax points out, "Watteau's use of a signboard within a signboard is in keeping with his use of a symbolic subtext as a commentary upon the activities depicted within the painting. Moreover, it was also in keeping with the visual and verbal wit often displayed in signboards of the seventeenth and eighteenth centuries" ("Antoine Watteau's Paintings and Cultural Politics," chap. 4, 124). In this chapter of her innovative and carefully documented dissertation, Plax pro-vides a convincing explanation for the success of this signboard among Watteau's contemporaries, and locates the work in its social milieu. She argues that "Wat-

teau carries the tactics he employed in [*L'Embarquement pour Cythère* and other fêtes galantes] even further in *L'Enseigne:* the playing of one painterly and cultural discourse against the other to create a visual dialogue which could more fully articulate the complex relationships which existed between culture and power and class during the early eighteenth century. By confounding the boundaries between high and low art and traditional genres, Watteau demonstrates their inadequacies in representing a whole range of lived experience, social practices and shared aspirations. Watteau's Signboard, for the first time, gives monumental form to a new class of collectors and dealers, and a system of artistic production and consumption existing outside the authority of official, state-controlled culture" (116).

16. Robert Neuman, "Watteau's *L'Enseigne de Gersaint* and Baroque Emblematic Tradition." See also Plax, "Antoine Watteau's Paintings and Cultural Politics," 123–24.

17. Gérard Le Coat, "Modern Enchantment and Traditional Didacticism in Watteau's *L'Enseigne de Gersaint* and Couperin's *Folies Françaises,*" *Gazette des Beaux-Arts* 41 (November 1978): 169–72; Oliver Banks, *Watteau and the North: Studies in the Dutch and Flemish Baroque on French Rococo Painting* (New York: Garland Press, 1977), 241–52. Surmounting the clock is a gilded statue of Fame, blowing a trumpet, while below the clock is a pair of lovers—the entire piece presumably an allegory of the undermining of Fame and Love by Time. On the same *vanitas* theme, we note the medal of the Ordre du Saint-Esprit, proudly displayed by Louis XIV.

18. In Aragon's essay, he recalls having seen *L'Enseigne* during a Paris exhibition in 1937. In "French Light" (in *L'Enseigne de Gersaint*, 36), as he recalls it, even the colors were different: "It had seemed to me that, here at home, those incomparable yellows had a different life from over there" (36–37). It would probably be best to withhold all judgments on Watteau's use of color in *L'Enseigne* until the painting has been cleaned.

19. "Adieu lumière de ma vie: L'Art de mourir d'Antoine Watteau," *Esprit* 93 (September 1984): 1–21.

20. Vidal, *Watteau's Painted Conversations*, 180.

21. According to Marianne Roland Michel, *L'Enseigne de Gersaint* is just an image of everyday life in Gersaint's shop, and one should therefore not "overload" the king's portrait "with too much significance" (*Watteau: An Artist of the Eighteenth Century* [New York: Alpine Fine Arts, 1984], 109).

22. In *Looking at Pictures* (New York: Holt, Rinehart and Winston, 1960), 75–87, Kenneth Clark calls the work a frivolous genre scene.

23. See my introduction, above.

24. Donald Posner relates the portrait of Louis XIV to Watteau's "easy acceptance" of the passage of time: "Each side of his picture . . . is focused on a scene of people looking at a painted image. The young couple entering the shop at the left confront a painting of an old monarch; the couple at the right, elderly, to judge

by the woman's costume, gaze upon a summertime scene of youthful bathers. At the left, the picture of the king is barely noticed. The woman just glances at it while the gentleman with her doesn't even see it, and for the workman it is an anonymous object to be crated. The picture at the right, however, is intently studied. Youth and beauty, not power and fame, genuinely fascinate" (Posner, *Antoine Watteau,* 276–77).

25. See Marin, *Portrait of the King* and *La Parole mangée.*

26. Vidal, *Watteau's Painted Conversations,* 182.

27. In 1712 Antoine Crozat (1655–1738) obtained from the king the exclusive privilege on commerce in French Louisiana. His brother Pierre (1661–1740)— who later became Trésorier de France—not only protected Watteau but also assembled a magnificent art collection, half of which was acquired by Catherine the Great and can now be found in the Hermitage Museum, St. Petersburg.

28. Thomas Crow, "Codes of Silence: Historical Interpretation and the Art of Watteau," *Representations* 12 (fall 1985): 5. Crow notes that for wealthy financiers like Crozat, who (decades after the cult of *honnêteté* was created) aspired to a life of theatricalized leisure, and who had begun to set the standard in matters of luxury and display, "the ideal of honnêteté was more easily available as representation, in the arabesque and fête galante, than as participatory performance. Moreover, these individuals tended to have precisely that expertise in painterly aesthetics disdained by the old nobility. Provision of that expertise had been Crozat's primary route to influence with the regent, and the Crozat household constituted at that moment an informal artistic academy, a haven for a guardian of technical and scholarly knowledge, during a period when the actual Academy of Painting had to a significant degree forsaken this role.

"What individuals like Crozat lacked in one kind of knowledge they made up for in another. And it was Watteau's extraordinary experience and talent that accomplished this crucial substitution for them. The fête galante as a genre in fact reaches its maximum popularity later in the century for patrons grown ever more distant from the bygone mode of life it memorializes but ever more accomplished as amateurs of art. The Crozat circle was the school in which Watteau learned to fit the multiple overlay of codes embodied in elite leisure and its decor with the higher demands for formal coherence, density, and integration embodied in the Italianate high-art tradition. This last matching of code to code constitutes Watteau's great achievement, and here I think we can see the professional and intellectual subculture of the artist and patron as locked in a crucial series of exchanges with other contiguous sectors of French society. These exchanges can lead us, quite concretely, from an apparently private, elite art toward the actively transformative sphere of urban popular culture on the one hand and toward the central locations of power within the state on the other" (13–14).

29. "Specular" as in "per speculum in aenigmate" ("through a glass darkly"): 1 Cor. 13.12.

30. Thomas Crow, *Painters and Public Life in Eighteenth-Century Paris* (New

Haven: Yale University Press, 1985), describes the institutions and artists that played the most important roles in the expansion of a public sphere for art works in the later seventeenth and eighteenth centuries. He shows how institutions such as the salons contributed to a market for art works that was independent of the patronage system. Although Crow devotes a chapter (chap. 2) to Watteau's place in the development of these institutions and related discourses, he does not comment specifically upon the relationship between them and *L'Enseigne de Gersaint*. However, Crow's findings inform Plax's argument about the semiotics of shop signs in "Antoine Watteau's Paintings and Cultural Politics." In both *Painters and Public Life* and "Codes of Silence," Crow establishes suggestive links among elite leisure, urban popular culture, and the exercise of state power.

31. Posner, *Antoine Watteau*, 277.

32. Huyghe, "L'Univers de Watteau," preface to Adhémar, *Watteau, sa vie, son œuvre*, 17. Huyghe notes that Watteau had a predilection for this **S**-shaped compositional form and preferred movement from right to left and front to back. He argues that this "unnatural" movement is linked to the theme of regression, of movement toward the past.

33. In her study of eighteenth-century French fashion, Madeleine Delpierre points out that at the beginning of the Regency, fashionable Parisian women began to wear hoop dresses outdoors and not just in their boudoirs. See Delpierre, *Se vêtir au XVIIIe siècle* (Paris: Adam Biro, 1996), 22. At several levels, *L'Enseigne* plays upon this ambiguity between inside and outside, old and new. See Delpierre's illuminating comments on the female fashion (illustrated in this painting) of wearing a minuscule, symbolic bonnet (55).

34. Ibid., 37–38.

35. "This couple's graceful, effortless gestures, dancelike poses, and fashionable clothes, have become something of a visual cliché; they are the embodiment of refined society, marking the difference between the realm of leisure and the realm of work" (Plax, "Antoine Watteau's Paintings," 118).

36. Posner, *Antoine Watteau*, 277.

37. Vidal, *Watteau's Painted Conversations*, 178.

38. "Above all the beholder's glance is eluded. In *Gersaint's Shopsign* the only glance that the beholder meets, comes from the portrait of Louis XIV, that is being packed up. In other paintings it is at best marginal figures who gaze at the beholder, who is thereby caught by surprise as it were" (Norbert Knopp, "Watteaus neue Bildform," in *Amici Amico: Festschrift für Werner Gross zu seinem 65. Geburtstag* [Munich: Fink Verlag, 1968], 243).

39. Posner, *Antoine Watteau*, 276.

40. Plax, "Antoine Watteau's Paintings," 154.

41. Delpierre, *Se vêtir au XVIIIe siècle*, 22–23. As Delpierre points out, in the *Enseigne* this older fashion is also worn by the young customer seated on the right, in front of the counter.

42. Plax, "Antoine Watteau's Paintings," 118; Vidal, *Watteau's Painted Con-*

versations, 188. Vidal argues that this erotic interest is framed by, and hence subordinated to, an interest in art. However, she does not go so far as to maintain that the viewer's pleasure is disinterested: "These anonymous connoisseurs, seen only from behind, study the image in a de Piles–like conversational fashion, stepping in close to appreciate the painter's artifice. (Even the initially engaging playfulness of the male viewer's attention to the nymphs is turned to the artist's account, for when we look closer, we realize that at such close range the man sees as much paint as he wants to see flesh.) The work of art is being absorbed by such pleasurable and knowledgeable viewing, but on the other hand, the painting also seems to absorb their bodies within the perimeter of the frame" (ibid).

43. In "Les Signes Galants: A Historical Reevaluation of Galanterie," *Yale French Studies* 92 (1997): 11–29, Alain Viala maps out the complex sociohistorical evolution of a few "signs" of *galanterie,* from the middle of the seventeenth century through Rousseau's *Lettre à d'Alembert* (1768).

44. Crow, "Codes of Silence," 5. In chapter 3 of "Watteau's Paintings and Cultural Politics," Plax examines the fête galante in a similar perspective. To my knowledge, only Knopp has criticized this position, in his excellent article "Watteaus neue Bildform." Knopp reads Watteau as a forerunner of modern artistic formalism. He argues that it is a mistake to associate Watteau with the theme of the fête galante, for the simple reason that Watteau subordinates all thematic concerns to a concern with the work of art itself (259). Although Knopp somewhat overstates the case for Watteau's modernity, I believe he is right to emphasize the artist's overriding concern with the work of art itself, rather than with any specific theme. Critics have been somewhat at a loss to explain how Watteau's career could have culminated in two great paintings—*Gilles* and *L'Enseigne de Gersaint*—that seem to stand apart from the project of the fête galante. Donald Posner, for example, stresses how unusual these canvases are: "[These two paintings] are so unusual, in themselves and in his career, that they cannot usefully be grouped with any other of his pictures for discussion. They are 'sports,' sudden deviations from expected types in Watteau's art, brought about by circumstances that are today imperfectly known" (*Antoine Watteau,* 266). At the end of this chapter (277), however, Posner does note certain compositional and thematic resemblances between *L'Enseigne de Gersaint* and the fête galante *L'Embarquement pour Cythère.* In fact, it is possible that both of these apparent deviations from Watteau's artistic project were meant to be shop signs. (Alluding to an article by Adhémar, Posner suggests that *Gilles* may have been "one of the two shopsigns made for cafés that the actor Belloni, upon retiring from the fairs, opened in 1718–19" [292n.78].) See Hélène Adhémar, "Watteau, les romans et l'imagerie de son temps," *Gazette des Beaux-Arts* 90 (1977): 165–72. The identification of *Gilles* with one of the Belloni shop signs is based upon the plausible assumption that Gilles and Pierrot were two versions of the same figure. The relationship between *Gilles* and the fête galante lies outside the scope of this chapter.

45. See René Démoris, "Les Fêtes Galantes chez Watteau et dans le roman contemporain," *Dix-huitième siècle* 3 (1971): 337–57. A summary of portions of this article follows. See also Crow, *Painters and Public Life:* "But if there is nothing imaginary about the subject matter of the fête galante, if the activities and costumes which Watteau depicts were present in his daily experience as a protégé of the Crozat circle, it would nevertheless be far too simple to see these pictures as a literal rendering of the life around him, however much accuracy of description they might contain. The genre is a frankly artificial one: it had to be if it was to add another, necessary layer of fiction over the life-as-fiction it portrays, that is, if it was to be in any way distinguishable as a mode of representation from the already existing lower genres" (56–57).

46. Although the experiment in aristocratic monarchy failed, as did the much more important fiscal experiment of John Law, the venture is nevertheless quite significant, since it marked a complete break with the royal policy of excluding the nobility and was the last attempt to restore the upper nobility to its mythical place of power at the king's side. See Robert Mandrou, *L'Europe absolutiste: Raison et raison d'État, 1649–1715* (Paris: Fayard, 1977), 133.

47. With its fêtes galantes, the aristocracy laid claim to its cultural superiority, in opposition to an increasingly wealthy urban bourgeoisie. By representing itself as a leisure class, whose costumed members disported themselves in a country setting, the aristocracy radically distinguished itself from the richest members of the Third Estate, while emphasizing its ancestral link to the land. In the words of Démoris, the fête galante "represents the moment of leisure, when the aristocrat can define himself as such, by the quality with which he is able to endow this leisure" (Démoris, "Les Fêtes galantes chez Watteau," 346).

48. Ibid., 347. Démoris explains that the classical hierarchy of subjects, diction, and genres did not allow a novelist to imitate the "low reality" of daily life in a plausible or serious way. *La vie quotidienne* was so diverse that no single form could encompass it, and was so inherently uneventful that the conventions of any narrative form would necessarily falsify it. For this reason, Démoris maintains, efforts to represent contemporary reality during this period resulted in works whose subject was absent or illusory, and in narrative techniques that emphasized the arbitrariness or artificiality of any narrative. In regard to the absence or illusory quality of action in these novels and their thematization of artifice, see ibid., 352.

49. Adhémar (*Watteau, sa vie, son œuvre,* 181) cites Caylus, who considered this lack of passion or action as a defect.

50. This lack of dramatic action and passion may have been a defect from the perspective of neoclassical aesthetics, but as Démoris points out, the aesthetics of the fête galante is incompatible with dramatic tension and with the expression of feelings. See Démoris, "Les Fêtes galantes chez Watteau," 355–56.

51. "Its own beauty is what justifies the presence of the fête galante, as a noble form of diversion. Thus it also serves to mask and satisfy desire. Whereas action

in [French classical] theater is so important as to make the scenery unessential, in Watteau the absence of human action confers upon nature the new function of object of desire" (ibid., 356).

52. Marin, *La Parole mangée*, 199.

53. In *A Theory of Semiotics* (Bloomington: Indiana University Press, 1975), Umberto Eco defines a sign as "everything that, on the grounds of a previously established social convention, can be taken as something standing for something else" (16).

54. See Knopp, "Watteaus neue Bildform." This observation apparently contradicts Gersaint's frequently quoted remark about the "natural" quality of Watteau's style in *L'Enseigne:* "the whole was done after nature; its attitudes were so true and easy, the organization so natural, the groups so well understood, that it attracted the eyes of passersby; and even the most accomplished painters came several times to admire it" (Champion, *Notes critiques*, 62). However, what Gersaint called the "natural" quality of Watteau's style had nothing to do with its capacity to render an extra-artistic "reality." On the contrary, this naturalness was obtained by combining traditional and nontraditional artistic models, or by recombining and reworking conventional types in an unconventional context. Huyghe discusses Watteau's compositional method at some length, in "L'Univers de Watteau." According to Caylus, for example (31), Watteau would dress people in theatrical costumes and then have them adopt untheatrical ("natural") poses. These references to "nature" in Watteau have to be read historically. According to Ballot de Sovrot, Watteau advised his student Lancret to follow his example, by looking at "the master of masters: Nature." In context, however, Watteau always transformed and recombined "nature," as clearly appears in Ballot de Sovrot's summary of Watteau's compositional method: "drawing some country scenes in the Paris area, then sketching the figures elsewhere, and combining them as he pleased, shaping them into a painting of his imagination and choice" (quoted in ibid., 31). In "Gersaint's Biography of Antoine Watteau," Plax stresses the importance of placing all Gersaint's biographical remarks about Watteau in their ideological context.

55. Vidal, *Watteau's Painted Conversations*, 185.

56. Knopp, "Watteaus neue Bildform," 242.

57. For example, commentators have identified the lady and gentleman behind the counter with M. and Mme. Gersaint. But Posner has convincingly argued that neither the characters in *L'Enseigne*, nor the art works, nor the shop itself are based on real models (*Antoine Watteau*, 273).

58. Domna Stanton discusses self-fashioning among French aristocrats in the seventeenth century in *The Aristocrat as Art* (New York: Columbia University Press, 1980). Andrew McClellan suggests that Watteau's shop sign provides even an art dealer like Gersaint with a medium for asserting his nobility. See McClellan, "Edmé Gersaint and the Marketing of Art in Eighteenth-Century Paris," *Eighteenth-Century Studies* 29, no. 2 (winter 1995–96): 218–22.

59. Plax, "Antoine Watteau's Paintings," 94.

60. Vidal, *Watteau's Painted Conversations*, 188–96.

61. See Giorgio Agamben, "La Camera delle meraviglie," in *L'Uomo senza contenuto* (Milan: Rizzoli, 1970), 49–64.

62. Ibid., 57–58.

63. Ibid., 61.

64. See Posner, *Antoine Watteau*, 276–77), as well as Norman Bryson's discussion of the way in which Watteau exploits the theatrical potential of "attention," *Word and Image: French Painting of the Ancien Régime* (Cambridge: Cambridge University Press, 1981), 82–88.

65. Posner, *Antoine Watteau*, 277.

66. Vidal, *Watteau's Painted Conversations*, 188.

67. See Georges Bataille, *La Part maudite* (Paris: Minuit, 1967).

68. See Michael Fried, *Absorption and Theatricality: Painting and Beholder in the Age of Diderot* (Berkeley: University of California Press, 1980).

69. I am, of course, alluding here to a notion that was used first in structural linguistics, and later in anthropology and semiotics (most famously by Roland Barthes). It is worth emphasizing that a "zero degree" sign is one that signifies the absence of any specific meaning, and not a sign without meaning.

70. See Posner, *Antoine Watteau*, 266–71.

71. An "affirmative" reading of Watteau's sign may also be anachronistic, although in a post-Romantic, modernist way. If (like Knopp) one emphasizes the self-referential aspect of *L'Enseigne* (arguing that it is a painting about painting, an art dealer's shop sign about the selling of art), one runs the risk of completely slighting all its "realistic" features, of overlooking the fact that this self-referential art also appeals to a reality outside of art. A modernist reading of Watteau's shop sign stresses art as "token" (in Jean-Joseph Goux's terms), at the expense of art as "sign."

Chapter Four

1. In a classic article on Diderot, Peter Szondi discusses the relationship between the *coup de théâtre* and feudal social relations: Szondi, "Tableau and *Coup de Théâtre*: On the Social Psychology of Diderot's Bourgeois Tragedy," in *On Textual Understanding and Other Essays* (Minneapolis: University of Minnesota Press, 1986). On Marivaux's investment in theatrical relations, see David Marshall, *The Surprising Effects of Sympathy: Marivaux, Diderot, Rousseau, and Mary Shelley* (Chicago: University of Chicago Press, 1988), 11–40.

2. Goux, *The Coiners of Language*, 17 (translation modified); *Les Monnayeurs du langage*, 29.

3. Translations from Molière are those of Richard Wilbur, *"The Misanthrope" and "Tartuffe"* (New York: Harcourt Brace Jovanovich, 1954).

4. Furetière, *Dictionnaire universel*, rev. ed. (Paris, 1694; first published 1690), s.v. (emphasis added).

5. "CRÉDIT se dit aussi de la puissance de l'autorité, des richesses qu'on acquiert par le moyen de cette réputation qu'on a acquise. Ce ministre a acquis un grand *crédit* à la cour sur l'esprit du Prince" (ibid.).

6. "[C]e *prest* naturel qui se fait d'argent & de marchandises, sur la réputation & solvabilité d'un négociant" (ibid., emphasis added).

7. "Ce banquier a bon *crédit* sur la place, sa banqueroute n'a gueres diminué son crédit" (ibid., emphasis added).

8. "On dit, Faire *crédit*, vendre *à crédit*, acheter *à crédit* pour dire, ne payer pas comptant ce qu'on achète. C'est *le crédit* que font les Marchands aux Grands Seigneurs qui ruine leur fortune, leur négoce" (ibid., emphasis added).

9. "A CREDIT se dit souvent pour dire, A plaisir, sans utilité, sans fondement. Cet homme s'est ruiné *à crédit*, à plaisir, *sans faire de dépense qui parût*" (ibid., emphasis added).

10. J. G. A. Pocock has discussed the debates on credit in England in the half-century after the Glorious Revolution, in *The Machiavellian Moment: Florentine Political Thought and the Atlantic Republican Tradition* (Princeton: Princeton University Press, 1975), chaps. 13–14. In *Virtue, Commerce, and History: Essays on Political Thought and History, Chiefly in the Eighteenth Century* (Cambridge: Cambridge University Press, 1985), 106–23, Pocock has also examined how the institutions of commercial capitalism—with its mobile forms of property—affected the public presentation of personality. Dewald places the debate on credit in a specifically French, aristocratic context: Dewald, *Aristocratic Experience*, 157–63.

11. See Jean-Jacques Rousseau, *Politics and the Arts: Letter to M. d'Alembert on the Theater*, edited and translated by Allan Bloom (Ithaca: Cornell University Press, 1960).

12. In *Molière: Une Aventure théâtrale* (Paris: Gallimard, 1963), Jacques Guicharnaud attributes Célimène's "fall" to the fact that no one else shares her understanding of these conventions.

13. It is important to distinguish *amour-propre*, in this aristocratic context, both from its older, Augustinian form ("Vx. Attachement exclusif à sa propre personne, à sa conservation et son développement," *Nouveau Petit Robert*) and from the modern form that appears in Marivaux. The most eloquent spokesman for the Augustinian conception of *amour-propre* is La Rochefoucauld, for whom (in the words of Pierre Force) "self-love is the engine of all human behavior" ("Self-Love, Identification, and the Origin of Political Economy," *Yale French Studies* 92 [1997]: 49). As Force points out (49–50), French classicism already connected this form of self-love with commerce. On the more modern form of self-love, see Michel Deguy, "Première apparition de l'amour-propre moderne," in *La Machine matrimoniale: ou Marivaux* (Paris: Gallimard, 1981), 36 and following, to which I shall return. As my numerous references to this text will imply, my own understanding of Marivaux has been immensely enriched by Deguy's essay.

14. Apostolidès, *Le Prince sacrifié*, 148 (emphasis added). In Apostolidès's view, the replacement of war metaphors by monetary metaphors in love rhetoric testifies to a historical transition: "Love itself is not experienced as a conquest, as it was in the courtly novels [romans galants] of the preceding generation, and now borrows monetary metaphors to express itself." He argues that M. Jourdain's attempts (in *Le Bourgeois gentilhomme*) to purchase honor exemplify the situation of all "bourgeois gentlemen": "This is, in fact, a commercial operation specific to the old regime—the conversion of commercial capital and annuity bonds [titres de rente] into noble titles. The use of monetary metaphors in elite discourse reveals movement between the theoretically separate hierarchies of honor and wealth" (149).

15. Ibid., 153. Apostolidès then seems to allude to the vocabulary of Jean-Joseph Goux, when he formulates the contrast between Alceste and Célimène as follows: "Although language may not be the gold that Alceste would like, neither is it the worthless paper money that Célimène would desire. While the former fetishizes the use-value of words, the latter fetishizes their exchange-value" (153–54).

16. This utopian form resembles the first ("sage," according to Faure) version of John Law's system.

17. *Le Siècle de Louis XIV* (Paris: Pléiade, 1957), chap. 29, 981 (emphasis added).

18. Goux, *The Coiners of Language*, 94; *Les Monnayeurs du langage*, 133.

19. Deguy, *La Machine matrimoniale*, 37.

20. Walter Benjamin, "On Some Motifs in Baudelaire," in *Illuminations* (New York: Harcourt, Brace and World, 1968), 198.

21. Deguy, *La Machine matrimoniale*, 37.

22. Ibid., 28–29.

23. Kavanagh, *Enlightenment and the Shadows of Chance*. From the perspective of his illuminating discussion of the rise of probability theory (and with it, the notion of the "average man" [21 and following]), it might be possible to rethink the now familiar issue of the "solitary individual" in the anonymous crowd.

24. "Si elle osait, elle m'appelerait une originale," says Silvia to Lisette in act I, scene 1.

25. *The Game of Love and Chance*, translated by David Cohen (Harmondsworth, Middlesex, England: Penguin, 1980), 318. All subsequent quotations from this play are taken from this translation. *Théâtre complet*, 2 vols (Paris: Bordas, 1989), vol. 1. All references to the French text of Marivaux's plays are taken from this edition, first prepared for Éditions Garnier by Frédéric Deloffre, and later revised by Françoise Rubelin.

26. For a contemporary work on the *honnête homme* in French classicism, see Emmanuel Bury, *Littérature et politesse: L'Invention de l'honnête homme* (Paris: Presses Universitaires de France, 1996).

27. See Deloffre's footnote to this passage: *Théâtre complet*, 1:1099.

28. Deguy, *La Machine matrimoniale*, 55. Deguy asks (54), "Could it be that there is no psychology in Marivaux?"

29. Ronald Rosbottom has underlined "the etymological connection between *speculation* and *spectator,* both coming from the Latin *speculare,*" in "Narrating the Regency," in *Romance Quarterly* 38, no. 3 (August 1991): 343.

30. The scientific, "experimental" dimension of Marivaux's theater is underlined by the title of Henri Coulet and Michel Gilot's classic *Marivaux: Un Humanisme expérimental* (Paris: Larousse, 1973), and by that of Deguy's later (1981) *La Machine matrimoniale.* However, Deguy emphasizes (24 and following) the difference between the spurious moral superiority of the "spectator" in Marivaux's journals, or the narrator in his novels, and the equality of his theatrical characters, all of whom are subject to the same errors and the same laws.

31. See Donald N. McCloskey's suggestive discussion in *The Rhetoric of Economics* (Madison: University of Wisconsin Press, 1985), especially chap. 4, "The Literary Character of Economic Science."

32. See act I, scenes 2 and 4.

33. Kavanagh, *Enlightenment and the Shadows of Chance,* chap. 1, "The Triumph of Probability Theory."

34. Deguy, *La Machine matrimoniale*, 63.

35. One of his late plays, *L'Épreuve* (1755), even bears the word *trial* in its title.

36. "Do whatever you want, under conditions implicitly imposed by me": definition of liberal discourse proposed by Roland Barthes at a seminar in 1972 at the École Pratique des Hautes Études, Paris.

37. See Pierre Voltz, *La Comédie* (Paris: Armand Colin, 1964), 108–20; Coulet and Gilot, *Marivaux: Un Humanisme expérimental.*

38. See Scott Bryson's analysis of how the spectator to bourgeois dramas of the late eighteenth century is at once liberated and disciplined: Bryson, *The Chastised Stage: Bourgeois Drama and the Exercise of Power* (Stanford: Anma Libri, 1991), especially chap. 3.

39. Deguy, *La machine matrimoniale*, 63.

40. Unless otherwise indicated, all English quotations from *Les Fausses confidences* are taken from the translation by Timberlake Wertenbaker, *False Admissions, Successful Strategies, La Dispute* (Bath: Absolute Press, 1989).

41. *Théâtre complet,* 2:342 and following. "The nervous and brilliant dialogues that constituted the famous *marivaudage* disappear" (343).

42. According to Richelet's *Dictionnaire français* (1680), the *intendant* is "[c]elui qui a soin des affaires d'une grande Maison, ou de quelque grand Seigneur."

43. As Deguy points out (*La Machine matrimoniale*, 56), although Dorante is one of the rare "passionate" characters in Marivaux's theater, he feels his passion before the curtain rises.

44. Ibid., 84 and following.

45. In fact, the Peruvian gold mines had been pretty much exhausted by the

early eighteenth century, but the discovery of precious metals in Brazil had begun to have a decisive effect upon European economies. See Pierre Vilar, *Or et monnaie dans l'histoire* (Paris: Flammarion, 1974), 275 and following.

46. "Il faut donc, comme le disait très bien Marivaux lui-même, que les acteurs *ne paraissent jamais sentir la valeur de ce qu'ils disent,* et qu'en même temps les spectateurs la sentent et la démêlent à travers l'espèce de nuage dont l'auteur a dû envelopper leurs discours" (D'Alembert, *Éloge de Marivaux,* cited in *Théâtre complet,* 2:984, emphasis in original).

47. In act I, scene 3, Dorante's uncle, M. Rémy, explains to him that Marton comes from the same social background as Dorante, but that her late father's business difficulties have reduced Marton to the status of *suivante,* or lady's companion. For similar reasons, Dorante has been forced to seek employment below his original rank, as an *intendant.*

48. See "Vérité et réalité dans *Les Fausses confidences,*" in *Mélanges d'histoire littéraire offerts à Daniel Mornet* (Paris: Nizet, 1951), 121; quoted by Roland Morisse in Marivaux, *Les Fausses confidences* (Paris: Nouveaux Classiques Larousse, 1973), 34.

49. Morisse, in Marivaux, *Les Fausses confidences,* 38.

50. "La lettre arrive toujours à destination" ("Séminaire sur *La Lettre volée,*" in *Écrits* [Paris: Seuil, 1966], 41).

51. *Théâtre complet,* 2:346.

52. Guicharnaud, *Molière: Une Aventure théâtrale,* 473.

53. Ibid., 470.

54. Ibid., 464 and following. "The 'tragic' character in *Le Misanthrope* is perhaps not Alceste, but Célimène, for it is really she who falls from a height" (473).

55. In act I, scene 2, of *Les Fausses confidences,* Dubois assures Dorante: "Nous sommes convenus de toutes nos actions, toutes nos mesures sont prises; je connais l'humeur de ma maîtresse, je sais votre mérite, je sais mes talents, je vous conduis; et on vous aimera, toute raisonnable que l'on est; et on vous enrichira, tout ruiné que vous êtes, entendez-vous?"

56. Deguy (*La Machine matrimoniale,* 61) remarks that servants like Dubois are needed, in Marivaux's theater, to guide their masters into Love.

57. Émile Benveniste, *Problèmes de linguistique générale,* vol. 1 (Paris: Gallimard, 1966), 255–56. Benveniste's "I" retains a strictly *linguistic* status; neither "I" nor "you" refers to the ontological reality of a person (1:254).

58. As Deguy explains, the *amour-propre* of Lucile (in *Les Serments indiscrets*) also requires her suitor to have recourse to indirect methods: "[Q]u'y a-t-il d'intolérable pour Lucile au seuil du mariage, au point de se révolter à l'idée même d'entrer en badinage . . . ? Elle a mis l'autre dans la condition de ne pouvoir faire sa cour, de ne pouvoir badiner avec l'amour. Tout devra être indirect" (*La Machine matrimoniale,* 70).

59. Françoise Meltzer, *Salomé and the Dance of Writing: Portraits of Mimesis in Literature* (Chicago: University of Chicago Press, 1987), 178. As I have done

in my present discussion of portraits in Watteau and Marivaux, Meltzer draws upon the seminal work of Louis Marin (177–80).

60. "Mme. de Clèves n'était pas peu embarrassée. La raison voulait qu'elle demandât son portrait; mais, en le demandant publiquement, c'était apprendre à tout le monde les sentiments que ce prince avait pour elle, et, en le lui demandant en particulier, c'était quasi l'engager à lui parler de sa passion" (*La Princesse de Clèves* [Paris: Garnier-Flammarion, 1966], 92).

61. *La Machine matrimoniale*, 28. The other conventional device, also repeatedly used in Marivaux, is "le coup du billet."

62. Meltzer, *Salomé and the Dance of Writing*, 182–83.

63. See Deguy's comments in *La Machine matrimoniale*, 84–86 ("L'amour et l'occident, ou le coup de foudre et le coup de fourbe").

64. Araminte absolves him in these words: "Ce trait de sincérité me charme, me paraît incroyable, et vous êtes le plus honnête homme du monde. Après tout, puisque vous m'aimez véritablement, ce que vous avez fait pour gagner mon coeur n'est point blâmable" (III, 12).

Chapter Five

1. English text from *History of My Life*, translated by Willard R. Trask, 6 vols. (Baltimore: Johns Hopkins University Press, 1967; rpt., 1997), 1:36 (emphasis added). Original French text from *Histoire de ma vie*, 3 vols. (Paris: Laffont/Bouquins, 1993), 1:9 (vol. 3, chap. 11). All subsequent citations will refer to the volume and page of this edition, with Casanova's volume and chapter divisions given parenthetically. In this edition, Francis Lacassin reproduces the only complete edition of Casanova's original manuscript, published by Brockhaus-Plon in 1960, with the notes to that edition (by Dr. and Mrs. Arthur Hübscher) and additional biographical notes from the 1924 edition by La Sirène.

2. Helmut Watzlawick discusses the history of Casanova's manuscripts in "Biographie d'un manuscrit" (*Histoire de ma vie*, 1:xv–xxvii).

3. Of course, one might also have heard about Casanova's famous escape from I Piombi prison in Venice, and want to read about it. If this first-person adventure narrative (1787) had not been so well received, Casanova probably would not have attempted a complete autobiography. The I Piombi narrative has often been reprinted separately from *Histoire de ma vie*.

4. The reputed impossibility of translating *jouissance* into English raises theoretical problems, some of which are discussed by Jane Gallop, "Beyond the *Jouissance* Principle," *Representations* 7 (summer 1984): 110–15. As Gallop points out, a certain nobility has been ascribed (in French feminism *and* in *Le Plaisir du texte* of Roland Barthes) to *jouissance*, in contrast to the more vulgar *plaisir*. She concludes that "if *jouissance* is defined, as it is by Barthes and the women, as a loss of self, disruption of comfort, loss of control, it cannot simply be claimed

as an ego-satisfying identity, but most also frighten those who 'know' it" (114).

5. Thomas Kavanagh, "Casanova's Autobiography of Chance," *Michigan Romance Studies* 14 (1994): 158.

6. Ibid., 156. This moment of bliss is what Kavanagh calls the "solipsistic present" in Casanova: "He speaks within a moment centered on and concerned only with the feelings, reactions, and desires of a story-telling voice simultaneously at the center and circumference of all that happens in the text" (153). Casanova implies that he once knew *jouissances* that had nothing vicarious about them, without mediation by represented experience, as experience by oneself, for oneself. As Kavanagh points out, however, a "story-telling voice" (or self) mediates the solipsistic present. The notion of unmediated experience implies the absence of any such voice, of any difference between self and other. This experience (if there can be "experience" without a self) would be that of a *jouissance* so intense as to be unrepresentable, a mystical state perhaps something like what Georges Bataille describes (in *L'Expérience intérieure*) as the absence of "interior dialogue."

7. *Histoire de ma vie*, 1:620–24 (vol. 3, chap. 11).

8. Casanova first arrived in Paris in June 1750, just after having become a Freemason at Lyons. He left Paris in the autumn of 1752.

9. For an evocation of *galanterie* in the theater world at this time, see Henri Lagrave, *Le Théâtre et son public à Paris de 1715 à 1750* (Paris: Klincksieck, 1972), part 4, chap. 3.

10. *Histoire de ma vie*, 1:620 (vol. 3, chap. 11).

11. Throughout Europe there was a difference between ideal or accounting money (in France, the livre tournois) and "real" money (the louis, the franc, the écu). During most of the eighteenth century, real French money was metallic, and the value of each coin depended to a large extent (but not exclusively) upon the value of the metal it contained (according to the *Nouveau Petit Robert*, the "intrinsic" value of the *billon* was insignificant). Edgar Faure argues (*La Banqueroute de Law*, 174–76) that when John Law introduced the *billet–écu de banque*, a paper note denominated in écus and livres ("real" money), he took the first step toward overcoming the discrepancy between real and ideal money (that is, by completely separating monetary value from metal). The louis was a gold coin, struck in the effigy of the French king and worth 10 livres (24 livres after 1726). The franc was also a gold coin, equivalent to 1 livre or 20 sous. The écu, or écu blanc, was a silver coin. Coinage also existed in copper and *billon* (copper, sometimes mixed with another metal). To summarize the most common equivalencies:

1 livre = 1 franc
1 (gold) louis = 24 livres/francs
1 (silver) petit écu = 3 livres/francs
1 (silver) gros écu (or "écu de six francs") = 6 livres/francs

Faure estimates that 1 livre or franc in 1750 was worth 5 French francs in 1977.

On that basis, one can estimate that 1 livre/franc in 1750 = 25 French francs ($5 U.S.) in 1996. This would mean that, for example, Victorine Murphy's price (2 louis) for spending the night with Patu and Casanova was 48 livres, or (25 × 48) 1,200 1996 French francs ($240 U.S.). According to Casanova, she set the asking price for her little sister's virginity at 600 livres (25 louis), or (25 × 600) 15,000 French francs ($3,000 U.S.), and the king had her paid 24,000 livres (1,000 louis = 600,000 1996 French francs = $120,000 U.S.) for having procured her little sister for his "seraglio" (*Histoire de ma vie*, 1:623 [vol. 3, chap. 11]).

Louis XIV's costly wars led him to make numerous changes in the value and metallic composition of "real" money. As we have seen, although Law's projects for fiscal reform were adopted in the hope of eliminating the Sun King's war debts, they caused tremendous upheavals. Measures taken in 1726 and 1733 stabilized the value of French currency at 24 livres for the louis and 6 livres for the écu. For a concise discussion of these issues, see Guy Cabourdin and Georges Viard, *Lexique historique de la France d'ancien régime* (Paris: Armand Colin, 1990), 220–21.

12. To pay a total of 300 livres at 12 livres a session, Casanova would have had to visit the Murphy girl twenty-five times (in two months).

13. See Kavanagh, "Casanova's Autobiography of Chance," 160.

14. The Boucher portrait of Miss Murphy is now in the Musée des Beaux-Arts, Reims. Gaston Capon suggests that the painting that circulates in this episode may have been done by a Swede. See *Histoire de ma vie*, 1:620n.1 (vol. 3, chap. 11). See also Casanova de Seingalt, *Casanova à Paris: Ses séjours racontés par lui-même, avec notes, additions, et commentaires de Gaston Capon* (Paris: Libraire Schemit, 1913), 107–14.

15. Compare Casanova's musings on beauty and the etymology of "form" in *Histoire de ma vie*, 2:392–94 (vol. 6, chap. 9).

16. Casanova, *Mémoires*, 3 vols. (Paris: Pléiade, 1951), 1:694.

17. *Casanova: Un voyage libertin* (Paris: Denoël, 1985), 136 (emphasis in original).

18. Georges Bataille underscores the link between miracles and laughter in "Les Larmes et les rois," *Botteghe oscure* 17 (1956): 42 and following.

19. Marin, *Portrait of the King*, 8. "The king's portrait . . . constitutes the sacramental body of the monarch."

20. In Casanova, the king's portrait and those of his subjects are based upon two conflicting and incompatible notions of representation. Like Rousseau's *Confessions*, Casanova's self-portrait is painted on the post-absolutist, post-classical assumption that an account of unique, individual experience is inherently more valuable, more interesting than the story of an exemplary life—that the *Histoire de ma vie*, a private story that nobody else knows, is worth more than a story like Augustine's *Confessions*, which retells what everyone should already know about the nature of human desire. The contemporary emergence of the novel in European literature testifies, as Gianni Celati has shown (in *Finzioni occidentali* [Turin: Einaudi, 1975]), to this same poetics of "indiscretion." In autobiography

as in the novel, "this is my body" loses its semiotically exemplary value, and becomes the watchword of countless narratives that seek to communicate the infinitely rich, complex world of individual experience. However, if "this is my body" is no longer interpreted in terms of transubstantiation, as if a body were actually present in its representation, then these autobiographies and novels must be understood as presenting facsimiles or fictions (Celati's *finzioni*) of individual experience. If the truth of experience, like the Protestant God, can only be known to a solitary individual, then that experience can only be known to others vicariously, in a generally recognizable or general form, which communicates the truth of individual experience to everyone. When individual experience becomes inherently more valuable than exemplary life, it is necessary to translate that experience into universally meaningful signs of value, into a common language, which is that of vicarious experience.

21. The dates (August 21–23) that Casanova assigns to his visits to Les Délices are probably incorrect, as the Hübschers explain in a footnote (*Histoire de ma vie*, 2:398n.3). From my perspective, the question of when these events took place, or what may "really" have happened, is less important than the historical fact that Casanova wrote this text at a specific time and place.

22. Ibid., 2:400 and n. 1 (vol. 6, chap. 9).

23. Ibid., 2:773–87 (vol. 8, chap. 4).

24. According to Haldenwang (ibid., 2:413n.3), one of these three young ladies, Jeanne-Christine de Fernex, descended from the ruined noble family that had given its name to the land, "Ferney," that Voltaire had bought in 1758.

25. Ibid., 2:414 (vol. 6, chap. 10).

26. When *Histoire de ma fuite*, Casanova's account of his escape (in 1756) from I Piombi, the infamous Venetian prison, was finally published in 1788, he had been embroidering the story orally for more than three decades. See the articles and documents collected in *Histoire de ma vie*, 2:1003–39 ("L'Evasion des Plombs de Venise"). With some minor modifications, he incorporated the adventure into his memoirs (1:859 and following).

27. Casanova's witty justification for Voltaire's having dropped the name Arouet (the alphabet belongs to everyone . . .) is well known (see chapter 2, above). On the other hand, Casanova says nothing about Voltaire's (and his own) adoption of the nobiliary particle (de Voltaire, de Seingalt). I shall return to their choice of names and to the issue of their self-styled (that is, self-written) nobility.

28. As Chantal Thomas brilliantly demonstrates, Louis XV is for Casanova (more than for anyone else) "le Bien-Aimé": Thomas, *Casanova: Un Voyage libertin*, 130. As Thomas has shown, Casanova loved Louis XV, in the way that a woman (or another man) can worship an ineffably charming, inaccessible man. For Casanova, she maintains, loving the king meant "wanting to be loved by the king" (130), imagining himself in a passive position, miraculously elected as the object of the monarch's desire. In fact, Thomas explains that Casanova's devotion to the ancien régime (and his hostility to the Revolution) had an erotic basis: his

fantasy life required that he imagine himself in a world where kings inhabited a higher sphere of being, inaccessible to their subjects ("an insurmountable exteriority" [136]). Thomas's essay appeared in the mid-1980s, as did François Roustang's *Le Bal masqué de Giacomo Casanova* (Paris: Editions de Minuit, 1984); translated into English by Anne Vila, *The Quadrille of Gender* (Stanford: Stanford University Press, 1987). Earlier discussions of Casanova had taken place almost exclusively in terms either of hagiography (Casanova as idol of self-styled heterosexual male admirers) or of positivism (where his memoirs were treated as a source of "facts" about eighteenth-century life). Thomas summarizes these trends in her first chapter, "Le Casanovisme" (59 and following). More recently, Lydia Flem has published *Casanova: The Man Who Really Loved Women* (New York: Farrar, Straus, and Giroux, 1997).

29. In the opinion of J. Rives Childs, *Casanova: A Biography Based on New Documents* (London: George Allen and Unwin, 1961), 128, Casanova and Voltaire first met "about July 5, 1760." As Rives Childs points out (133), the only allusion to this encounter in Voltaire's correspondence occurs in a letter to his friend Thieriot, dated 7 July [1760]. See also E. Maynial's discussion (with R. Vèze) of Casanova's visit to Les Délices, in *La Fin d'un aventurier: Casanova après les Mémoires* (Paris, 1952). Casanova's account of the meeting can be found in *Histoire de ma vie*, 2:400–425 (vol. 6, chap. 10). Among the many published discussions of the encounter, perhaps the most amusing is that of Henri de Régnier, *Casanova chez Voltaire* (Paris: Plon, 1929). See also the earlier titles cited by Raoul Vèze, in a note to the Laffont/Bouquins edition (2:401)—for example, "Voltaire aux Délices," an account of this meeting by Desnoireterres, published in 1842. Chantal Thomas, *Casanova: Un Voyage libertin*, 15, remarks that Casanova visited Voltaire the way that, a century later, one would visit the pyramids.

30. See Chantal Thomas, "Le français, langue du libertinage," in *Casanova: Un Voyage libertin*, 76 and following.

31. *Histoire de ma vie*, 2:424 (vol. 6, chap. 10). After twelve years of exile from Venice, Casanova began publicly criticizing Voltaire, perhaps in the hope of placating the Venetian inquisitors. In *Essai sur les mœurs* (chaps. 106 and 186), Voltaire's praise for Venice (whose history he discusses in considerable detail) had been mitigated by criticism of the overwhelming power of its patricians. Later, in the *Dictionnaire philosophique* (article "Venise"), Voltaire apparently reversed his position, although probably not because of anything that Casanova had said. In any case, Casanova publicly criticized Voltaire in the *Confutazione della Storia del Governo veneto di Amelot de Houssaie . . .* , vol. 2 (Amsterdam [Lugano], 1769), and the *Scrutinio del libro, Eloges de M. de Voltaire* (Venice, 1779). In *Candide* (chaps. 24–26) Voltaire portrays Pococurante's Venice as a boring and sad place.

32. Besterman, *Voltaire's Correspondence*, vol. 42, May–July 1760, letter *D* 9044 (*P* 6078).

33. In *Casanova chez Voltaire*, Régnier sets the scene for the encounter between Voltaire and Casanova, by contrasting the nervous energy of the chronic insom-

niac Voltaire ("He slept poorly" [1]) with the naturally happy disposition of Casanova, the good sleeper ("M. Casanova sleeps well" [16]).

34. See Thomas, *Casanova: Un Voyage libertin*, 82.

35. Ibid. In this respect, the encounter between Casanova and Voltaire resembles the meeting between the Nephew and Myself in Diderot's *Neveu de Rameau*.

36. Ibid., 80.

37. Ibid., 94. As Thomas says, the happiest moments of his life are those when he has what actors call "presence": the ability to fill a room, as they say in the business, to "work the audience" like a master.

38. "Casanova's single abiding choice is to trust his luck at every moment of a present which, freed from past and future, is experienced as richer and more vital than any continuity" (Kavanagh, "Casanova's Autobiography of Chance," 153).

39. See ibid., 166.

40. See Thomas, *Casanova: Un Voyage libertin*, 82.

41. See ibid., 77 and following.

42. This is the last sentence of vol. 6, chap. 9 (emphasis added). The Laforgue-Casanova text (the "édition originale"—that is, the first version of Casanova's memoirs to be published in French) is in print, in both the three-volume Pléiade edition and the single-volume Arléa (Paris: Seuil, 1993) edition. See note 16, above.

43. As Kavanagh points out, *Enlightenment and the Shadows of Chance*, 58–59, the model for the current French Loterie Nationale is the Loterie de l'École Militaire, established by Casanova in 1757, thanks to the influence of Cardinal Bernis. Casanova's extraordinary account of the circumstances in which he became acquainted with Bernis (between 1753 and 1755, while Bernis was ambassador to the republic of Venice) is contained in the story of his adventures with the nuns "M. M." and "C. C." (see particularly vol. 4, chaps. 3–4). This part of Casanova's text can be read as an extended commentary on the politics of representation. In "Casanova's Autobiography of Chance," Kavanagh discusses what it meant (philosophically, politically) for Casanova to represent his life as the systematically discontinuous story of successive chance events. I shall return below to some of the issues Kavanagh raises in this article.

44. See the preface to *Histoire de ma vie*, written in 1797, where Casanova defines the select character of his intended audience (1:xi).

45. For example, Italo Calvino cites almost the entire passage in his edition of excerpts from the poem. See *Orlando furioso di Ludovico Ariosto raccontato da Italo Calvino con una scelta del poema* (Milan: Einaudi, 1970), 128–36.

46. In the previous chapter of Casanova's memoirs (2:391), a gentleman in Lausanne tells him that Voltaire tyrannically insisted that participants in amateur productions of his plays shed real tears. For Voltaire, real tears are sincere: they stand for, or represent, an interior state. This fairly conventional notion of crying is quite different from that of Diderot's great actor, the *comédien insensible*, who

always remains detached from whatever emotion he conveys. In semiotic terms, for Voltaire a tear is a sign, while for Diderot's great actor, it is only a token.

47. *Epître à l'auteur du livre des Trois Imposteurs* (1769).

48. Thomas, *Casanova: Un Voyage libertin*, 121.

49. Ibid.

50. Of course, by speaking of superstition as "necessary," Casanova does not mean that it is "unavoidable, or fatally determined." As Chantal Thomas has noted (ibid., 121–22), Casanova could not stand the idea of necessity, except insofar as it applied to the physical world.

51. "Superstition," in *Dictionnaire philosophique* (Paris: Classiques Garnier, 1967), 394 and following, especially 396.

52. Thomas, *Casanova: Un Voyage libertin*, 114.

53. "Scarcely had he fallen when the student Ginés jumped upon him, and taking the basin [Quixote's "helmet"] from his head, gave him three or four blows with it on the shoulders and then struck it repeatedly on the ground, almost breaking it into pieces" (Cervantes, *Don Quixote*, translated by Walter Starkie [New York: Penguin, 1964], part 1, chap. 22, 218). With this reference to Quixote's "helmet" Casanova also implicitly casts Voltaire's philosophical project in the mock-heroic register of Folengo's *Secchia rapita* ("stolen bucket"), which Voltaire had called "des bêtises."

Conclusion

1. "By Voltaire's time the sacrificed king had turned into a ridiculous ghost. . . . It had become impossible to give credence to the reality of tragic action" (Caplan, "1759, 23 April: Clearing the Stage," 473).

2. Henri Lagrave, "*Irène*," in *Inventaire Voltaire*, 733.

3. See chapter 5, note 47, above.

4. Henri Lagrave, "Tragédies," in *Inventaire Voltaire*, 1334.

5. Ibid.

6. Goux, *The Coiners of Language*, 29.

7. Apostolidès, *Le Prince sacrifié*, 32 and following.

8. Unlike his immediate predecessors, Louis XV sat in the *corbeille*, or "circle," a practice that French heads of state continued until quite recently. In contrast, German and Italian princes in the eighteenth century continued to build theaters organized around the prince's loge (directly opposite the stage, in the first balcony). See Pierre Pougnaud, *Théâtres: Quatre siècles d'architectures et d'histoire* (Paris: Éditions du Moniteur, 1980), 21–22.

9. Apostolidès has argued that the models of subjectivity and value that have dominated the late twentieth century were already emerging in Diderot's *Encyclopédie*. See Apostolidès, "Le Paradoxe de l'*Encyclopédie*," *Stanford French Review* 14, no. 3 (winter 1990): 47–63.

Index

absolutism, 1–2, 126, 137; death of, 72–74; and division of subject, 39–40, 160; ideology of, 157–58, 186n. 80; Oedipus figure in, 49–51; and royal body, 15–19; and theory of king's two bodies, 17; Voltaire's rejection of, 59–60. *See also* culture, post-absolutist

Académie Française, 155

Adhémar, Hélène, 75–76, 187n. 8, 192n. 44, 193n. 49

aesthetics: medieval, 91–92; modernist, 159; post-absolutist, 87–95

Agamben, Giorgio, 91–92

agency, post-absolutist, in Voltaire's *Œdipe*, 69–72

Alfassa, Pierre, 187n. 5

amour-propre, 196n. 13; in Marivaux, 105–7, 110, 111–12, 122, 125, 199n. 58

Apostolidès, Jean-Marie, 17, 73, 103–4, 160, 169n. 18, 197nn. 14, 15, 206n. 9

Aragon, Louis, 187n. 5, 189n. 18

archetypes, as bearers of exchange value, 133–38

Argenson, Marquis d', 15, 31

Ariosto, Ludovico, *Orlando furioso*, 147–48

aristocracy: Casanova and, 146; and fête galante, 87–90, 193n. 47; and self-fashioning, 90, 194n. 58. *See also* nobility

Arouet, François, 44

Arouet, François-Marie. *See* Voltaire (François-Marie Arouet)

artifice and desire, in Watteau's fêtes galantes, 88–90

art world: and nobility, 86, 90–91, 194n. 58; and patronage system, 190n. 30; in Watteau's *L'Enseigne de Gersaint*, 89–90, 92–95, 97, 159

assignats, 165n. 15

Athalie (Racine), 41

athletic contest, Casanova's meeting with Voltaire as, 142–44

audience: Casanova and, 142–44; theatrical, 54–57, 115–16, 160, 183n. 59

Augustine, St., 140, 202n. 20

Auslander, Leora, 163n. 1

Baldus, Il (Folengo), 141–42

bank notes. *See* currency

Banque Générale (Banque Royale), 3, 4

Barthes, Roland, 195n. 69, 198n. 36

bastards, royal, 37, 46, 50, 170n. 24; and "Minority" *lit de justice* of 1718, 11–12, 37; and Regency Council meeting of August 26, 1718, 29–36; Saint-Simon and, 20

Bataille, Georges, 201n. 6, 202n. 18

beauty, ideal, of Miss "O-Morphi," 130–31, 133–35, 138

Benjamin, Walter, 106

Benveniste, Émile, 121–22

Bernis, Cardinal, 205n. 43

Besterman, Theodore, 59

Bloch, Marc, 168n. 9

blood: circulation of, as economic metaphor, 3; priority of, *vs.* rule of law, 36, 38–40, 82–83, 157, 160

body, royal: in absolutist culture, 15–19; theory of king's two bodies, 17